THE GOON™

WICKED INCLINATIONS

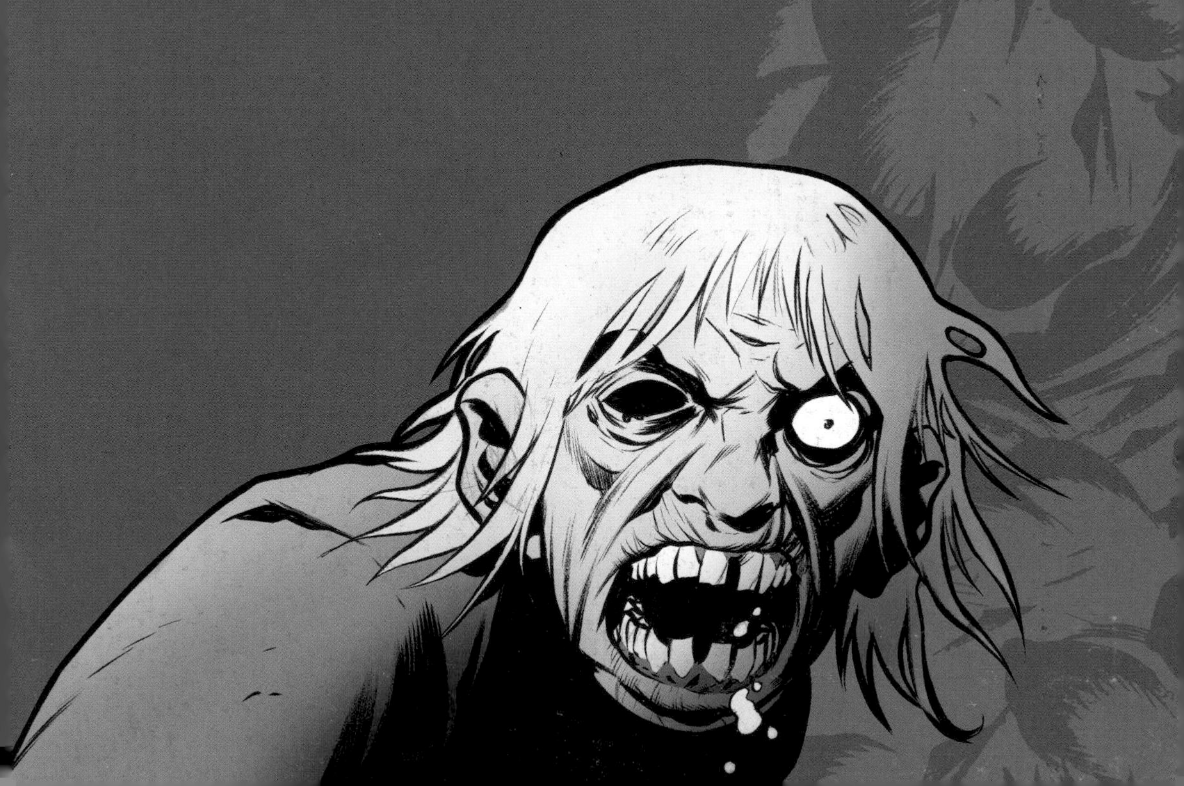

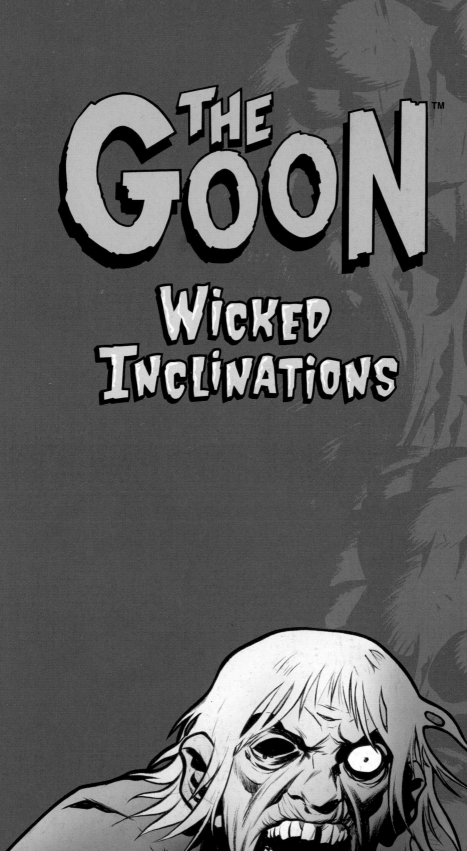

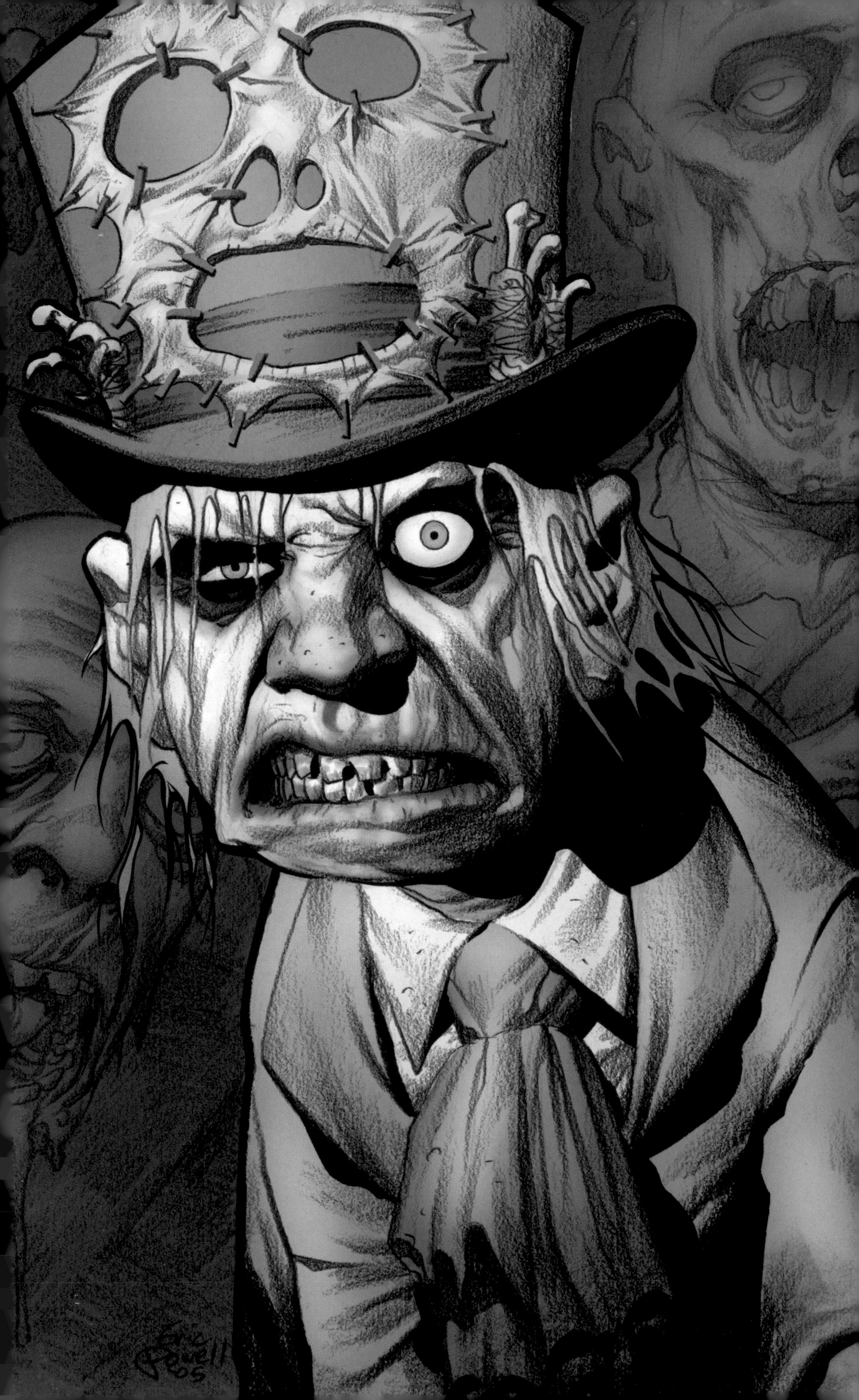

THE GOON™

WICKED INCLINATIONS

by Eric Powell

editor
Matt Dryer

assistant editor
Rachel Edidin

designer
Amy Arendts

art director
Lia Ribacchi

publisher
Mike Richardson

Zombies provided by Jethro & Earl Zombie Wranglerin' Inc.
and The Adopt-A-Zombie Foundation

Live animals provided by **Scott Allie**

Dark Horse Books™

Dedicated to Bill and Alicia Schenk. Thanks for everything.

The Goon™: Wicked Inclinations. Published by Dark Horse Comics, Inc., 10956
SE Main Street, Milwaukie, OR, 97222. The Goon™ & © 2006 Eric Powell. The
Albatross Exploding Funny Book Studio™ Logo is a trademark of Eric Powell. All
rights reserved. The stories, institutions, and characters in this publication are
fictional. Any resemblance to actual persons (living, dead, or undead), events, institutions, or locales, without satiric intent, is purely coincidental. No portion of
this book may be reproduced or transmitted, in any form, or by any means, without
express written permission from the copyright holder. Dark Horse Books™ is a
trademark of Dark Horse Comics, Inc. All rights reserved.

This volume collects issues 14-18 of the Dark Horse Comics ongoing series *The Goon*.

Published by
Dark Horse Books
A division of
Dark Horse Comics, Inc.
10956 SE Main Street
Milwaukie, OR 97222

darkhorse.com

First Edition: December 2006
ISBN-10: 1-59307-646-0
ISBN-13: 978-1-59307-646-7

1 3 5 7 9 10 8 6 4 2
Printed in China

Introduction by Michael Allred

MAN, OH MAN, do I dig *The Goon*! But I came late to the show on this one. I can usually pride myself on finding great chunks of art and entertainment ahead of the curve. But not so with Eric Powell and his killer cool creation. Why? My explanation may just reveal what a fragile, petty ego I have. I'll let you, dear friends and readers, decide.

My tale begins way back in 1992, when I'd just convinced Kevin "Teenage Mutant Ninja Turtles" Eastman to pay me ridiculous sums of money to publish my new creation, *The Spook*. That's right. *The Spook*: a mostly white creation with black markings suggesting skeletal features, an "exclamation bolt," and a name that I intended to pay homage to Will Eisner's *The Spirit*. Kevin had just started a new "creator friendly" publishing entity called Tundra, and I was a benefactor. In the process of trademarking my *Spook* character, Tundra discovered an "intent to use" on the name, and I was sent scrambling to find a new one. I was stumped. Glow-in-the-dark *Spook* T-shirts had been made, along with buttons and other promotional goodies. What a bummer! I brainstormed desperately, as advertising deadlines approached. I finally came up with the perfect new name for my thrilling creation. Wait for it . . . *The Goon*. *The Goon*?! That's right, *THE GOON*! I made a new logo (which you just may see here, folks), sent it off to Tundra, and exhaled. Soon, the new wave of promotional releases would herald the coming of my first big book. *The Goon* would be a series of three forty-eight-page square-bound books, with "flip action" animated corners. But this was not to be, and according to Eric, HIS *Goon* would never have been if comic book history had taken this path. He told me, "I'm glad you didn't call it *The Goon*. Otherwise I would have never made *The Goon*. I wanted to do something with a big monster as the main character, and then the title 'Goon' popped into my head. The word just made me think '30s noir. So I smashed that into all my monster/sci-fi ideas, and that's the book I ended up with."

Fortunately for both of us, and for lovers of crazed comics, when I was reading *Catcher in the Rye* on a flight to a comic book show, the name "Madman" popped off the page like a billboard. I immediately called the publisher with the switch, and at the last second my *Goon* became *Madman* (and the skeletal features fell away). Whew! Soon, Tundra became a brief happy memory. *Madman* found a home and family with Dark Horse Comics, and my invitation to join seven of the greatest comic book creators ever (!) with the LEGEND imprint exploded my career. Dark Horse and my legendary editor Bob Schreck made *Madman* a phenomenon.

Cut to the 21rst century. Not unlike the prodigal son, I had left my happy, prosperous Dark Horse family to find my way in the immediacy of self-publishing. My wife Laura and I created AAA Pop Comics, and I co-created a new batch of Marvel Mutants (you know, for the kids). Now, here comes the "fragile petty ego" part. In my absence (metaphorically off to college?), my Dark Horse family brought in a new sibling, the much cuter, fresher-smelling Eric Powell and his Toy . . . something called . . . *THE GOON*?! The praise was deafening. Awards rolled in. I turned away like a jealous older brother. I didn't want to hear anything about it. Goon, shmoon!

Still, sometimes something is so good it becomes virtually impossible to avoid it. In this case, in a lull between writing a *Madman* movie treatment and a screenplay, I was convinced by my art dealer to do a few commissions, something I've always avoided like the plague. But it was fun. Especially when I was asked to draw Madman with this "Goon" guy. *Aw, Man!* Okay, why not. Let's take a look at what this Eric Powell fella does. What's all the hubbub, Bub?

Soz, I goes and gets the *Goon Fancy Pants Edition* from a generous sibling at my Dark Horse family. And I'm faced with the obvious: Wow, this is terrific stuff! I immediately went online (Hello, 21st century!) to snatch up all the collections. I left my beloved refuge on the Oregon coast to hit the comics shops and hunt down everything Eric Powell had done (love those obsessive hunts. I know you can relate, gang!).

Around this time, Laura and I were in San Francisco at our favorite convention, Wonder-Con. We swung by The Comic Book Art Museum, only to be hit between the eyes by an original Eric Powell *Goon* painting. It was huge. It was stunning. It was beautiful. Here comes the blurb, folks . . . Eric Powell is this generation's Frank Frazetta! I actually love Frazetta's comic strip work every bit as much as, and sometimes even more than, his iconic paintings. The point is he can do it all, seemingly effortlessly. It's a rare gift. And Eric Powell has it. When Eric is on target, pencil, ink, or paint, there's no one today who can

do it any better. I was, and am, humbled. I'm an idiot. I don't know how long I stood in front of that painting with my mouth hanging open, or how much saliva drooled out of my mouth, but I was hooked.

Laura and I were celebrating the anniversary of my proposing to her under the Golden Gate Bridge a quarter of a century before (we were just babies), and so we only stayed at the convention for our commitments. After getting back home to Lakeside, Oregon, I finally looked at the convention program to find that Eric Powell had also been a guest. Idiot! It was time to make things right. I didn't know if Eric knew or cared who I was, but I had to pile on and share my affection for his work. In retrospect, I guess I'm glad I was such a brat about ignoring *The Goon*. What a thrill it finally was to have all that great material in front of me in one rush. And what an inspiration. Eric's work renewed my love for the pencil, bringing my own work to its biggest leap in years.

And so, I'm going to pull a "long story short" here and tell you that Dark Horse gave me his contact info and we began an exchange of words and work ultimately resulting in us gifting each other pinups with our characters together on the page. And now, happily, enthusiastically, I am accepting Eric's invitation to write the intro for the latest masterful collection of HIS *Goon*. So, if you dig Eric Powell's *The Goon* as much as I do . . . you're welcome.

Mike Allred's 1992 Goon logo

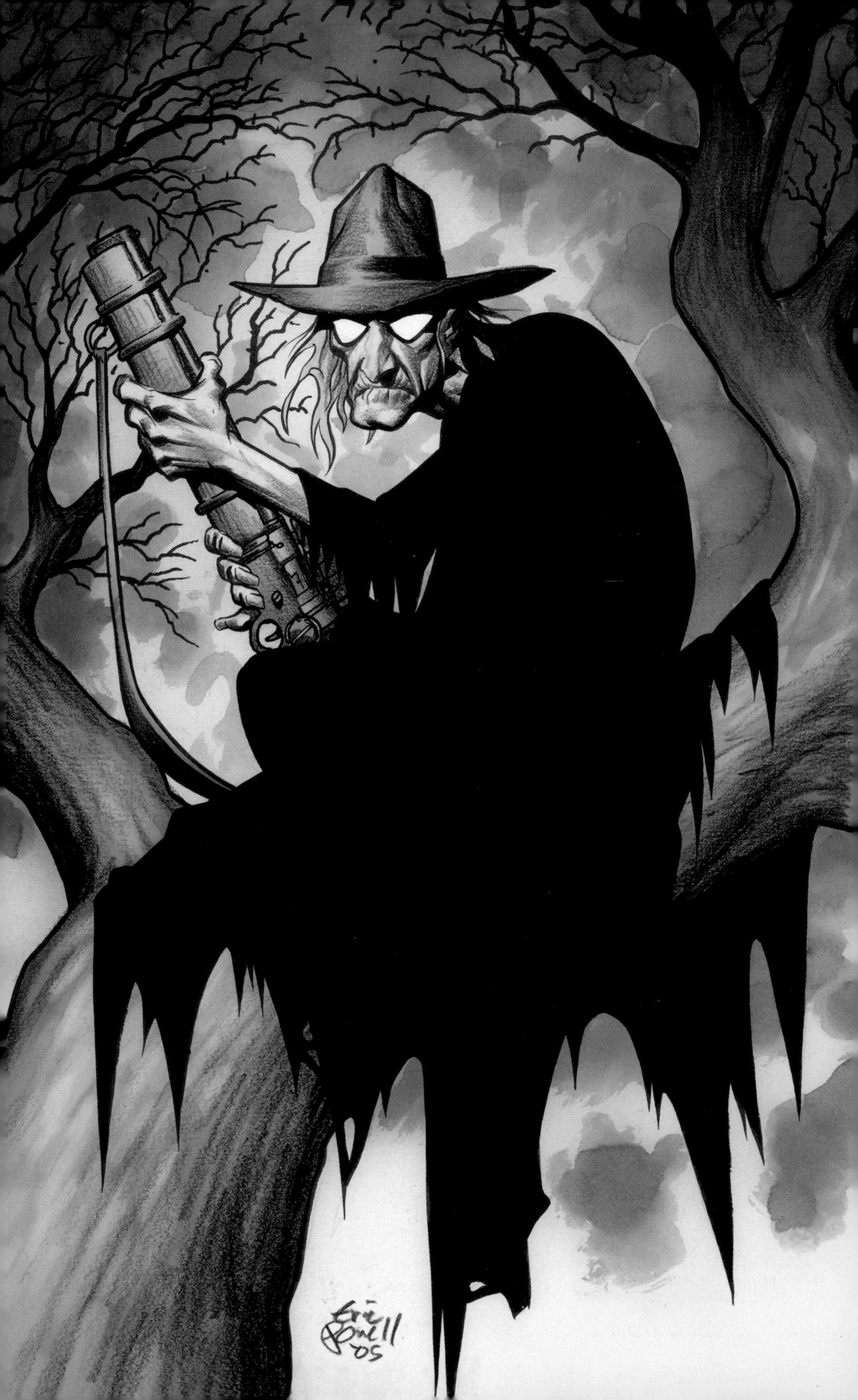

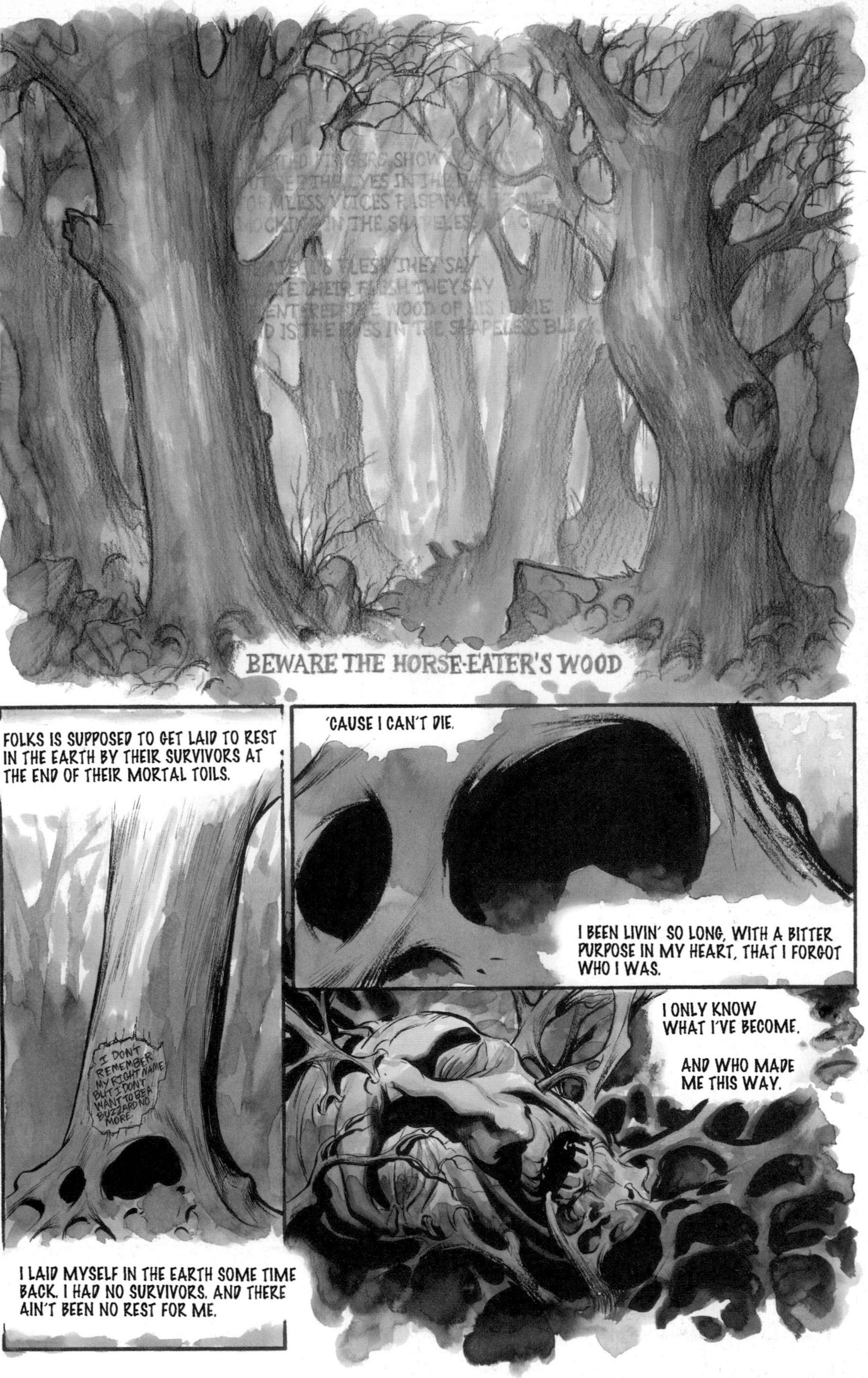
BEWARE THE HORSE-EATER'S WOOD
FOLKS IS SUPPOSED TO GET LAID TO REST IN THE EARTH BY THEIR SURVIVORS AT THE END OF THEIR MORTAL TOILS.
I DON'T REMEMBER MY RIGHT NAME BUT I DON'T WANT TO BE A BUZZARD NO MORE.
I LAID MYSELF IN THE EARTH SOME TIME BACK. I HAD NO SURVIVORS. AND THERE AIN'T BEEN NO REST FOR ME.
'CAUSE I CAN'T DIE.
I BEEN LIVIN' SO LONG, WITH A BITTER PURPOSE IN MY HEART, THAT I FORGOT WHO I WAS.
I ONLY KNOW WHAT I'VE BECOME.
AND WHO MADE ME THIS WAY.

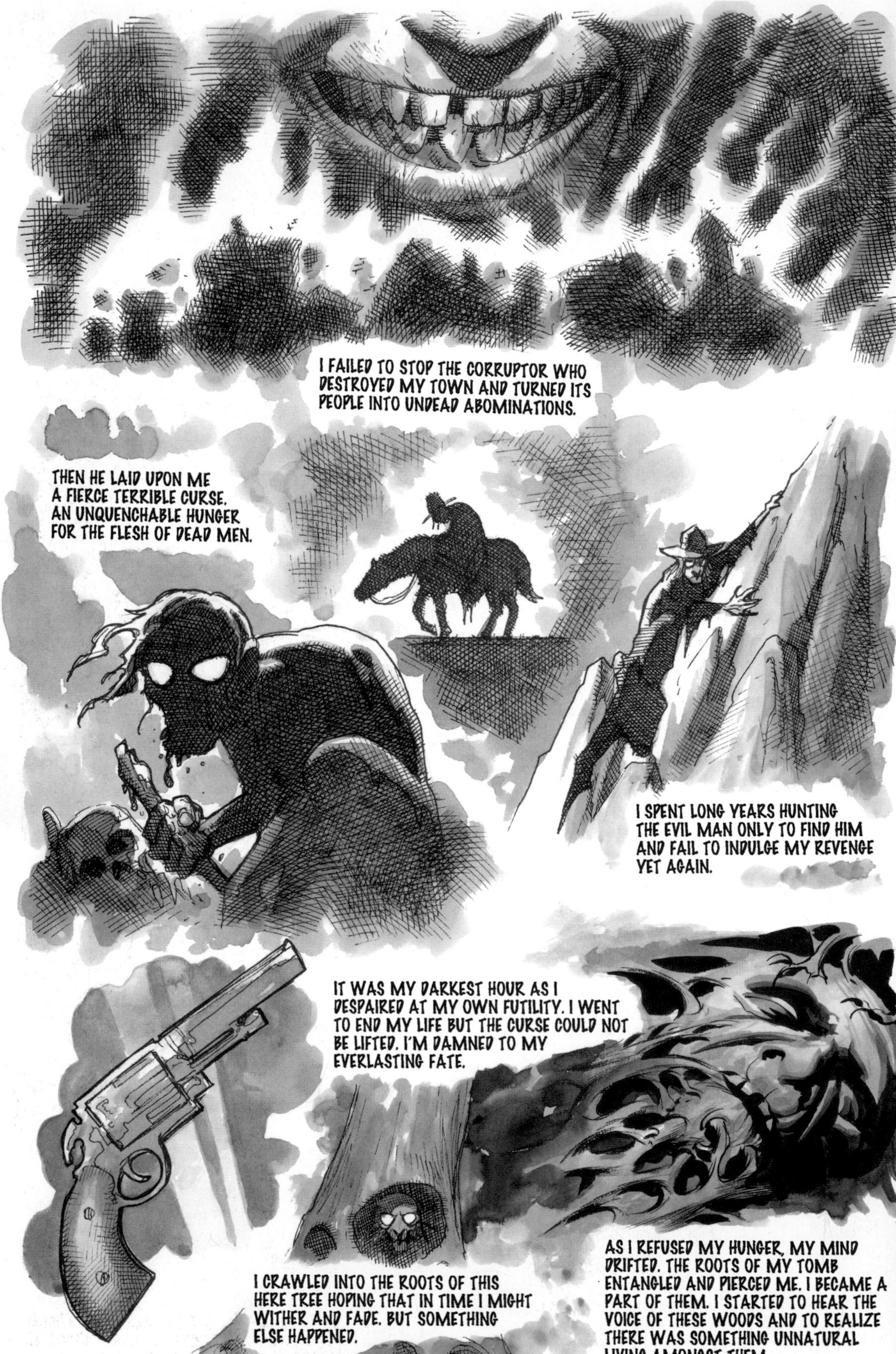
I FAILED TO STOP THE CORRUPTOR WHO DESTROYED MY TOWN AND TURNED ITS PEOPLE INTO UNDEAD ABOMINATIONS.
THEN HE LAID UPON ME A FIERCE TERRIBLE CURSE. AN UNQUENCHABLE HUNGER FOR THE FLESH OF DEAD MEN.
I SPENT LONG YEARS HUNTING THE EVIL MAN ONLY TO FIND HIM AND FAIL TO INDULGE MY REVENGE YET AGAIN.
IT WAS MY DARKEST HOUR AS I DESPAIRED AT MY OWN FUTILITY. I WENT TO END MY LIFE BUT THE CURSE COULD NOT BE LIFTED. I'M DAMNED TO MY EVERLASTING FATE.
I CRAWLED INTO THE ROOTS OF THIS HERE TREE HOPING THAT IN TIME I MIGHT WITHER AND FADE. BUT SOMETHING ELSE HAPPENED.
AS I REFUSED MY HUNGER, MY MIND DRIFTED. THE ROOTS OF MY TOMB ENTANGLED AND PIERCED ME. I BECAME A PART OF THEM. I STARTED TO HEAR THE VOICE OF THESE WOODS AND TO REALIZE THERE WAS SOMETHING UNNATURAL LIVING AMONGST THEM.

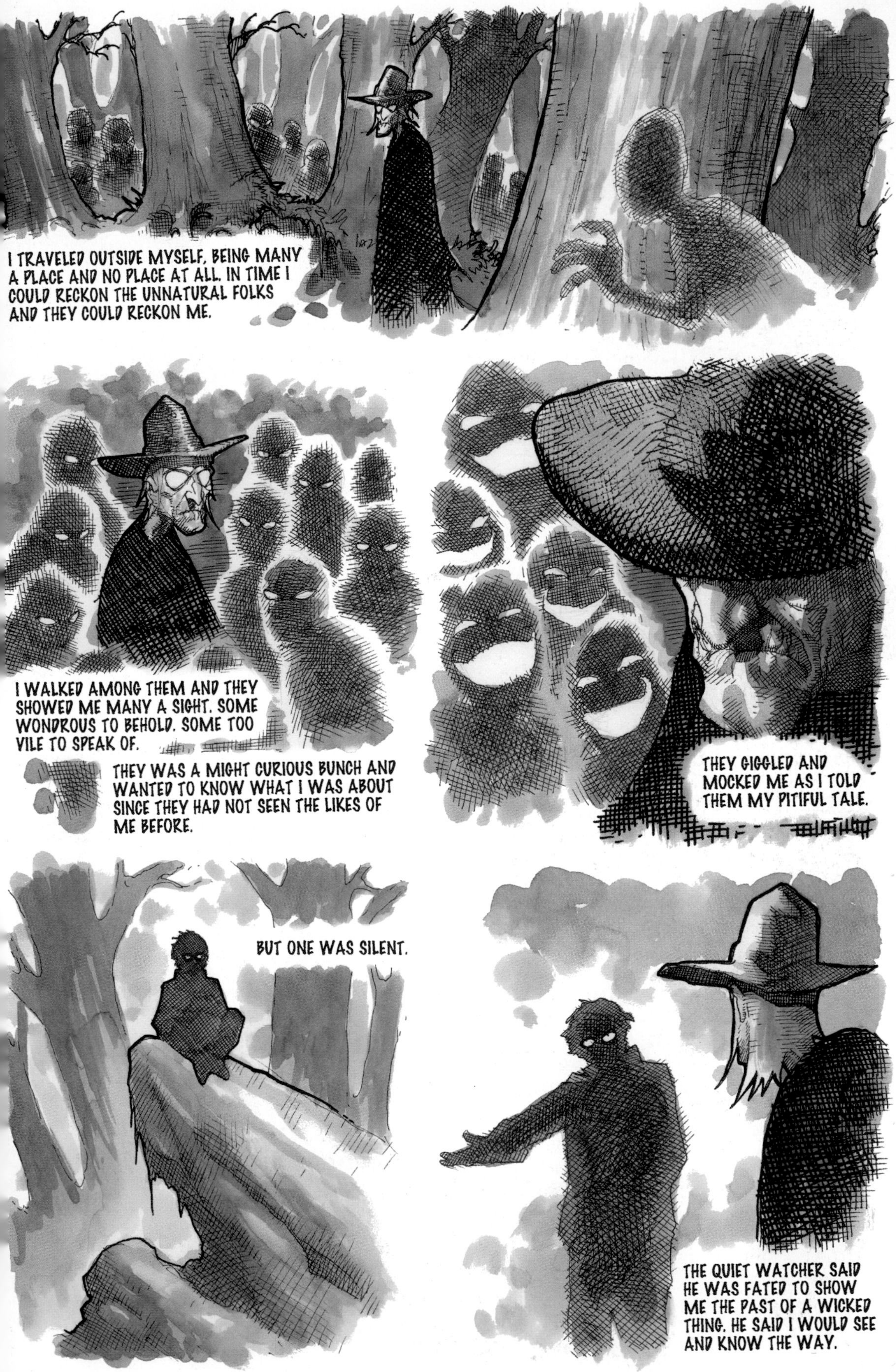
I TRAVELED OUTSIDE MYSELF, BEING MANY A PLACE AND NO PLACE AT ALL. IN TIME I COULD RECKON THE UNNATURAL FOLKS AND THEY COULD RECKON ME.
I WALKED AMONG THEM AND THEY SHOWED ME MANY A SIGHT. SOME WONDROUS TO BEHOLD. SOME TOO VILE TO SPEAK OF.
THEY WAS A MIGHT CURIOUS BUNCH AND WANTED TO KNOW WHAT I WAS ABOUT SINCE THEY HAD NOT SEEN THE LIKES OF ME BEFORE.
THEY GIGGLED AND MOCKED ME AS I TOLD THEM MY PITIFUL TALE.
BUT ONE WAS SILENT.
THE QUIET WATCHER SAID HE WAS FATED TO SHOW ME THE PAST OF A WICKED THING. HE SAID I WOULD SEE AND KNOW THE WAY.

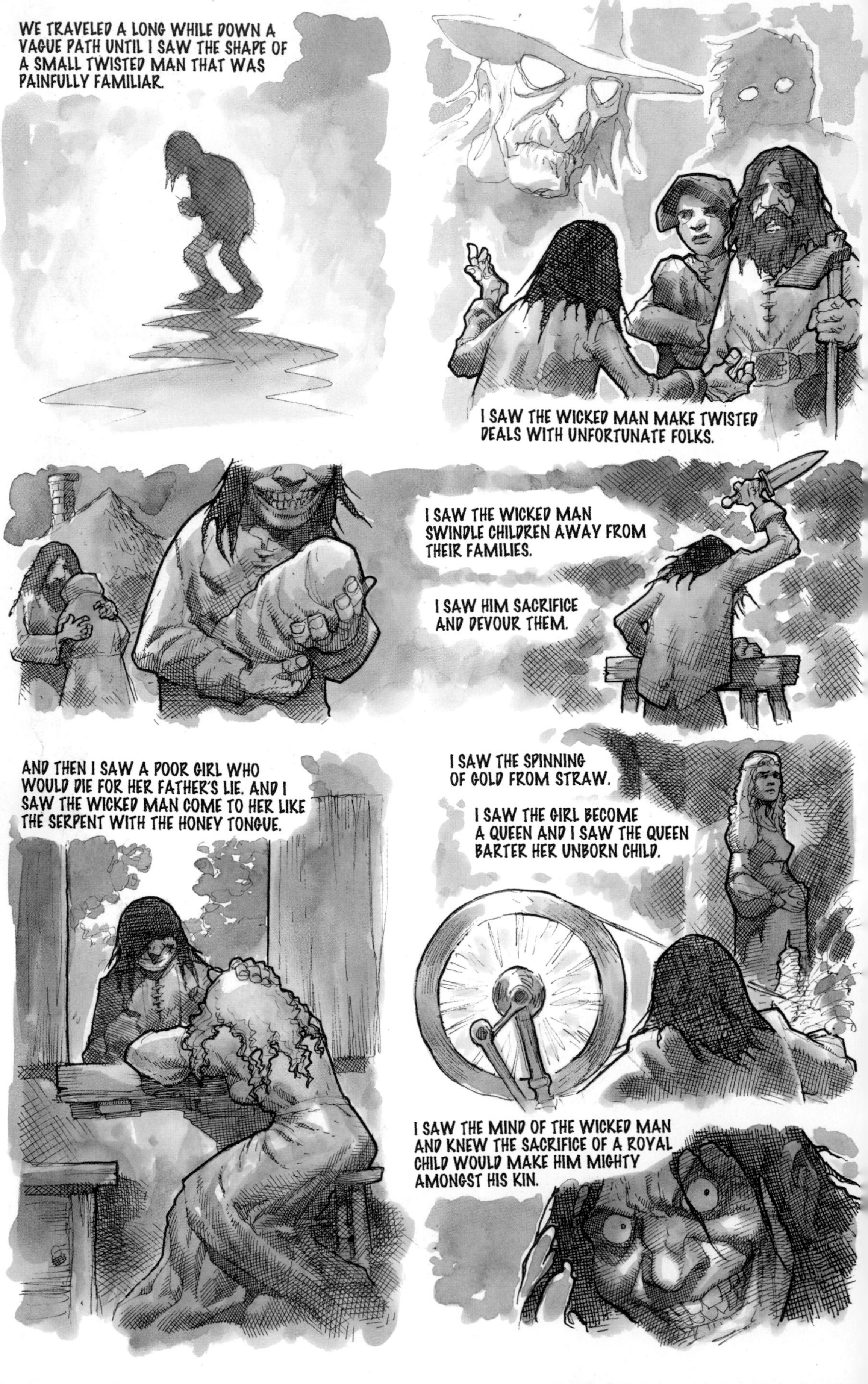

WE TRAVELED A LONG WHILE DOWN A VAGUE PATH UNTIL I SAW THE SHAPE OF A SMALL TWISTED MAN THAT WAS PAINFULLY FAMILIAR.
I SAW THE WICKED MAN MAKE TWISTED DEALS WITH UNFORTUNATE FOLKS.
I SAW THE WICKED MAN SWINDLE CHILDREN AWAY FROM THEIR FAMILIES.
I SAW HIM SACRIFICE AND DEVOUR THEM.
AND THEN I SAW A POOR GIRL WHO WOULD DIE FOR HER FATHER'S LIE. AND I SAW THE WICKED MAN COME TO HER LIKE THE SERPENT WITH THE HONEY TONGUE.
I SAW THE SPINNING OF GOLD FROM STRAW.
I SAW THE GIRL BECOME A QUEEN AND I SAW THE QUEEN BARTER HER UNBORN CHILD.
I SAW THE MIND OF THE WICKED MAN AND KNEW THE SACRIFICE OF A ROYAL CHILD WOULD MAKE HIM MIGHTY AMONGST HIS KIN.

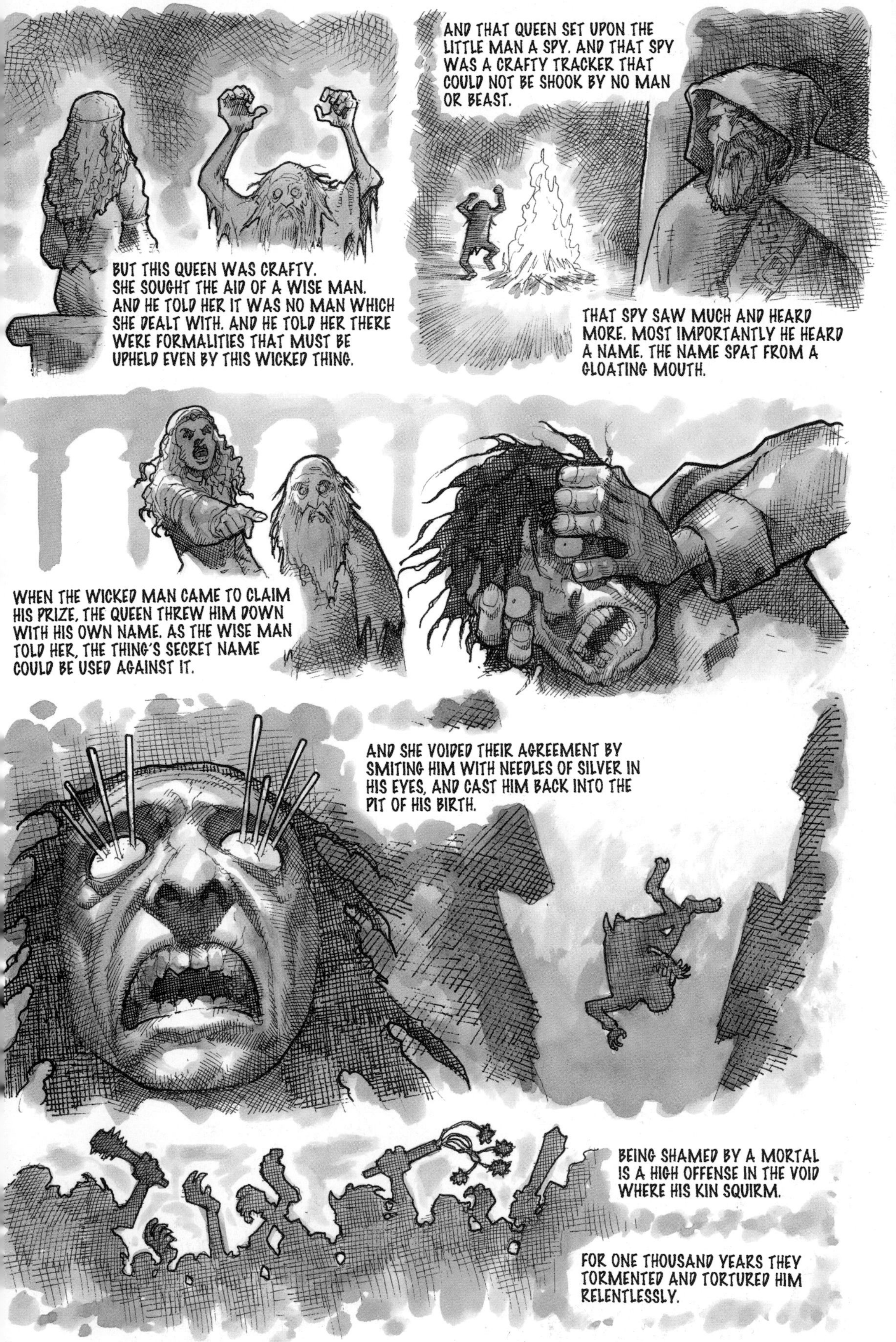
BUT THIS QUEEN WAS CRAFTY.
SHE SOUGHT THE AID OF A WISE MAN.
AND HE TOLD HER IT WAS NO MAN WHICH SHE DEALT WITH. AND HE TOLD HER THERE WERE FORMALITIES THAT MUST BE UPHELD EVEN BY THIS WICKED THING.
AND THAT QUEEN SET UPON THE LITTLE MAN A SPY. AND THAT SPY WAS A CRAFTY TRACKER THAT COULD NOT BE SHOOK BY NO MAN OR BEAST.
THAT SPY SAW MUCH AND HEARD MORE. MOST IMPORTANTLY HE HEARD A NAME. THE NAME SPAT FROM A GLOATING MOUTH.
WHEN THE WICKED MAN CAME TO CLAIM HIS PRIZE, THE QUEEN THREW HIM DOWN WITH HIS OWN NAME. AS THE WISE MAN TOLD HER, THE THING'S SECRET NAME COULD BE USED AGAINST IT.
AND SHE VOIDED THEIR AGREEMENT BY SMITING HIM WITH NEEDLES OF SILVER IN HIS EYES, AND CAST HIM BACK INTO THE PIT OF HIS BIRTH.
BEING SHAMED BY A MORTAL IS A HIGH OFFENSE IN THE VOID WHERE HIS KIN SQUIRM.
FOR ONE THOUSAND YEARS THEY TORMENTED AND TORTURED HIM RELENTLESSLY.

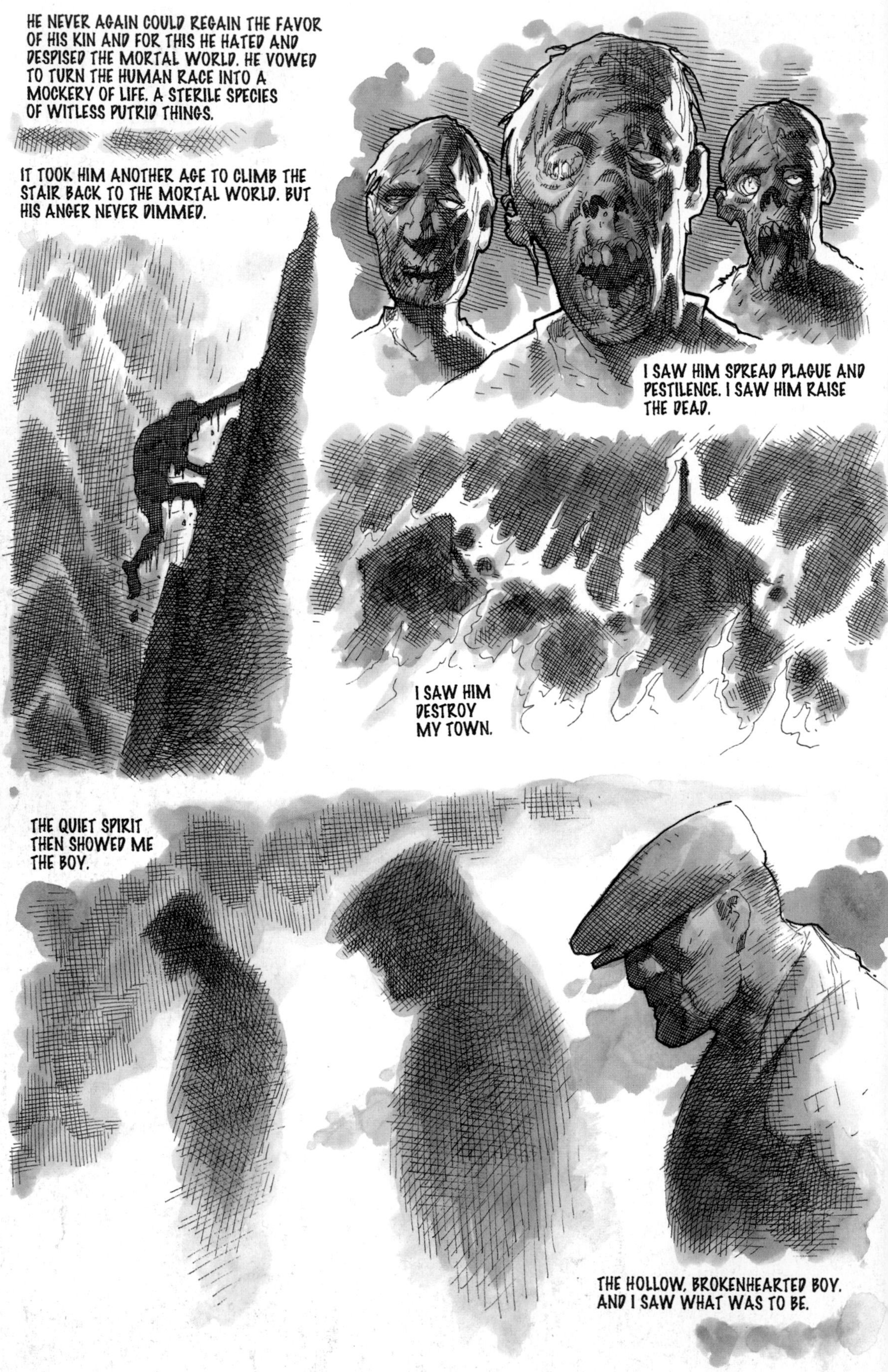
HE NEVER AGAIN COULD REGAIN THE FAVOR OF HIS KIN AND FOR THIS HE HATED AND DESPISED THE MORTAL WORLD. HE VOWED TO TURN THE HUMAN RACE INTO A MOCKERY OF LIFE. A STERILE SPECIES OF WITLESS PUTRID THINGS.
IT TOOK HIM ANOTHER AGE TO CLIMB THE STAIR BACK TO THE MORTAL WORLD. BUT HIS ANGER NEVER DIMMED.
I SAW HIM SPREAD PLAGUE AND PESTILENCE. I SAW HIM RAISE THE DEAD.
I SAW HIM DESTROY MY TOWN.
THE QUIET SPIRIT THEN SHOWED ME THE BOY.
THE HOLLOW, BROKENHEARTED BOY. AND I SAW WHAT WAS TO BE.

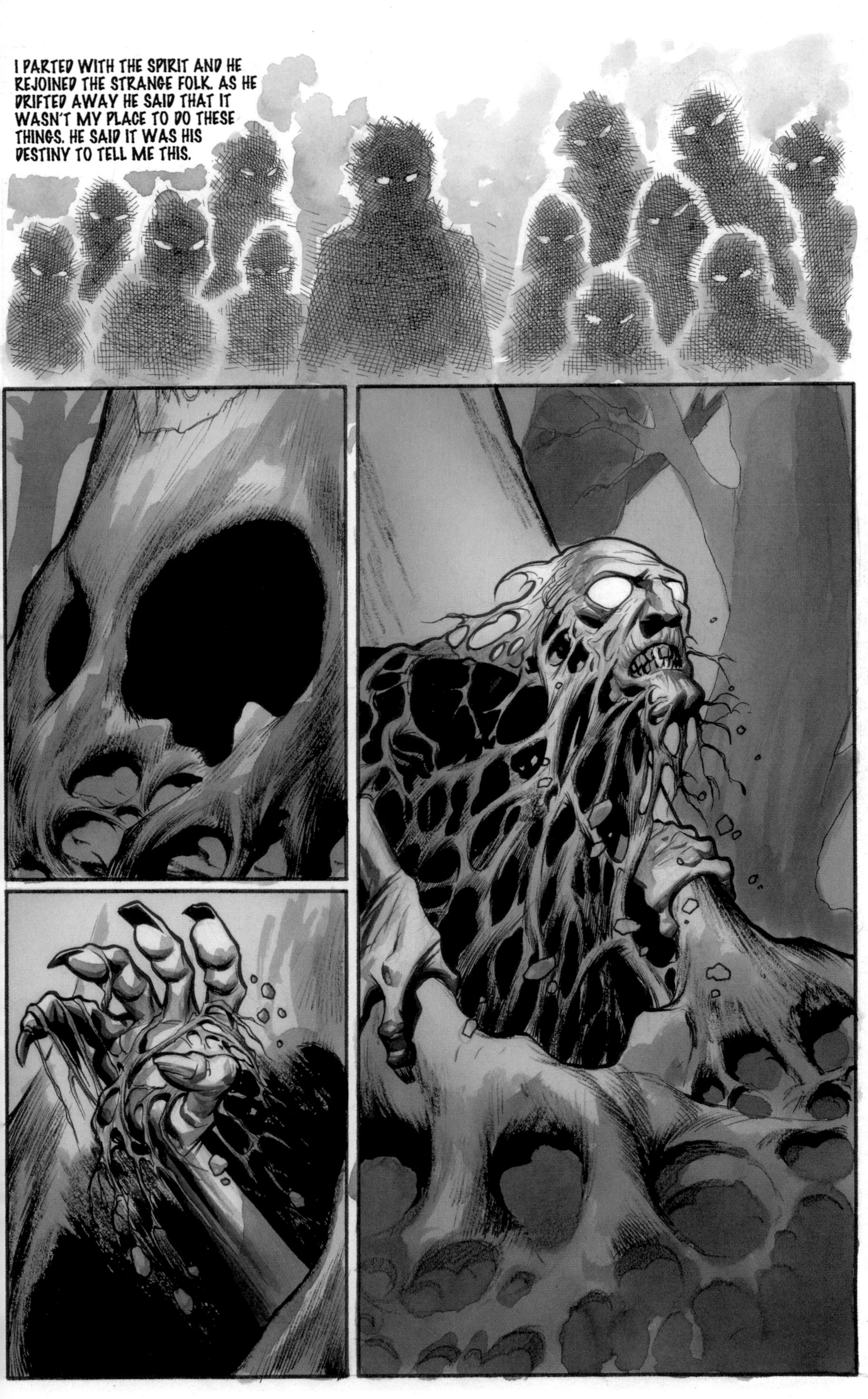
I PARTED WITH THE SPIRIT AND HE REJOINED THE STRANGE FOLK. AS HE DRIFTED AWAY HE SAID THAT IT WASN'T MY PLACE TO DO THESE THINGS. HE SAID IT WAS HIS DESTINY TO TELL ME THIS.

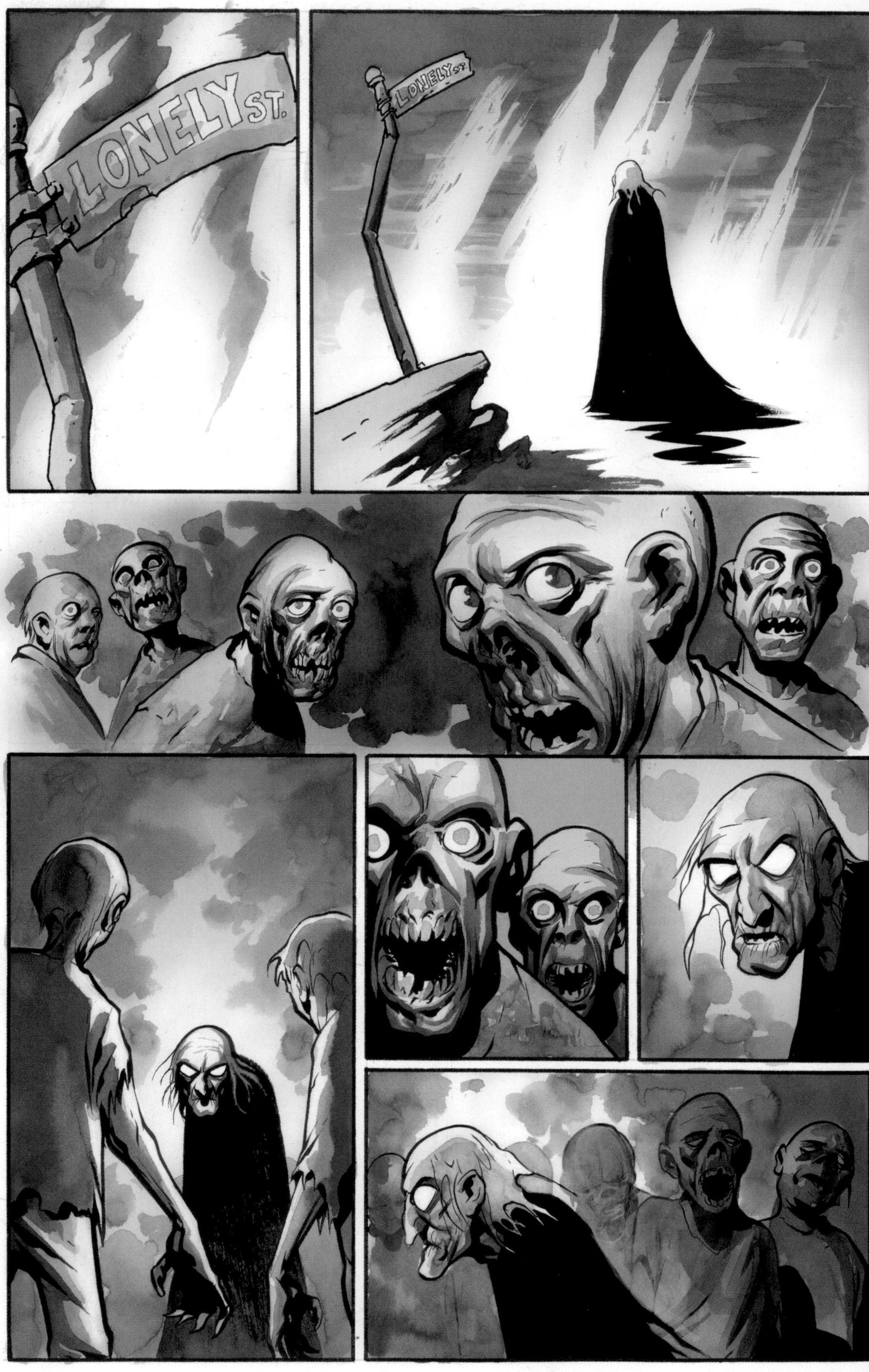
LONELY ST.
LONELY ST.

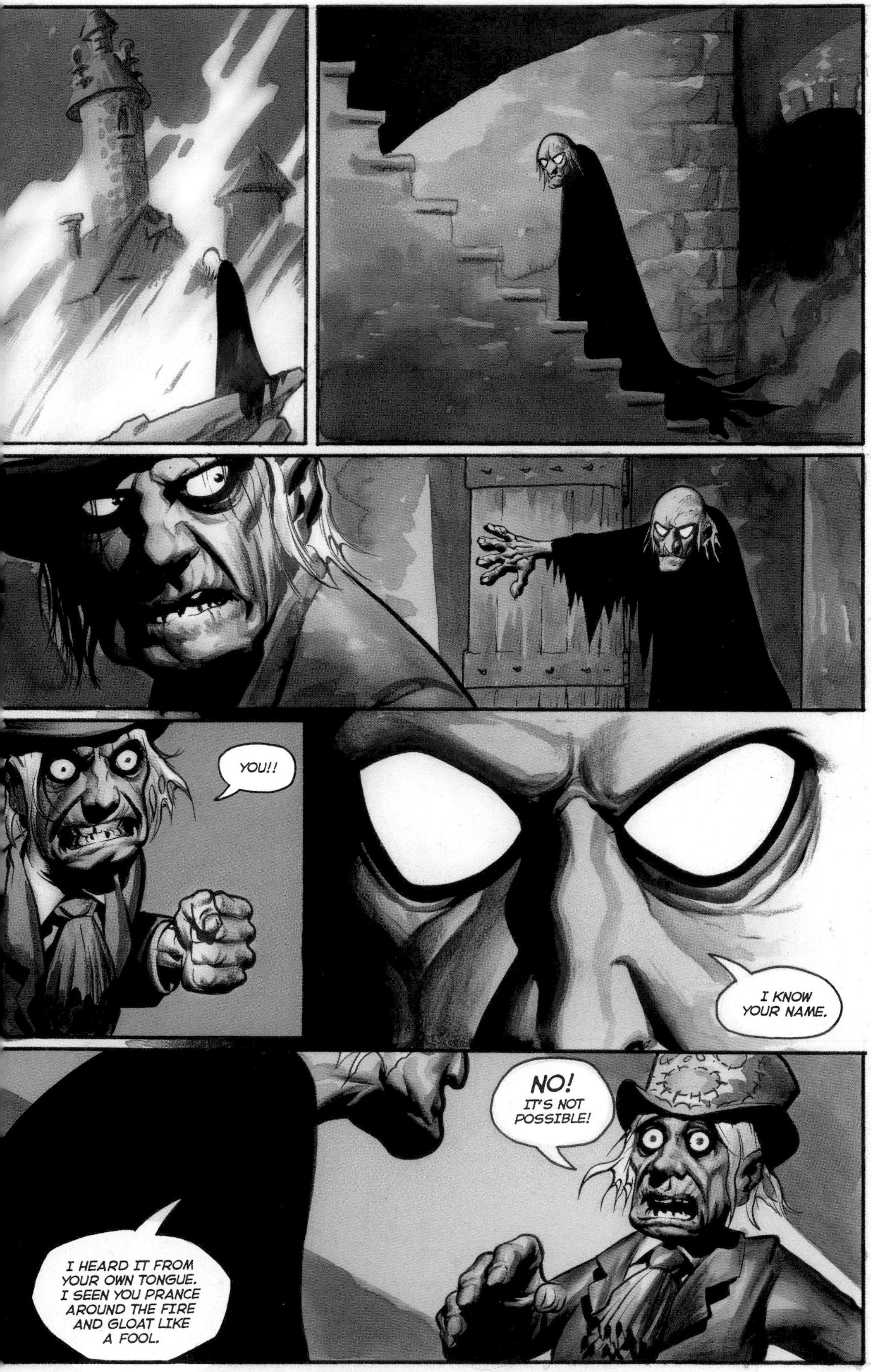
YOU!!
I KNOW YOUR NAME.
NO! IT'S NOT POSSIBLE!
I HEARD IT FROM YOUR OWN TONGUE. I SEEN YOU PRANCE AROUND THE FIRE AND GLOAT LIKE A FOOL.

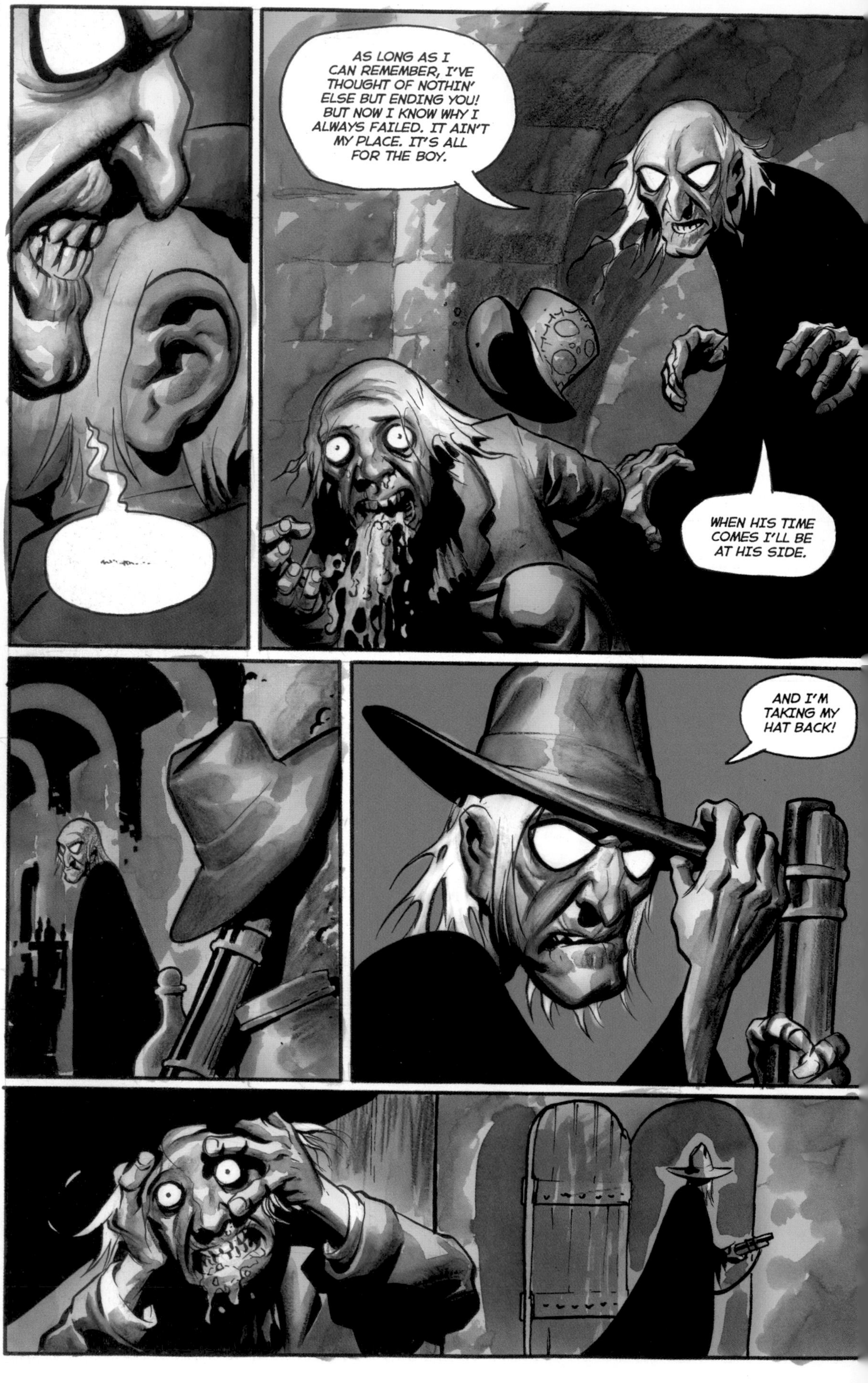
AS LONG AS I CAN REMEMBER, I'VE THOUGHT OF NOTHIN' ELSE BUT ENDING YOU! BUT NOW I KNOW WHY I ALWAYS FAILED. IT AIN'T MY PLACE. IT'S ALL FOR THE BOY.
WHEN HIS TIME COMES I'LL BE AT HIS SIDE.
AND I'M TAKING MY HAT BACK!

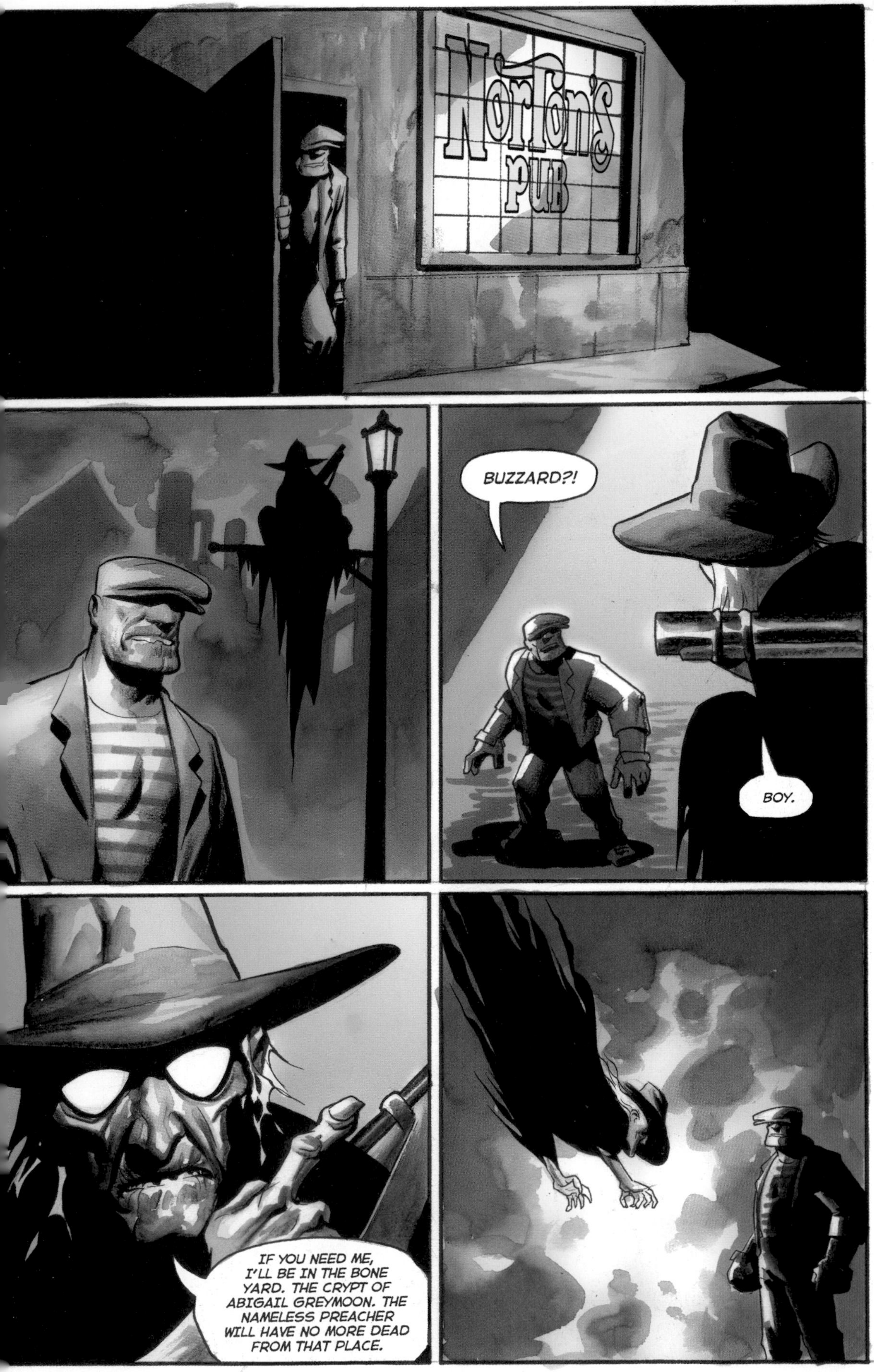
NORTON'S
PUB
BUZZARD?!
BOY.
IF YOU NEED ME, I'LL BE IN THE BONE YARD. THE CRYPT OF ABIGAIL GREYMOON. THE NAMELESS PREACHER WILL HAVE NO MORE DEAD FROM THAT PLACE.

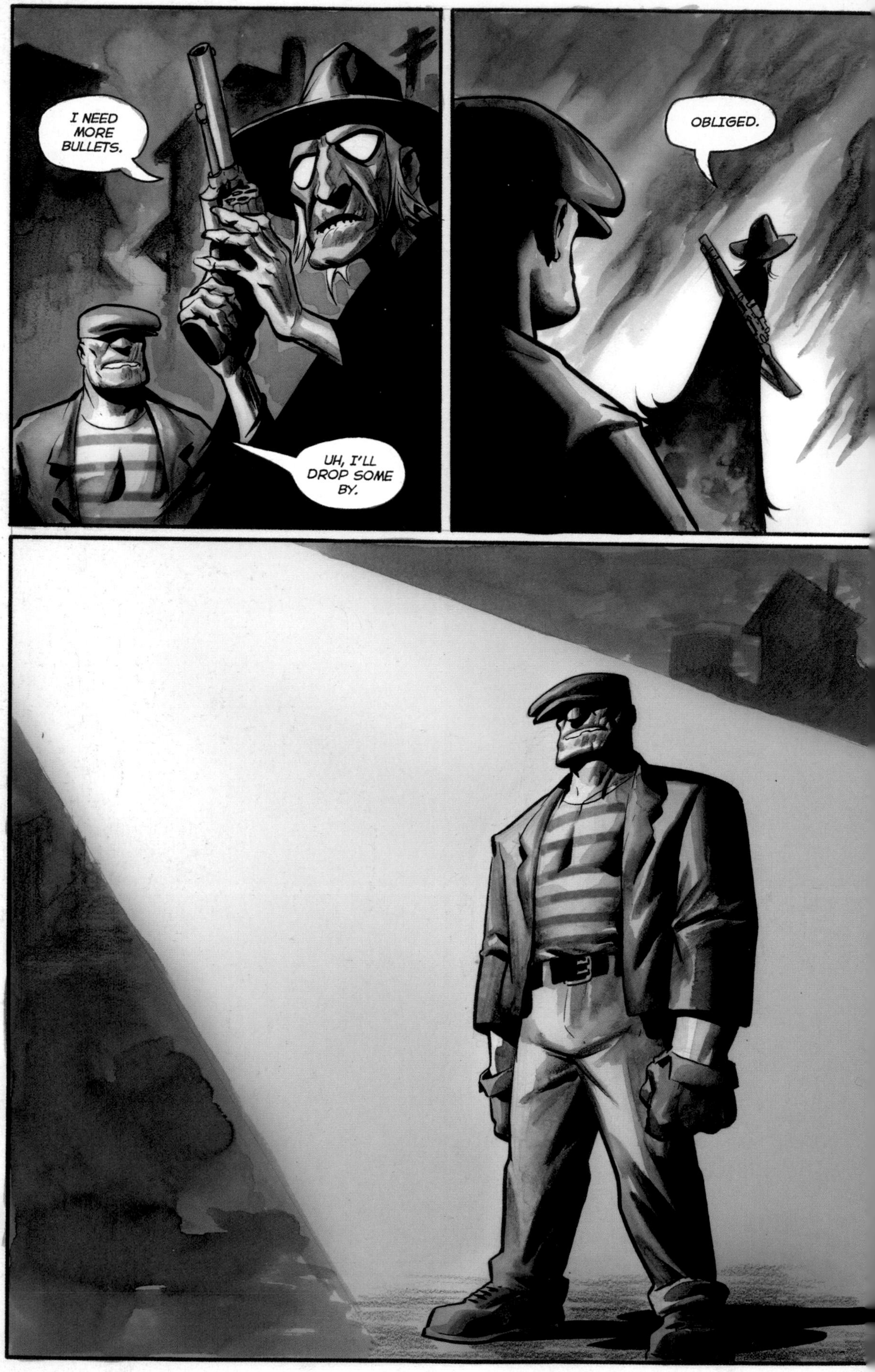
I NEED MORE BULLETS.
UH, I'LL DROP SOME BY.
OBLIGED.

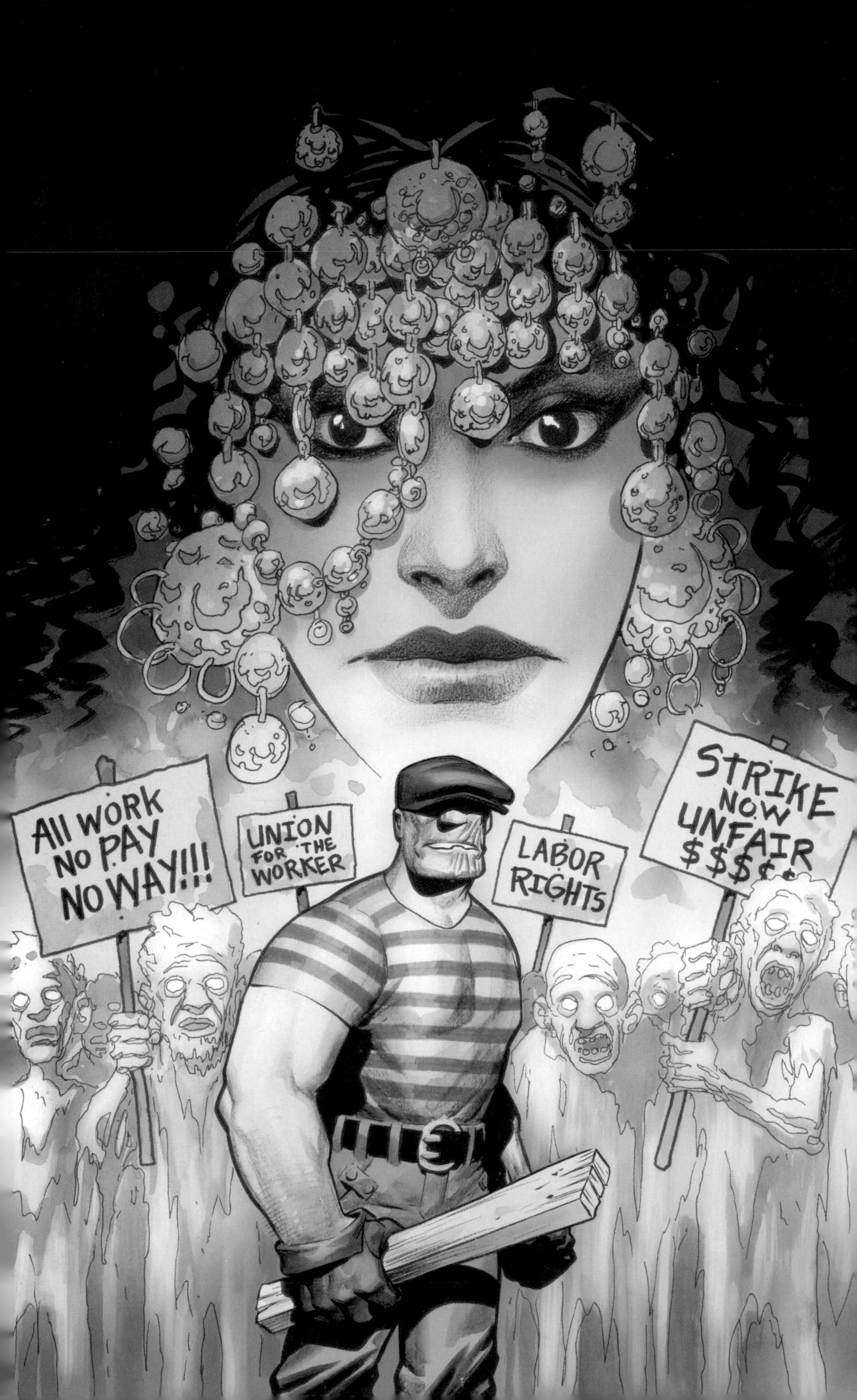
All WORK NO PAY NO WAY!!!
UNION FOR THE WORKER
LABOR RIGHTS
STRIKE NOW UNFAIR $$$¢¢

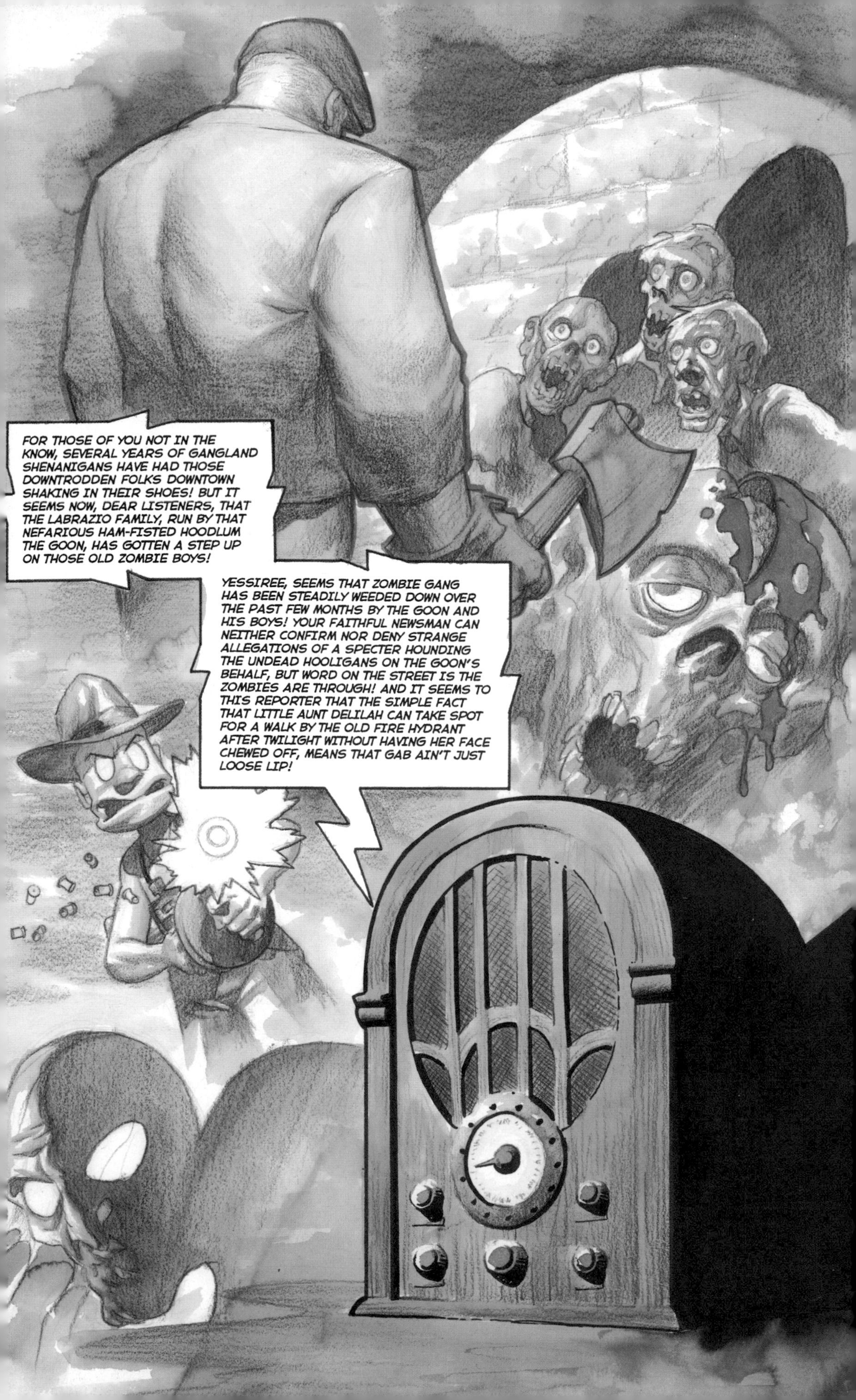
FOR THOSE OF YOU NOT IN THE KNOW, SEVERAL YEARS OF GANGLAND SHENANIGANS HAVE HAD THOSE DOWNTRODDEN FOLKS DOWNTOWN SHAKING IN THEIR SHOES! BUT IT SEEMS NOW, DEAR LISTENERS, THAT THE LABRAZIO FAMILY, RUN BY THAT NEFARIOUS HAM-FISTED HOODLUM THE GOON, HAS GOTTEN A STEP UP ON THOSE OLD ZOMBIE BOYS!
YESSIREE, SEEMS THAT ZOMBIE GANG HAS BEEN STEADILY WEEDED DOWN OVER THE PAST FEW MONTHS BY THE GOON AND HIS BOYS! YOUR FAITHFUL NEWSMAN CAN NEITHER CONFIRM NOR DENY STRANGE ALLEGATIONS OF A SPECTER HOUNDING THE UNDEAD HOOLIGANS ON THE GOON'S BEHALF, BUT WORD ON THE STREET IS THE ZOMBIES ARE THROUGH! AND IT SEEMS TO THIS REPORTER THAT THE SIMPLE FACT THAT LITTLE AUNT DELILAH CAN TAKE SPOT FOR A WALK BY THE OLD FIRE HYDRANT AFTER TWILIGHT WITHOUT HAVING HER FACE CHEWED OFF, MEANS THAT GAB AIN'T JUST LOOSE LIP!

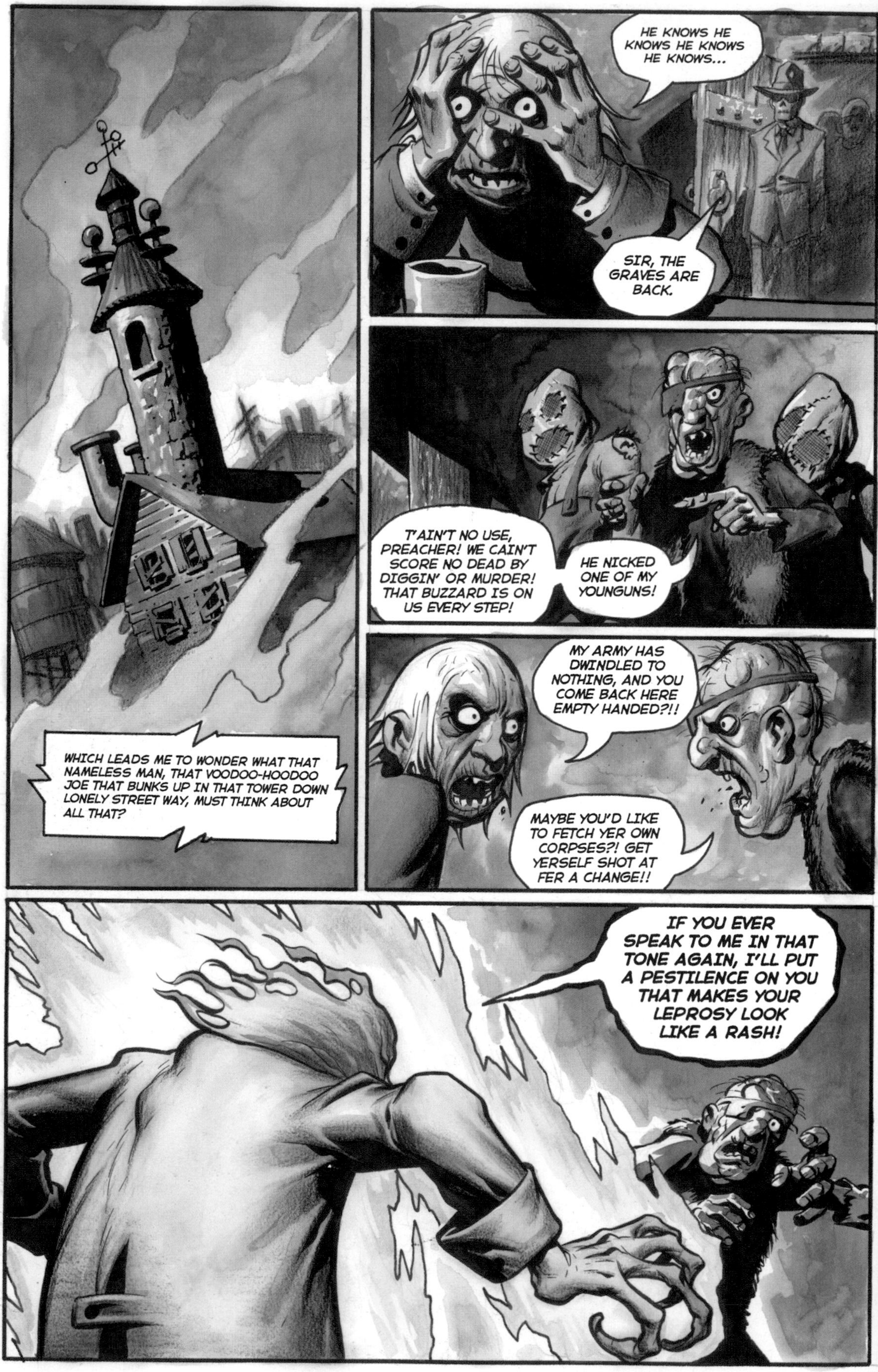
WHICH LEADS ME TO WONDER WHAT THAT NAMELESS MAN, THAT VOODOO-HOODOO JOE THAT BUNKS UP IN THAT TOWER DOWN LONELY STREET WAY, MUST THINK ABOUT ALL THAT?
HE KNOWS HE KNOWS HE KNOWS HE KNOWS...
SIR, THE GRAVES ARE BACK.
T'AIN'T NO USE, PREACHER! WE CAIN'T SCORE NO DEAD BY DIGGIN' OR MURDER! THAT BUZZARD IS ON US EVERY STEP!
HE NICKED ONE OF MY YOUNGUNS!
MY ARMY HAS DWINDLED TO NOTHING, AND YOU COME BACK HERE EMPTY HANDED?!!
MAYBE YOU'D LIKE TO FETCH YER OWN CORPSES?! GET YERSELF SHOT AT FER A CHANGE!!
IF YOU EVER SPEAK TO ME IN THAT TONE AGAIN, I'LL PUT A PESTILENCE ON YOU THAT MAKES YOUR LEPROSY LOOK LIKE A RASH!

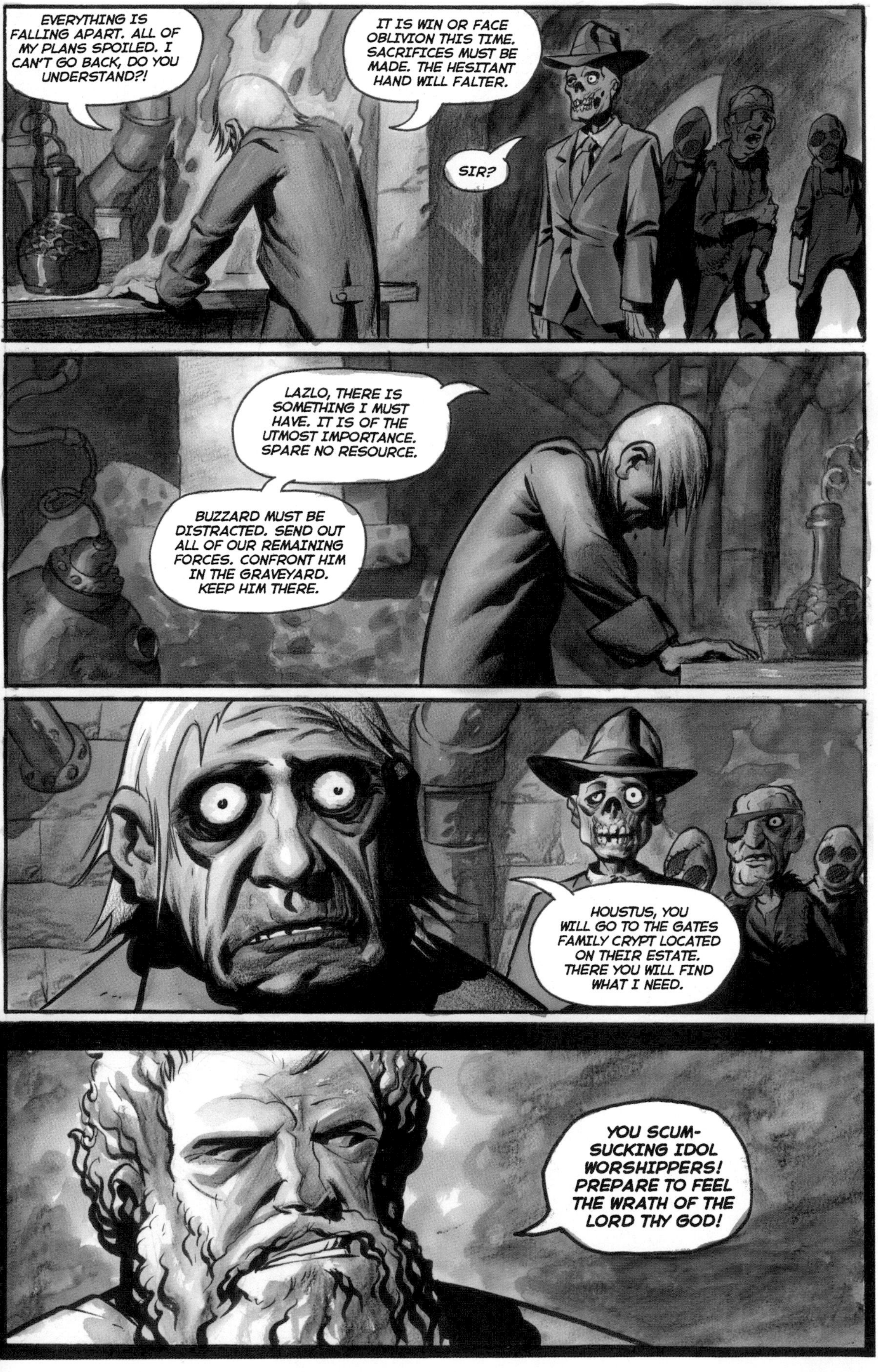
EVERYTHING IS FALLING APART. ALL OF MY PLANS SPOILED. I CAN'T GO BACK, DO YOU UNDERSTAND?!
IT IS WIN OR FACE OBLIVION THIS TIME. SACRIFICES MUST BE MADE. THE HESITANT HAND WILL FALTER.
SIR?
LAZLO, THERE IS SOMETHING I MUST HAVE. IT IS OF THE UTMOST IMPORTANCE. SPARE NO RESOURCE.
BUZZARD MUST BE DISTRACTED. SEND OUT ALL OF OUR REMAINING FORCES. CONFRONT HIM IN THE GRAVEYARD. KEEP HIM THERE.
HOUSTUS, YOU WILL GO TO THE GATES FAMILY CRYPT LOCATED ON THEIR ESTATE. THERE YOU WILL FIND WHAT I NEED.
YOU SCUM-SUCKING IDOL WORSHIPPERS! PREPARE TO FEEL THE WRATH OF THE LORD THY GOD!

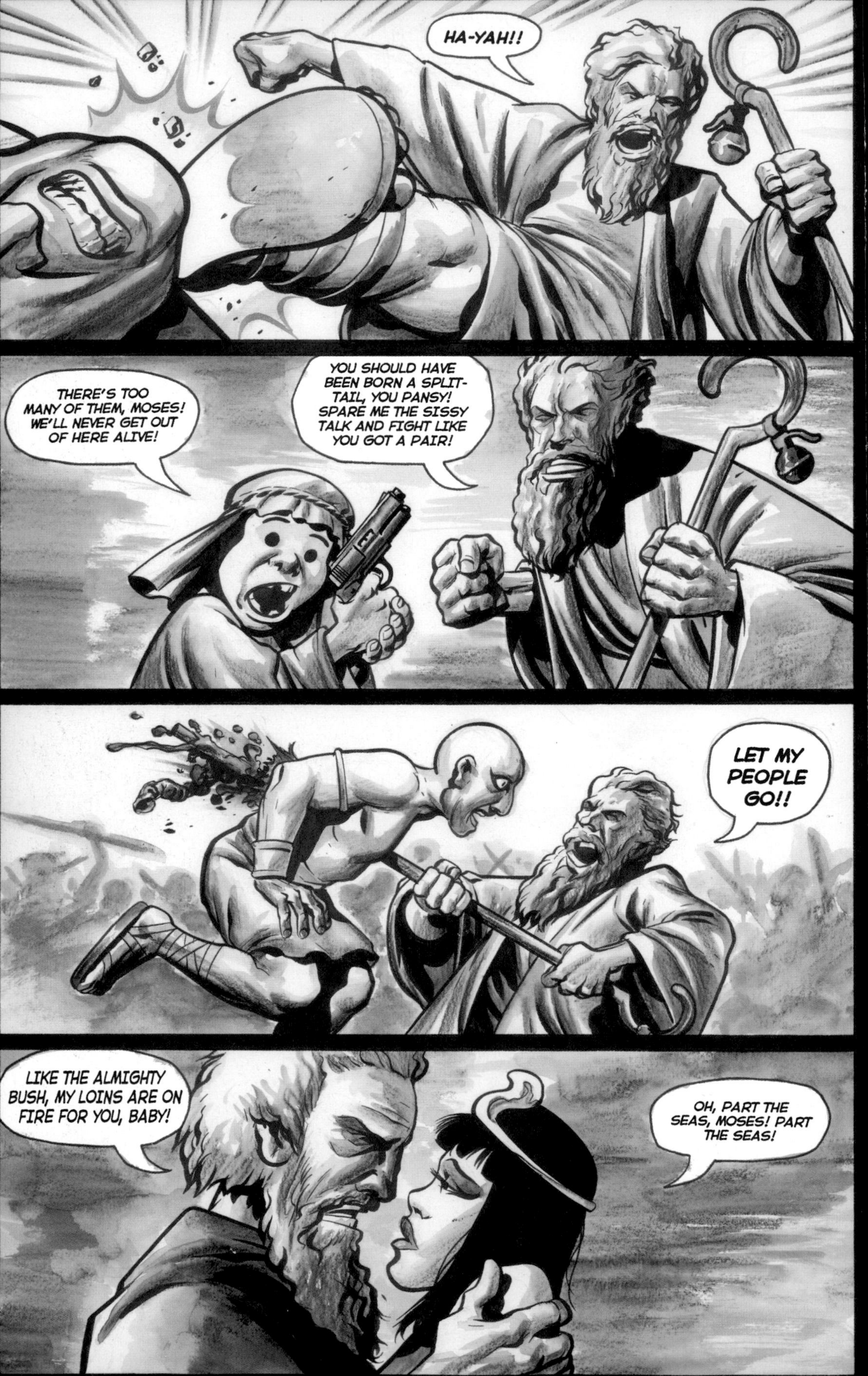
HA-YAH!!
THERE'S TOO MANY OF THEM, MOSES! WE'LL NEVER GET OUT OF HERE ALIVE!
YOU SHOULD HAVE BEEN BORN A SPLIT-TAIL, YOU PANSY! SPARE ME THE SISSY TALK AND FIGHT LIKE YOU GOT A PAIR!
LET MY PEOPLE GO!!
LIKE THE ALMIGHTY BUSH, MY LOINS ARE ON FIRE FOR YOU, BABY!
OH, PART THE SEAS, MOSES! PART THE SEAS!

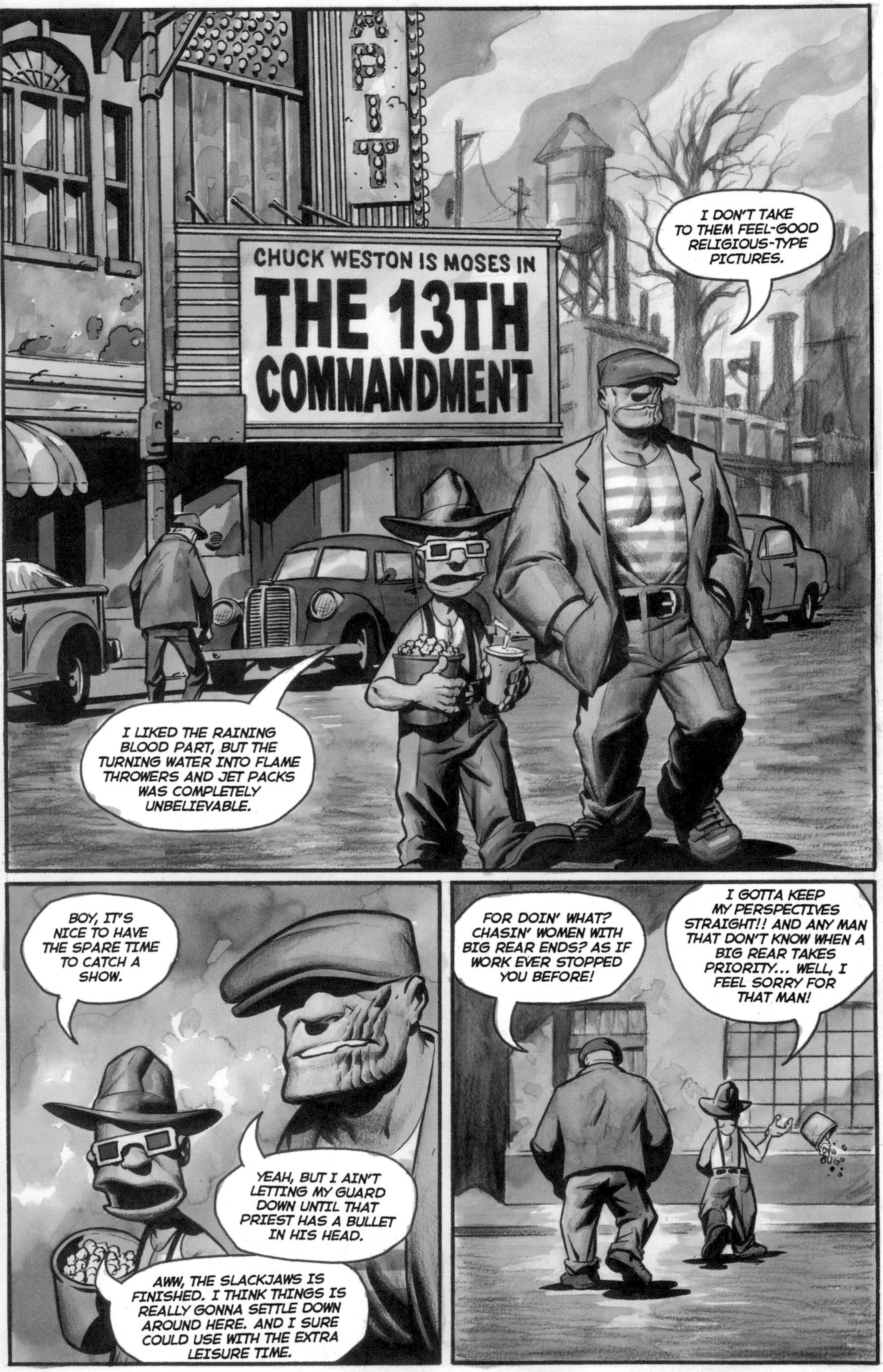
CHUCK WESTON IS MOSES IN
THE 13TH COMMANDMENT
I DON'T TAKE TO THEM FEEL-GOOD RELIGIOUS-TYPE PICTURES.
I LIKED THE RAINING BLOOD PART, BUT THE TURNING WATER INTO FLAME THROWERS AND JET PACKS WAS COMPLETELY UNBELIEVABLE.
BOY, IT'S NICE TO HAVE THE SPARE TIME TO CATCH A SHOW.
YEAH, BUT I AIN'T LETTING MY GUARD DOWN UNTIL THAT PRIEST HAS A BULLET IN HIS HEAD.
AWW, THE SLACKJAWS IS FINISHED. I THINK THINGS IS REALLY GONNA SETTLE DOWN AROUND HERE. AND I SURE COULD USE WITH THE EXTRA LEISURE TIME.
FOR DOIN' WHAT? CHASIN' WOMEN WITH BIG REAR ENDS? AS IF WORK EVER STOPPED YOU BEFORE!
I GOTTA KEEP MY PERSPECTIVES STRAIGHT!! AND ANY MAN THAT DON'T KNOW WHEN A BIG REAR TAKES PRIORITY... WELL, I FEEL SORRY FOR THAT MAN!

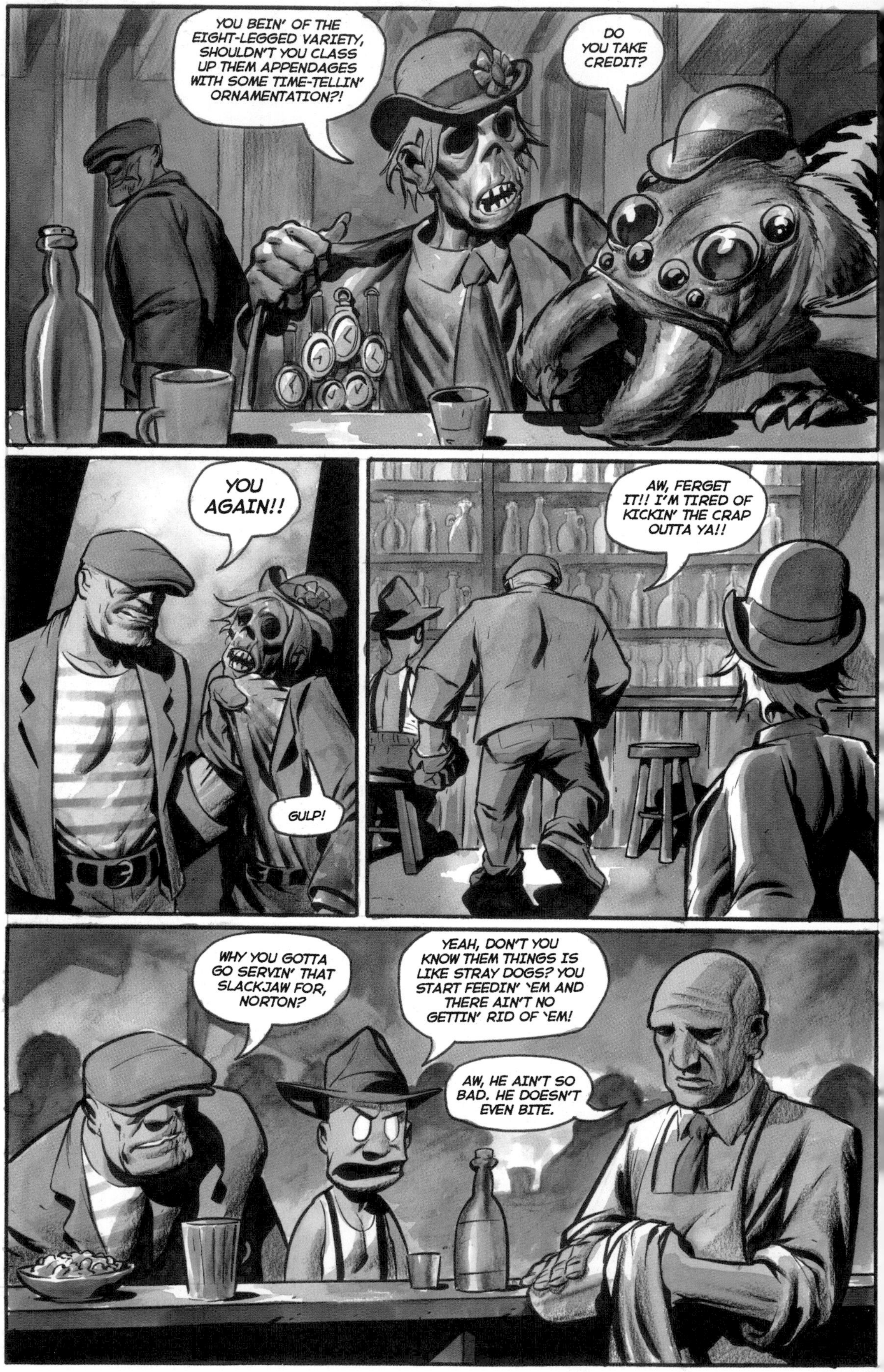
YOU BEIN' OF THE EIGHT-LEGGED VARIETY, SHOULDN'T YOU CLASS UP THEM APPENDAGES WITH SOME TIME-TELLIN' ORNAMENTATION?!
DO YOU TAKE CREDIT?
YOU AGAIN!!
GULP!
AW, FERGET IT!! I'M TIRED OF KICKIN' THE CRAP OUTTA YA!!
WHY YOU GOTTA GO SERVIN' THAT SLACKJAW FOR, NORTON?
YEAH, DON'T YOU KNOW THEM THINGS IS LIKE STRAY DOGS? YOU START FEEDIN' 'EM AND THERE AIN'T NO GETTIN' RID OF 'EM!
AW, HE AIN'T SO BAD. HE DOESN'T EVEN BITE.

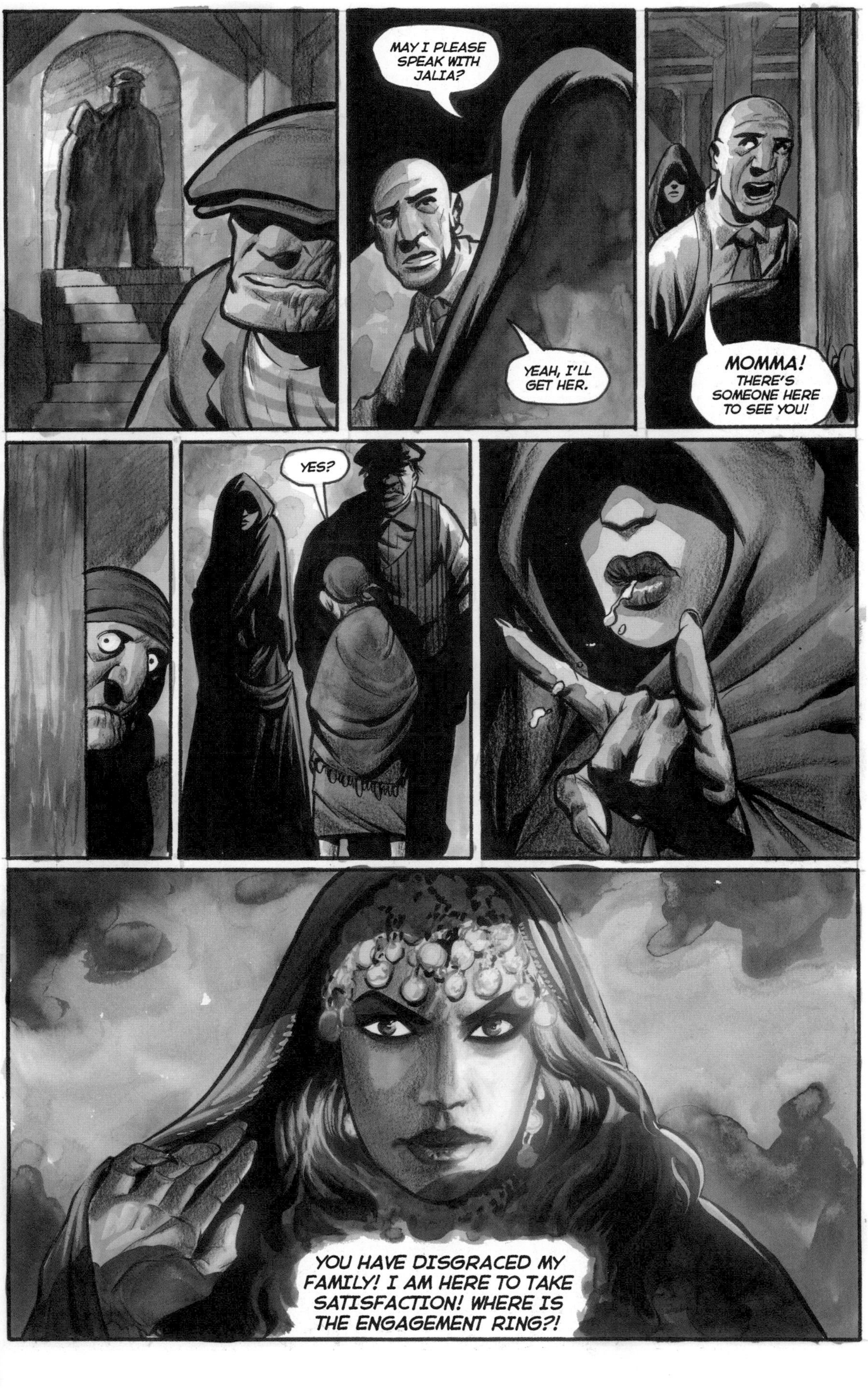
MAY I PLEASE SPEAK WITH JALIA?
YEAH, I'LL GET HER.
MOMMA! THERE'S SOMEONE HERE TO SEE YOU!
YES?
YOU HAVE DISGRACED MY FAMILY! I AM HERE TO TAKE SATISFACTION! WHERE IS THE ENGAGEMENT RING?!

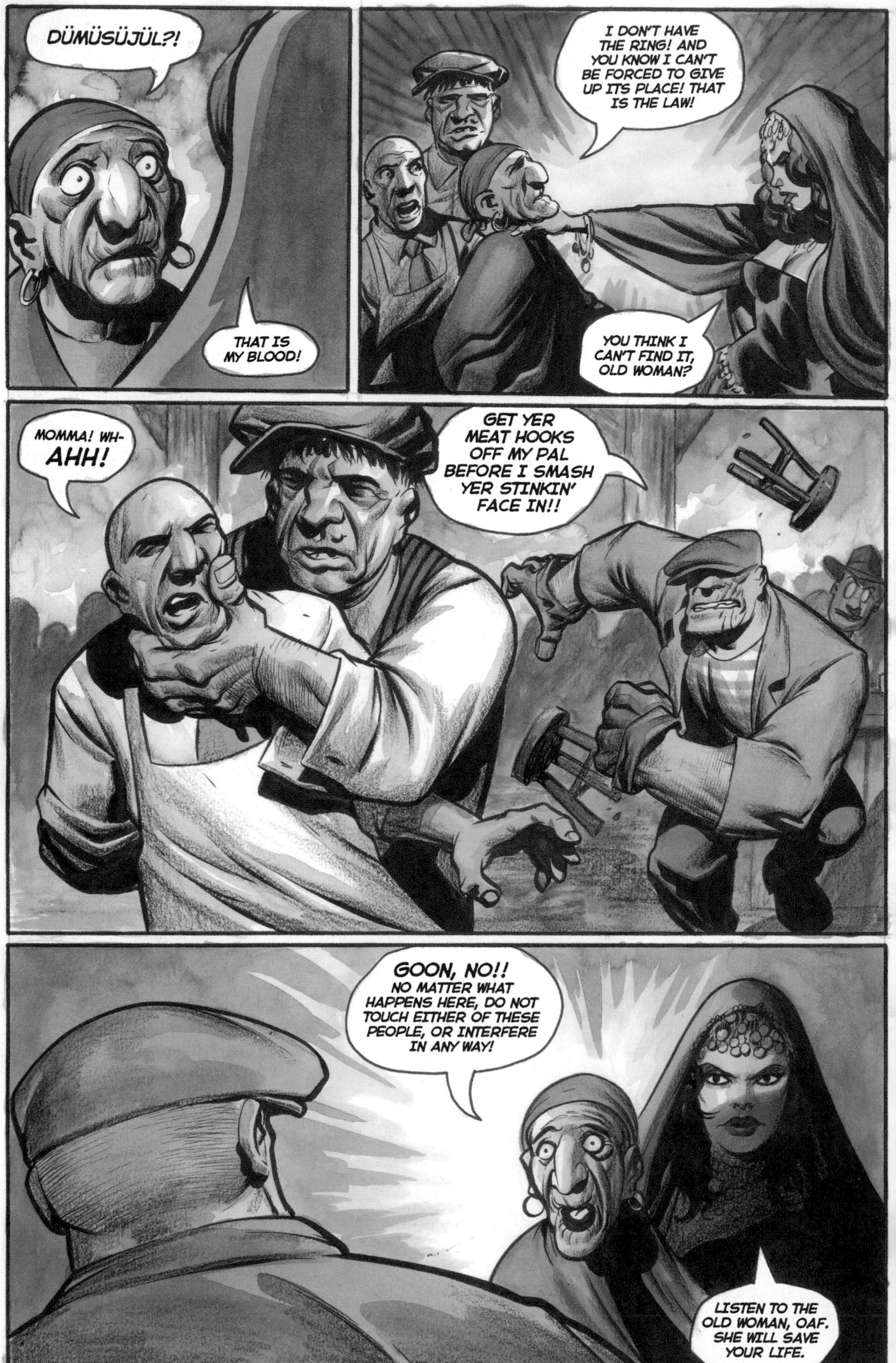
DÜMÜSÜJÜL?!
THAT IS MY BLOOD!
I DON'T HAVE THE RING! AND YOU KNOW I CAN'T BE FORCED TO GIVE UP ITS PLACE! THAT IS THE LAW!
YOU THINK I CAN'T FIND IT, OLD WOMAN?
MOMMA! WH- AHH!
GET YER MEAT HOOKS OFF MY PAL BEFORE I SMASH YER STINKIN' FACE IN!!
GOON, NO!! NO MATTER WHAT HAPPENS HERE, DO NOT TOUCH EITHER OF THESE PEOPLE, OR INTERFERE IN ANY WAY!
LISTEN TO THE OLD WOMAN, OAF. SHE WILL SAVE YOUR LIFE.

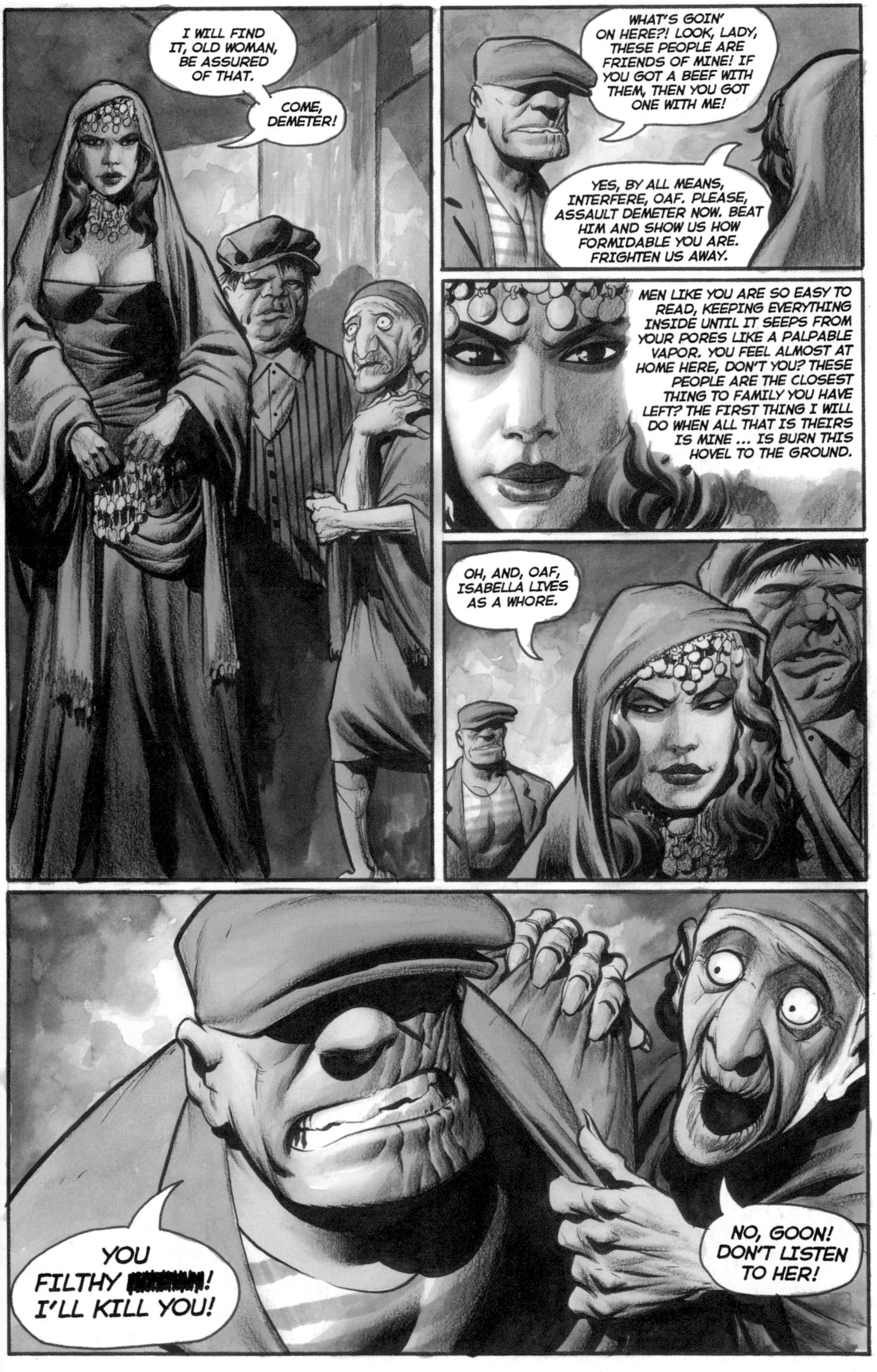
I WILL FIND IT, OLD WOMAN, BE ASSURED OF THAT.
COME, DEMETER!
WHAT'S GOIN' ON HERE?! LOOK, LADY, THESE PEOPLE ARE FRIENDS OF MINE! IF YOU GOT A BEEF WITH THEM, THEN YOU GOT ONE WITH ME!
YES, BY ALL MEANS, INTERFERE, OAF. PLEASE, ASSAULT DEMETER NOW. BEAT HIM AND SHOW US HOW FORMIDABLE YOU ARE. FRIGHTEN US AWAY.
MEN LIKE YOU ARE SO EASY TO READ, KEEPING EVERYTHING INSIDE UNTIL IT SEEPS FROM YOUR PORES LIKE A PALPABLE VAPOR. YOU FEEL ALMOST AT HOME HERE, DON'T YOU? THESE PEOPLE ARE THE CLOSEST THING TO FAMILY YOU HAVE LEFT? THE FIRST THING I WILL DO WHEN ALL THAT IS THEIRS IS MINE ... IS BURN THIS HOVEL TO THE GROUND.
OH, AND, OAF, ISABELLA LIVES AS A WHORE.
YOU FILTHY [redacted]! I'LL KILL YOU!
NO, GOON! DON'T LISTEN TO HER!

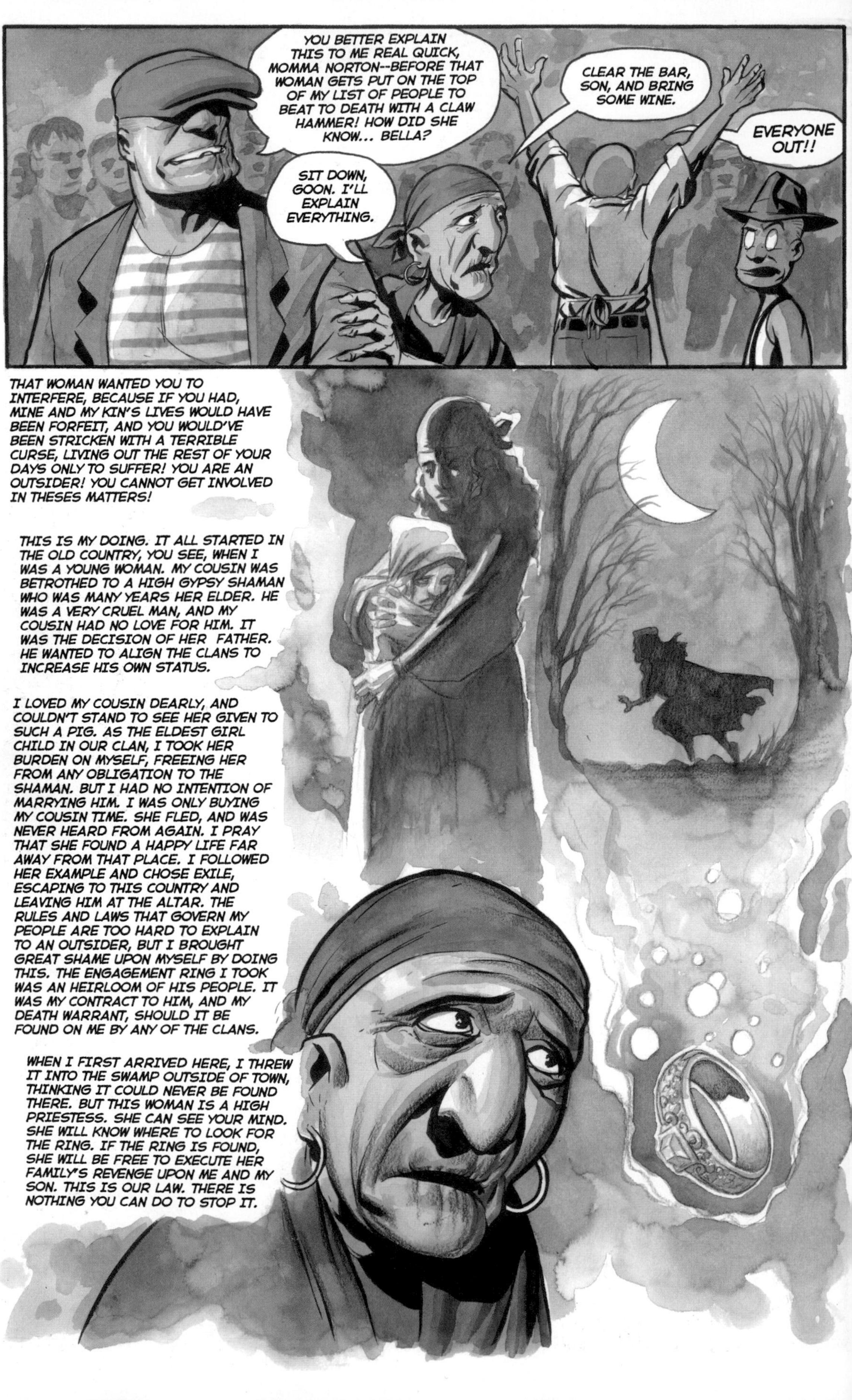
YOU BETTER EXPLAIN THIS TO ME REAL QUICK, MOMMA NORTON--BEFORE THAT WOMAN GETS PUT ON THE TOP OF MY LIST OF PEOPLE TO BEAT TO DEATH WITH A CLAW HAMMER! HOW DID SHE KNOW... BELLA?
SIT DOWN, GOON. I'LL EXPLAIN EVERYTHING.
CLEAR THE BAR, SON, AND BRING SOME WINE.
EVERYONE OUT!!
THAT WOMAN WANTED YOU TO INTERFERE, BECAUSE IF YOU HAD, MINE AND MY KIN'S LIVES WOULD HAVE BEEN FORFEIT, AND YOU WOULD'VE BEEN STRICKEN WITH A TERRIBLE CURSE, LIVING OUT THE REST OF YOUR DAYS ONLY TO SUFFER! YOU ARE AN OUTSIDER! YOU CANNOT GET INVOLVED IN THESES MATTERS!
THIS IS MY DOING. IT ALL STARTED IN THE OLD COUNTRY, YOU SEE, WHEN I WAS A YOUNG WOMAN. MY COUSIN WAS BETROTHED TO A HIGH GYPSY SHAMAN WHO WAS MANY YEARS HER ELDER. HE WAS A VERY CRUEL MAN, AND MY COUSIN HAD NO LOVE FOR HIM. IT WAS THE DECISION OF HER FATHER. HE WANTED TO ALIGN THE CLANS TO INCREASE HIS OWN STATUS.
I LOVED MY COUSIN DEARLY, AND COULDN'T STAND TO SEE HER GIVEN TO SUCH A PIG. AS THE ELDEST GIRL CHILD IN OUR CLAN, I TOOK HER BURDEN ON MYSELF, FREEING HER FROM ANY OBLIGATION TO THE SHAMAN. BUT I HAD NO INTENTION OF MARRYING HIM. I WAS ONLY BUYING MY COUSIN TIME. SHE FLED, AND WAS NEVER HEARD FROM AGAIN. I PRAY THAT SHE FOUND A HAPPY LIFE FAR AWAY FROM THAT PLACE. I FOLLOWED HER EXAMPLE AND CHOSE EXILE, ESCAPING TO THIS COUNTRY AND LEAVING HIM AT THE ALTAR. THE RULES AND LAWS THAT GOVERN MY PEOPLE ARE TOO HARD TO EXPLAIN TO AN OUTSIDER, BUT I BROUGHT GREAT SHAME UPON MYSELF BY DOING THIS. THE ENGAGEMENT RING I TOOK WAS AN HEIRLOOM OF HIS PEOPLE. IT WAS MY CONTRACT TO HIM, AND MY DEATH WARRANT, SHOULD IT BE FOUND ON ME BY ANY OF THE CLANS.
WHEN I FIRST ARRIVED HERE, I THREW IT INTO THE SWAMP OUTSIDE OF TOWN, THINKING IT COULD NEVER BE FOUND THERE. BUT THIS WOMAN IS A HIGH PRIESTESS. SHE CAN SEE YOUR MIND. SHE WILL KNOW WHERE TO LOOK FOR THE RING. IF THE RING IS FOUND, SHE WILL BE FREE TO EXECUTE HER FAMILY'S REVENGE UPON ME AND MY SON. THIS IS OUR LAW. THERE IS NOTHING YOU CAN DO TO STOP IT.

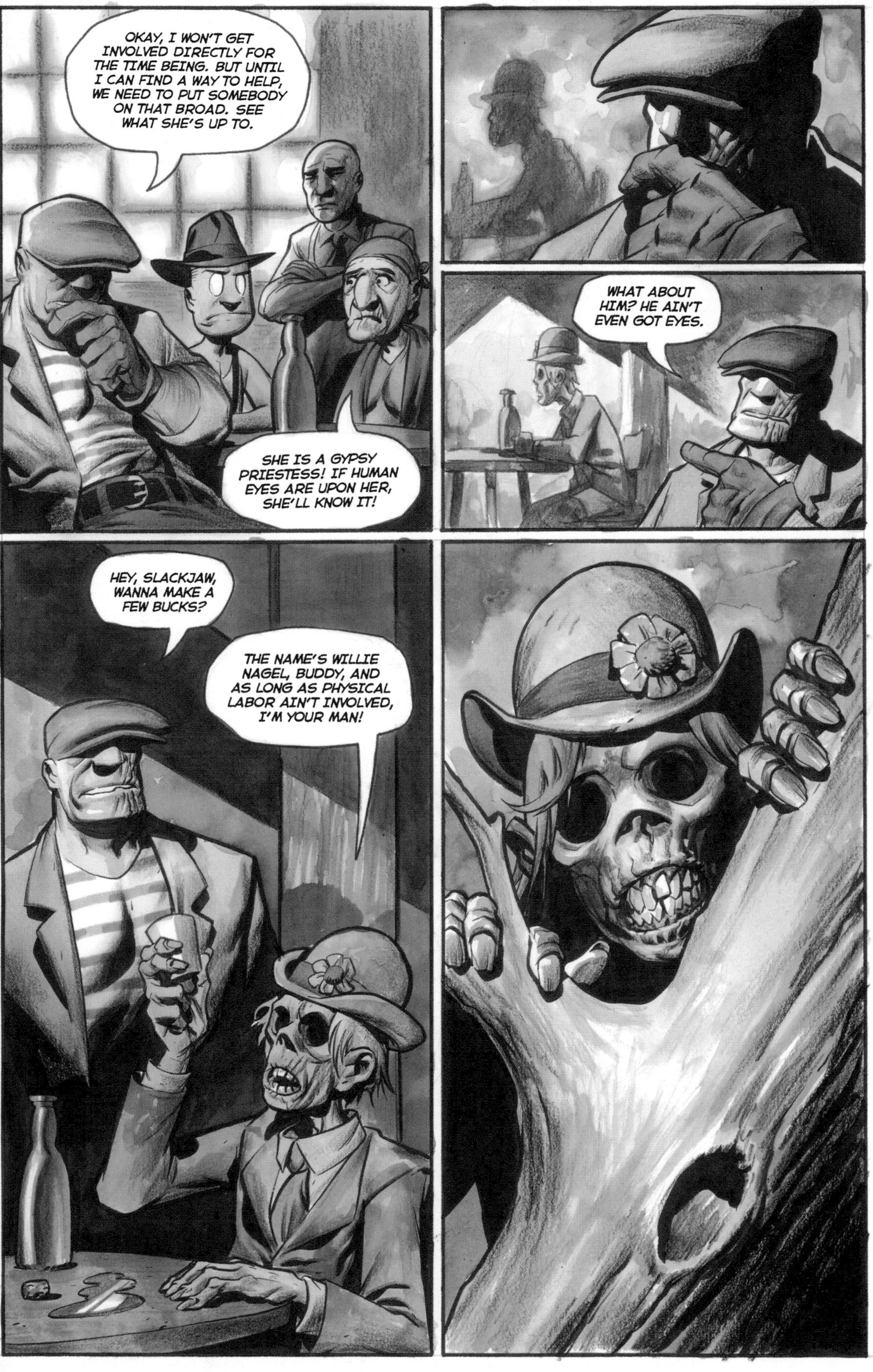
OKAY, I WON'T GET INVOLVED DIRECTLY FOR THE TIME BEING. BUT UNTIL I CAN FIND A WAY TO HELP, WE NEED TO PUT SOMEBODY ON THAT BROAD. SEE WHAT SHE'S UP TO.
SHE IS A GYPSY PRIESTESS! IF HUMAN EYES ARE UPON HER, SHE'LL KNOW IT!
WHAT ABOUT HIM? HE AIN'T EVEN GOT EYES.
HEY, SLACKJAW, WANNA MAKE A FEW BUCKS?
THE NAME'S WILLIE NAGEL, BUDDY, AND AS LONG AS PHYSICAL LABOR AIN'T INVOLVED, I'M YOUR MAN!

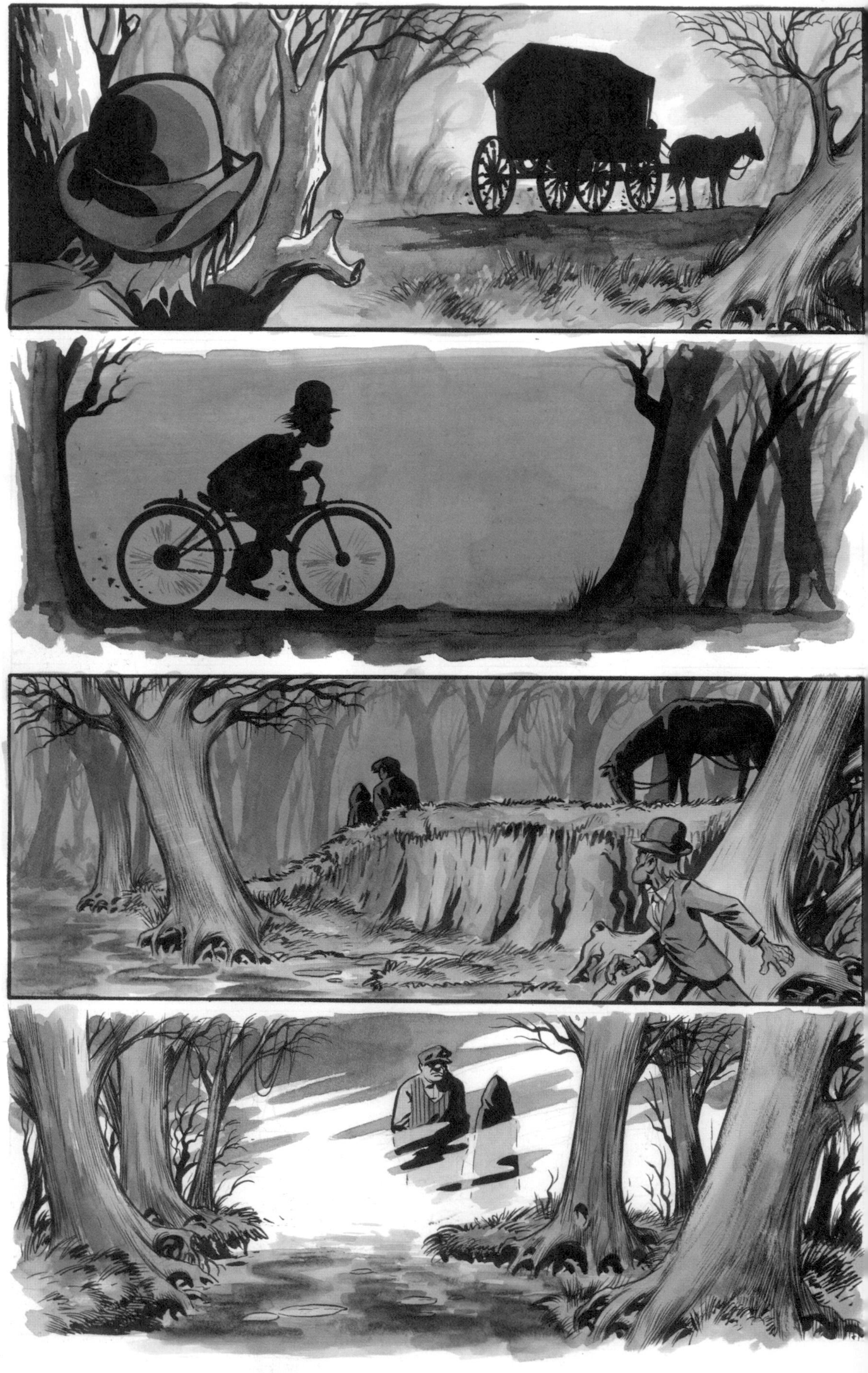

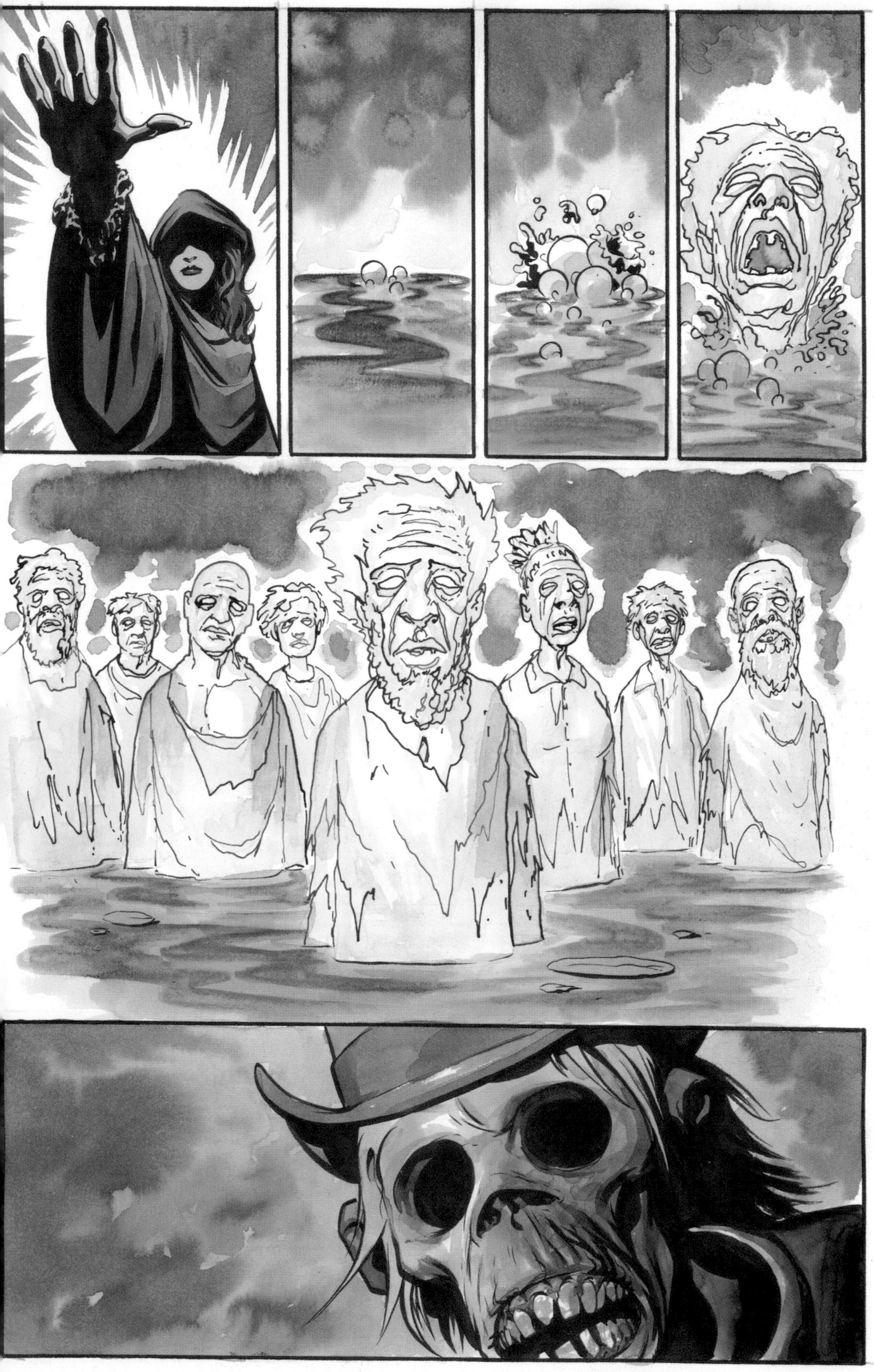

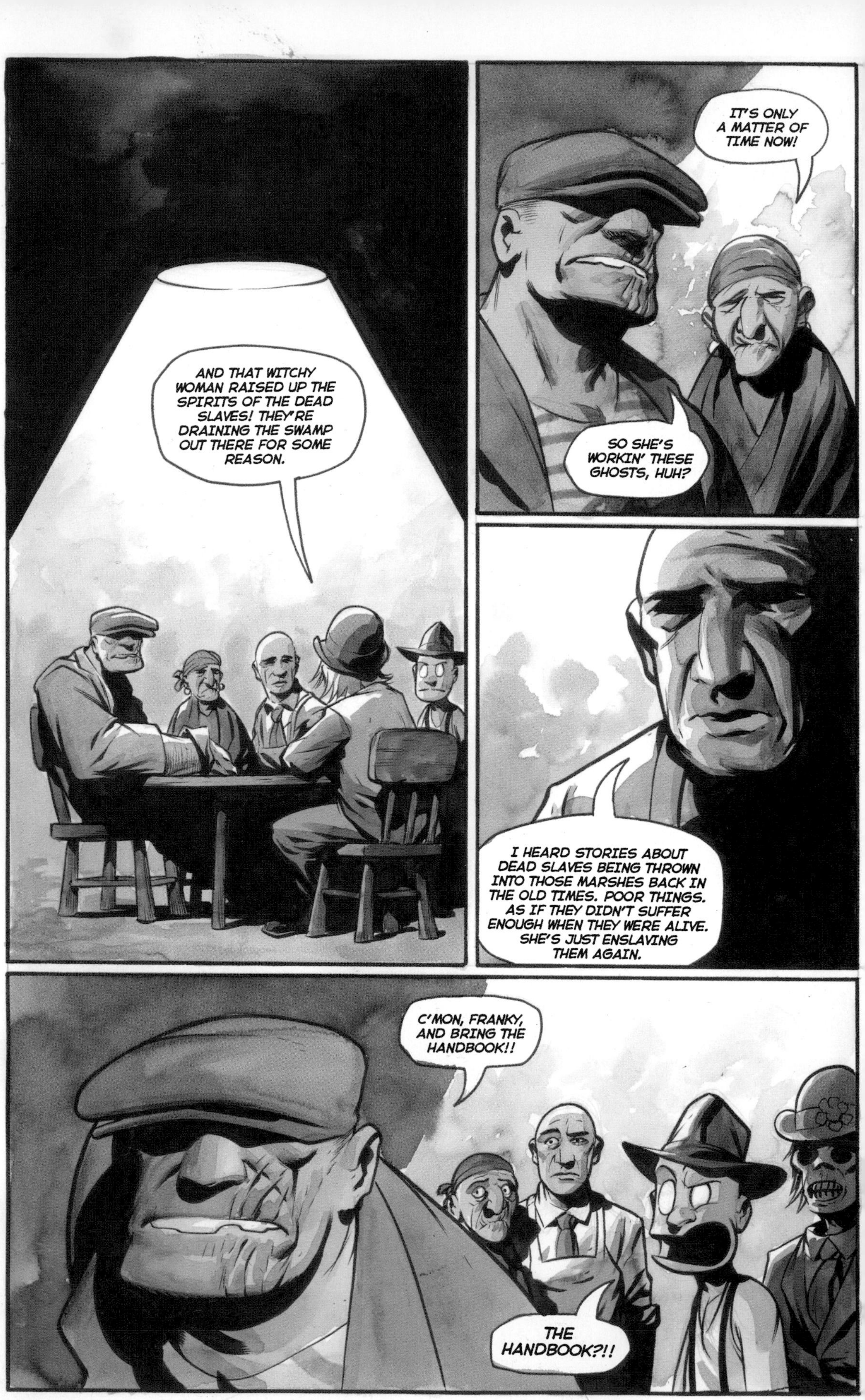
AND THAT WITCHY WOMAN RAISED UP THE SPIRITS OF THE DEAD SLAVES! THEY'RE DRAINING THE SWAMP OUT THERE FOR SOME REASON.
IT'S ONLY A MATTER OF TIME NOW!
SO SHE'S WORKIN' THESE GHOSTS, HUH?
I HEARD STORIES ABOUT DEAD SLAVES BEING THROWN INTO THOSE MARSHES BACK IN THE OLD TIMES. POOR THINGS. AS IF THEY DIDN'T SUFFER ENOUGH WHEN THEY WERE ALIVE. SHE'S JUST ENSLAVING THEM AGAIN.
C'MON, FRANKY, AND BRING THE HANDBOOK!!
THE HANDBOOK?!!

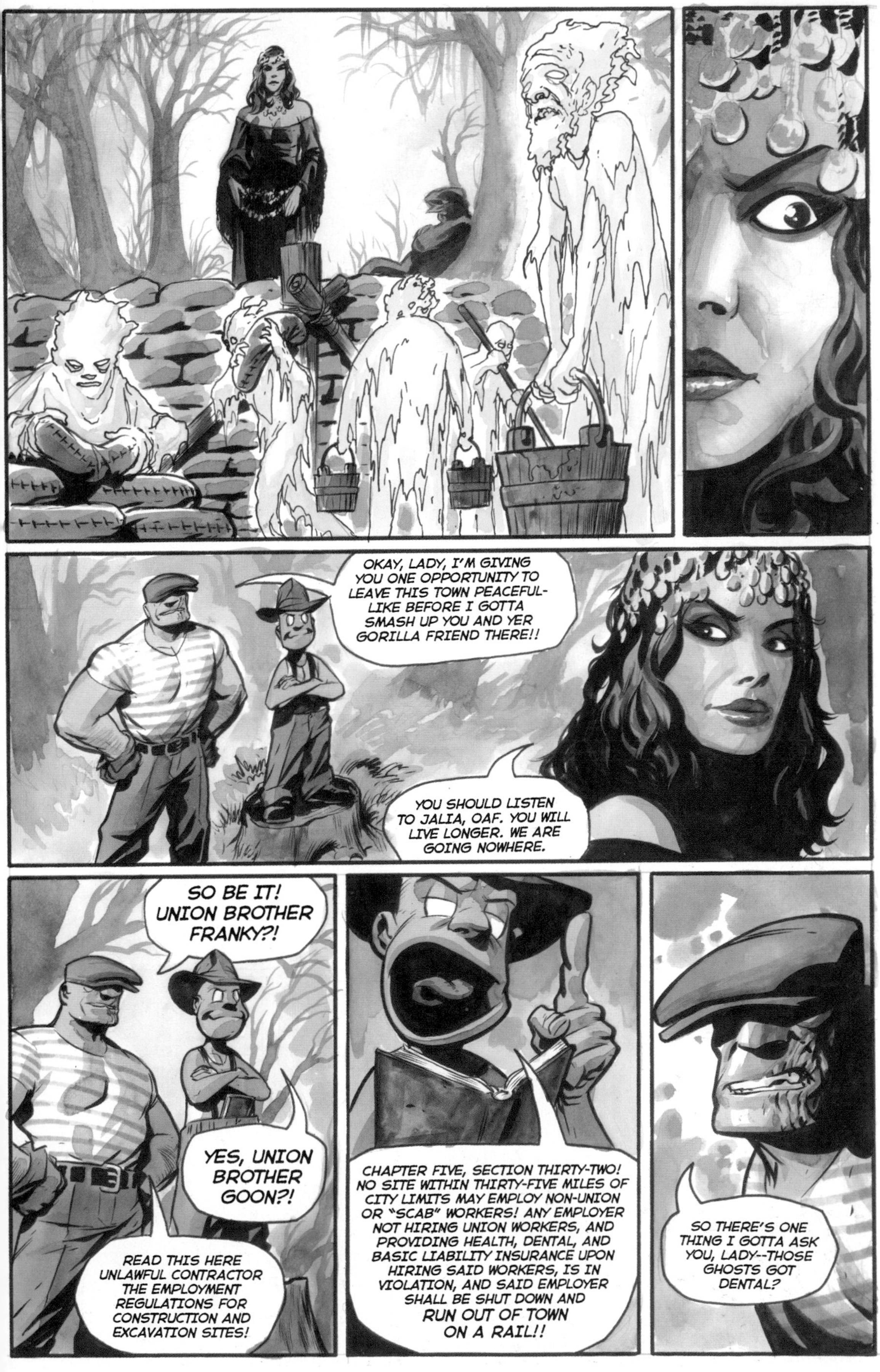
OKAY, LADY, I'M GIVING YOU ONE OPPORTUNITY TO LEAVE THIS TOWN PEACEFUL-LIKE BEFORE I GOTTA SMASH UP YOU AND YER GORILLA FRIEND THERE!!
YOU SHOULD LISTEN TO JALIA, OAF. YOU WILL LIVE LONGER. WE ARE GOING NOWHERE.
SO BE IT! UNION BROTHER FRANKY?!
YES, UNION BROTHER GOON?!
READ THIS HERE UNLAWFUL CONTRACTOR THE EMPLOYMENT REGULATIONS FOR CONSTRUCTION AND EXCAVATION SITES!
CHAPTER FIVE, SECTION THIRTY-TWO! NO SITE WITHIN THIRTY-FIVE MILES OF CITY LIMITS MAY EMPLOY NON-UNION OR "SCAB" WORKERS! ANY EMPLOYER NOT HIRING UNION WORKERS, AND PROVIDING HEALTH, DENTAL, AND BASIC LIABILITY INSURANCE UPON HIRING SAID WORKERS, IS IN VIOLATION, AND SAID EMPLOYER SHALL BE SHUT DOWN AND RUN OUT OF TOWN ON A RAIL!!
SO THERE'S ONE THING I GOTTA ASK YOU, LADY--THOSE GHOSTS GOT DENTAL?

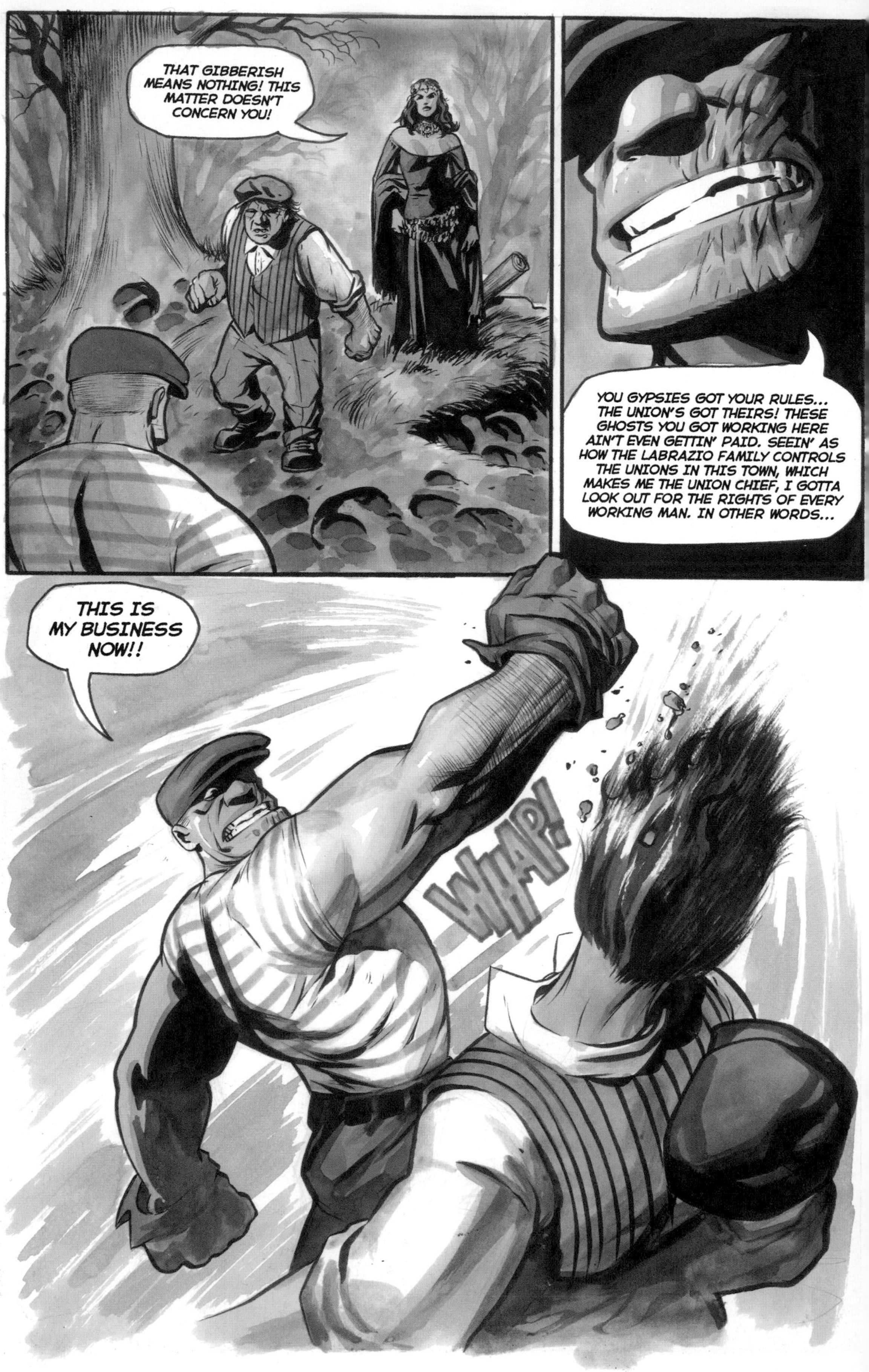
THAT GIBBERISH MEANS NOTHING! THIS MATTER DOESN'T CONCERN YOU!
YOU GYPSIES GOT YOUR RULES... THE UNION'S GOT THEIRS! THESE GHOSTS YOU GOT WORKING HERE AIN'T EVEN GETTIN' PAID. SEEIN' AS HOW THE LABRAZIO FAMILY CONTROLS THE UNIONS IN THIS TOWN, WHICH MAKES ME THE UNION CHIEF, I GOTTA LOOK OUT FOR THE RIGHTS OF EVERY WORKING MAN. IN OTHER WORDS...
THIS IS MY BUSINESS NOW!!
WHAP!

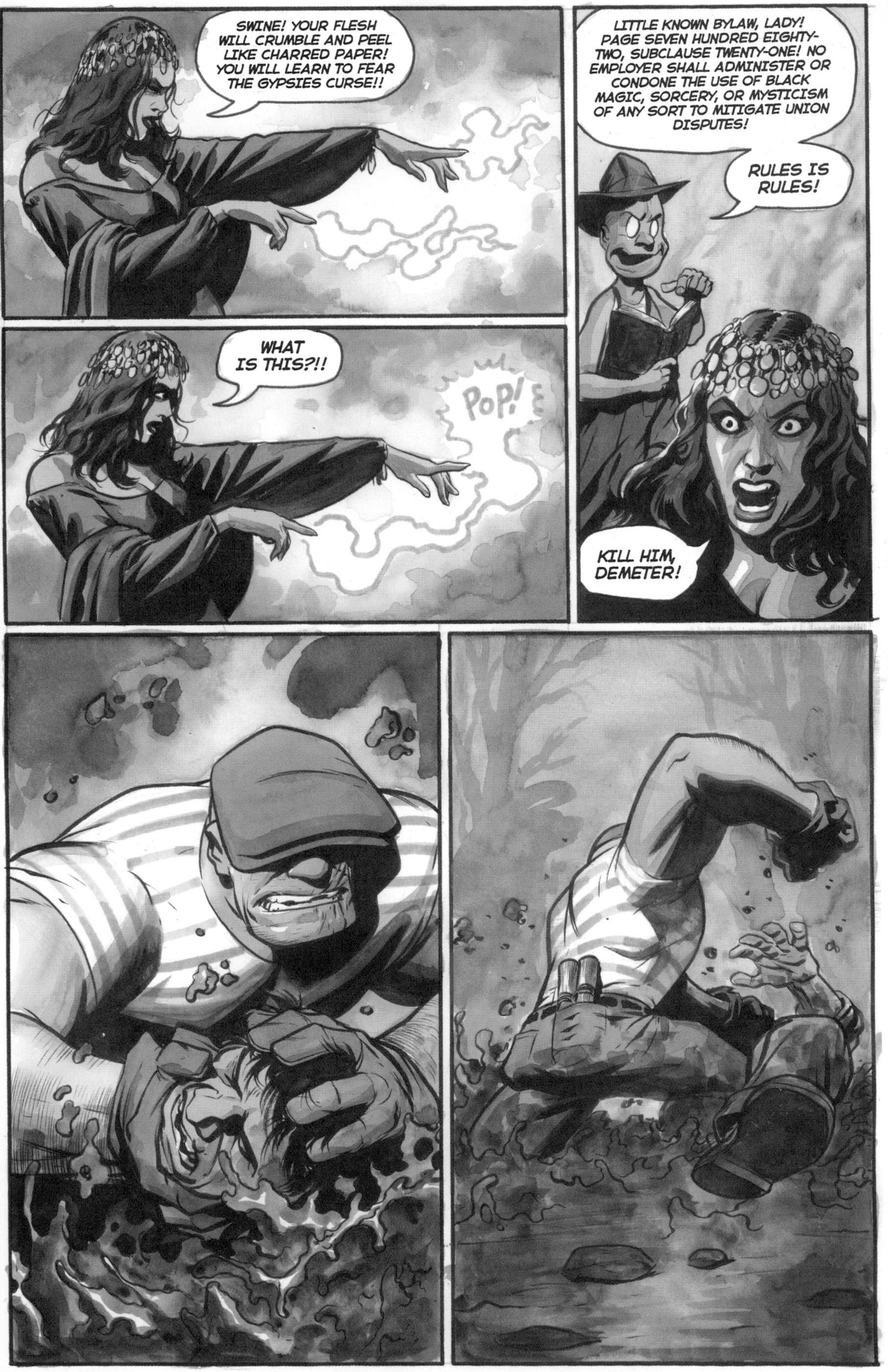
SWINE! YOUR FLESH WILL CRUMBLE AND PEEL LIKE CHARRED PAPER! YOU WILL LEARN TO FEAR THE GYPSIES CURSE!!
LITTLE KNOWN BYLAW, LADY! PAGE SEVEN HUNDRED EIGHTY-TWO, SUBCLAUSE TWENTY-ONE! NO EMPLOYER SHALL ADMINISTER OR CONDONE THE USE OF BLACK MAGIC, SORCERY, OR MYSTICISM OF ANY SORT TO MITIGATE UNION DISPUTES!
RULES IS RULES!
WHAT IS THIS?!!
POP!
KILL HIM, DEMETER!

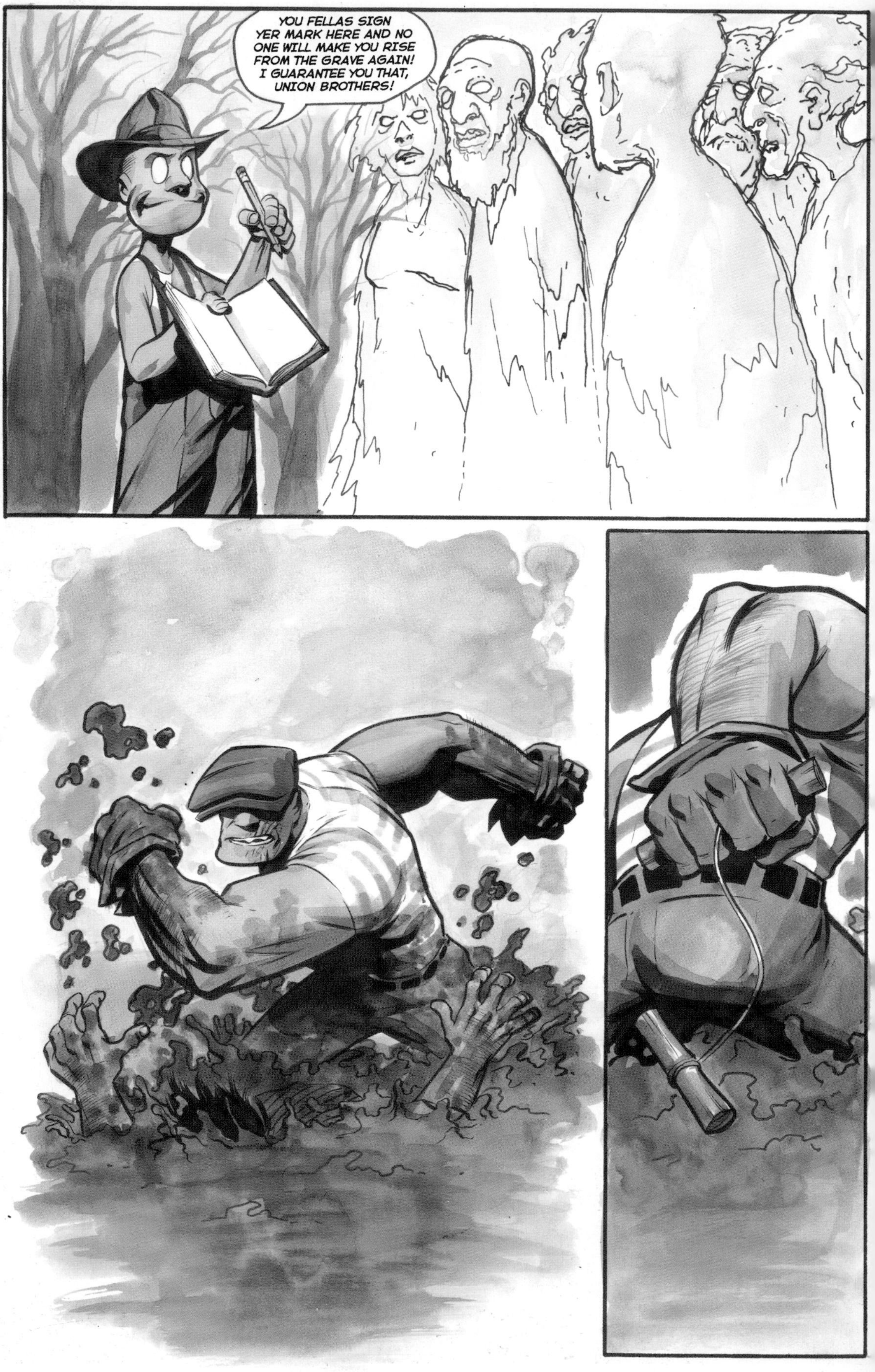
YOU FELLAS SIGN YER MARK HERE AND NO ONE WILL MAKE YOU RISE FROM THE GRAVE AGAIN! I GUARANTEE YOU THAT, UNION BROTHERS!

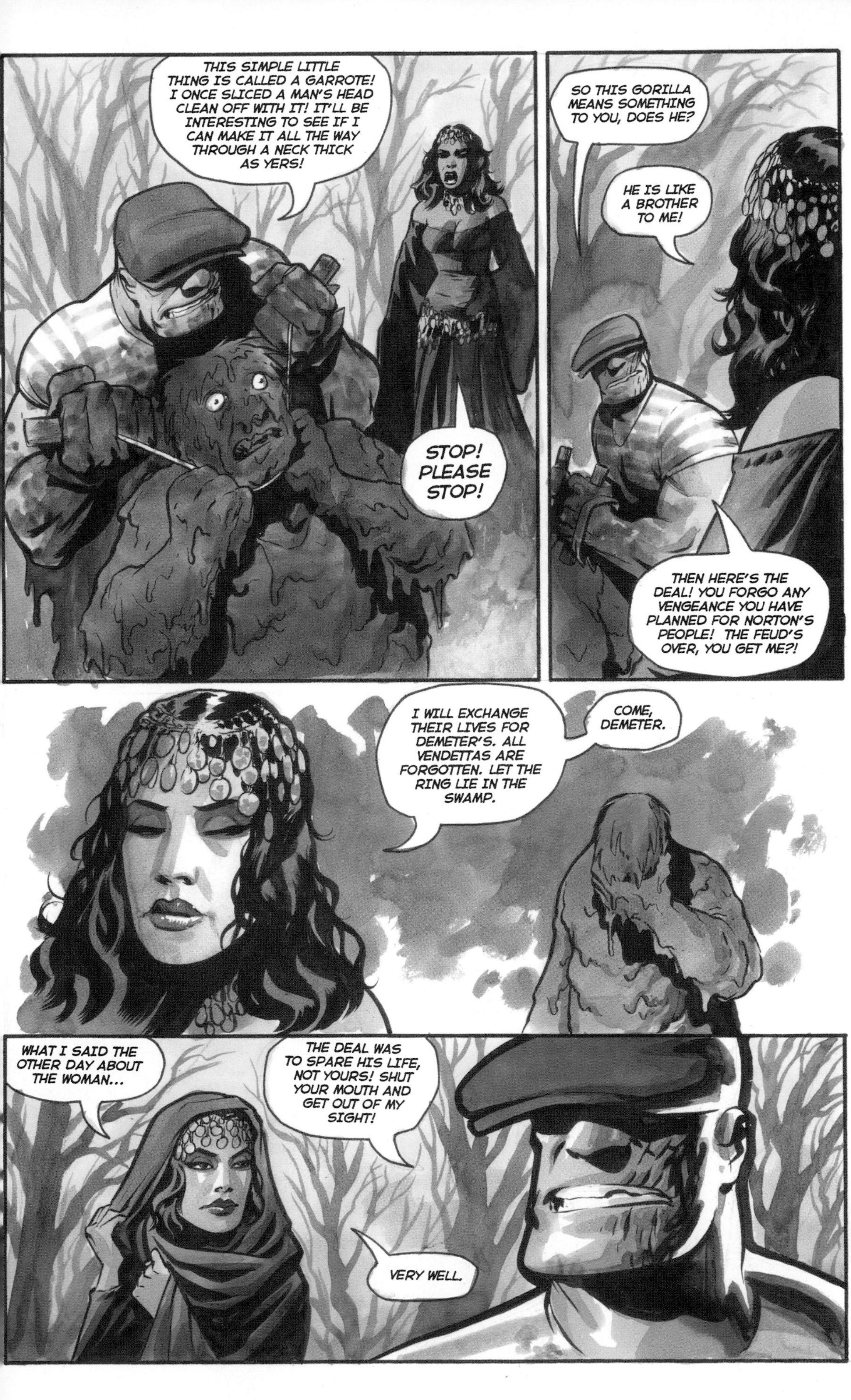
THIS SIMPLE LITTLE THING IS CALLED A GARROTE! I ONCE SLICED A MAN'S HEAD CLEAN OFF WITH IT! IT'LL BE INTERESTING TO SEE IF I CAN MAKE IT ALL THE WAY THROUGH A NECK THICK AS YERS!
STOP! PLEASE STOP!
SO THIS GORILLA MEANS SOMETHING TO YOU, DOES HE?
HE IS LIKE A BROTHER TO ME!
THEN HERE'S THE DEAL! YOU FORGO ANY VENGEANCE YOU HAVE PLANNED FOR NORTON'S PEOPLE! THE FEUD'S OVER, YOU GET ME?!
I WILL EXCHANGE THEIR LIVES FOR DEMETER'S. ALL VENDETTAS ARE FORGOTTEN. LET THE RING LIE IN THE SWAMP.
COME, DEMETER.
WHAT I SAID THE OTHER DAY ABOUT THE WOMAN...
THE DEAL WAS TO SPARE HIS LIFE, NOT YOURS! SHUT YOUR MOUTH AND GET OUT OF MY SIGHT!
VERY WELL.

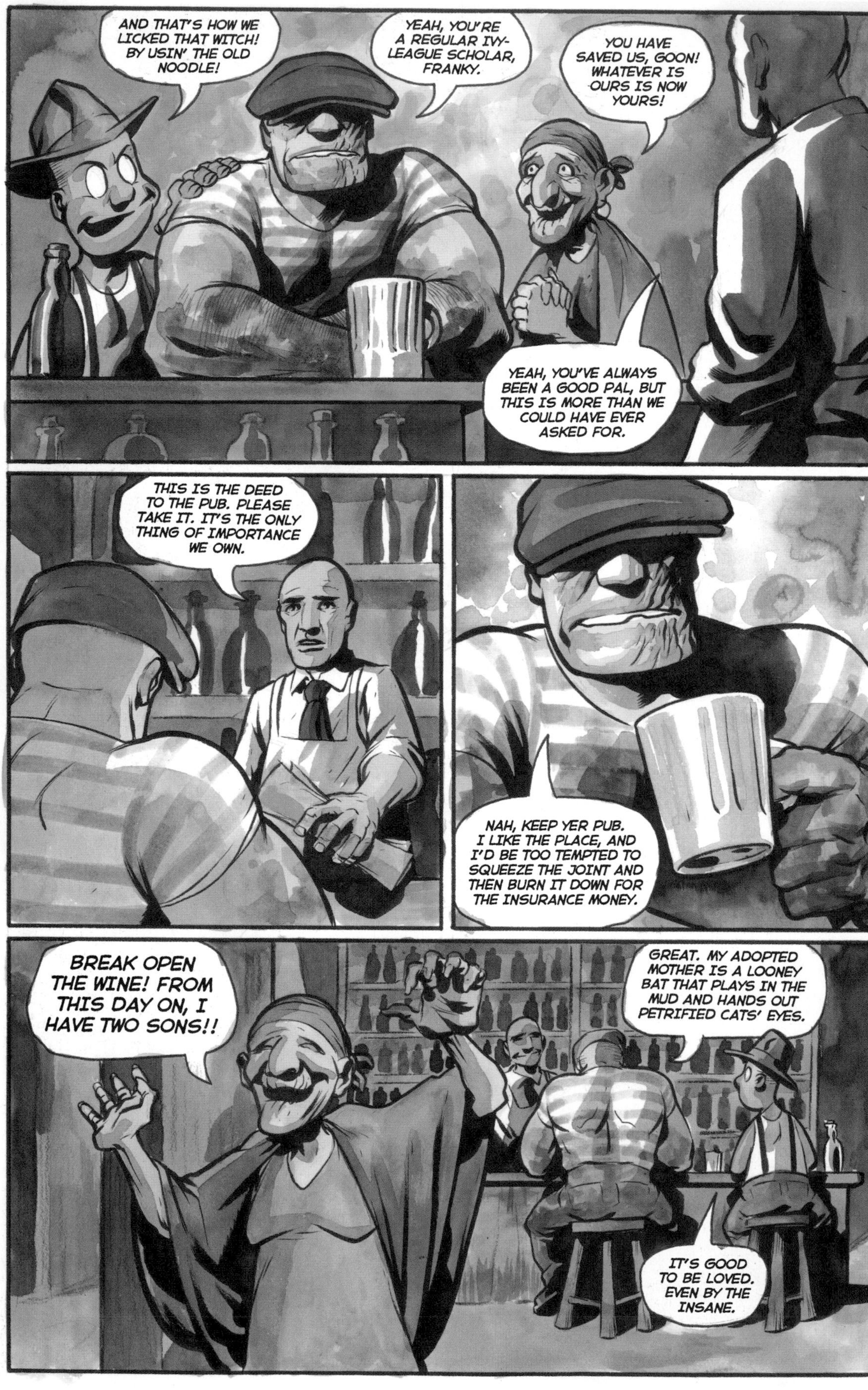
AND THAT'S HOW WE LICKED THAT WITCH! BY USIN' THE OLD NOODLE!
YEAH, YOU'RE A REGULAR IVY-LEAGUE SCHOLAR, FRANKY.
YOU HAVE SAVED US, GOON! WHATEVER IS OURS IS NOW YOURS!
YEAH, YOU'VE ALWAYS BEEN A GOOD PAL, BUT THIS IS MORE THAN WE COULD HAVE EVER ASKED FOR.
THIS IS THE DEED TO THE PUB. PLEASE TAKE IT. IT'S THE ONLY THING OF IMPORTANCE WE OWN.
NAH, KEEP YER PUB. I LIKE THE PLACE, AND I'D BE TOO TEMPTED TO SQUEEZE THE JOINT AND THEN BURN IT DOWN FOR THE INSURANCE MONEY.
BREAK OPEN THE WINE! FROM THIS DAY ON, I HAVE TWO SONS!!
GREAT. MY ADOPTED MOTHER IS A LOONEY BAT THAT PLAYS IN THE MUD AND HANDS OUT PETRIFIED CATS' EYES.
IT'S GOOD TO BE LOVED. EVEN BY THE INSANE.

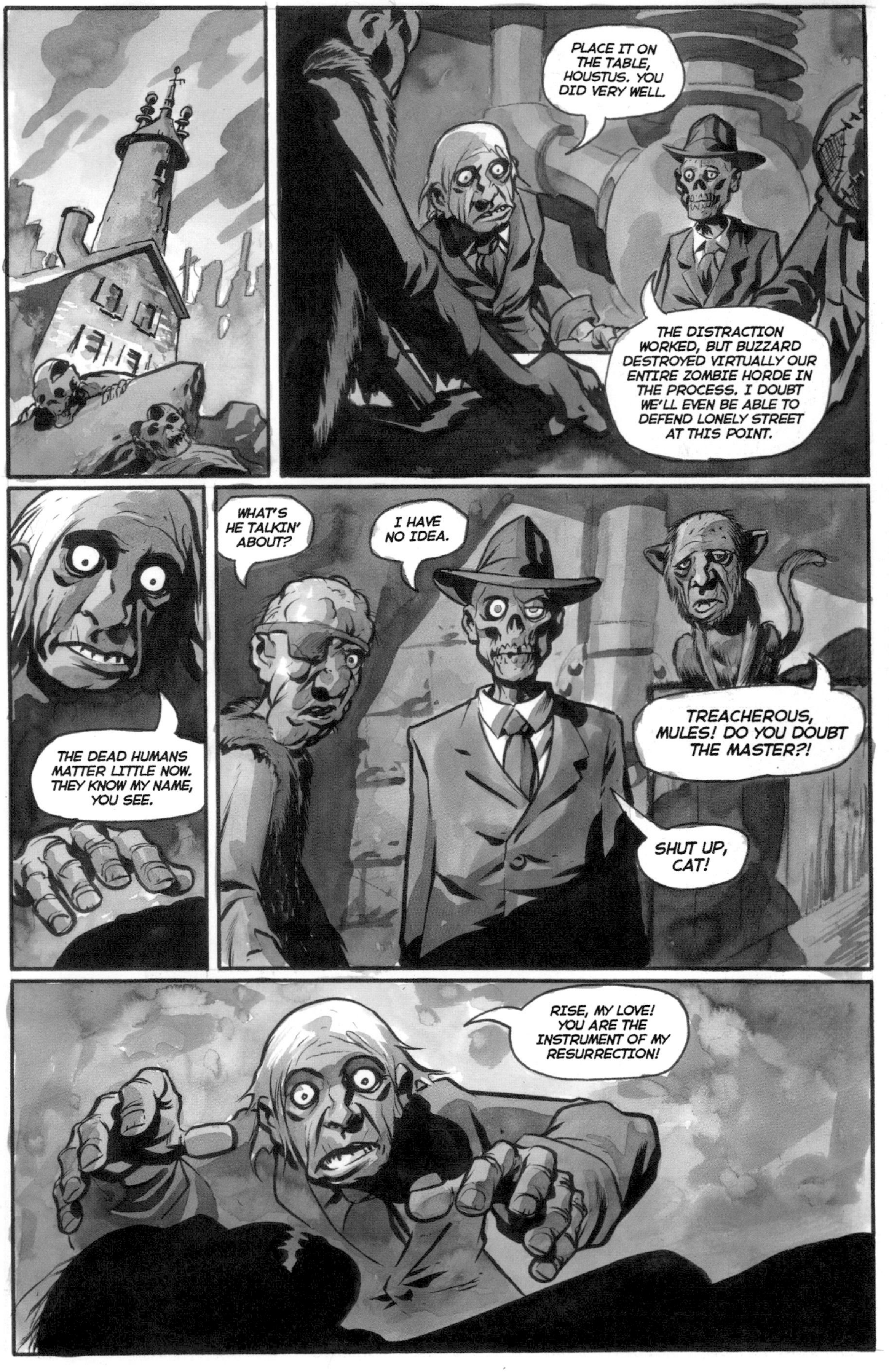
PLACE IT ON THE TABLE, HOUSTUS. YOU DID VERY WELL.
THE DISTRACTION WORKED, BUT BUZZARD DESTROYED VIRTUALLY OUR ENTIRE ZOMBIE HORDE IN THE PROCESS. I DOUBT WE'LL EVEN BE ABLE TO DEFEND LONELY STREET AT THIS POINT.
THE DEAD HUMANS MATTER LITTLE NOW. THEY KNOW MY NAME, YOU SEE.
WHAT'S HE TALKIN' ABOUT?
I HAVE NO IDEA.
TREACHEROUS, MULES! DO YOU DOUBT THE MASTER?!
SHUT UP, CAT!
RISE, MY LOVE! YOU ARE THE INSTRUMENT OF MY RESURRECTION!

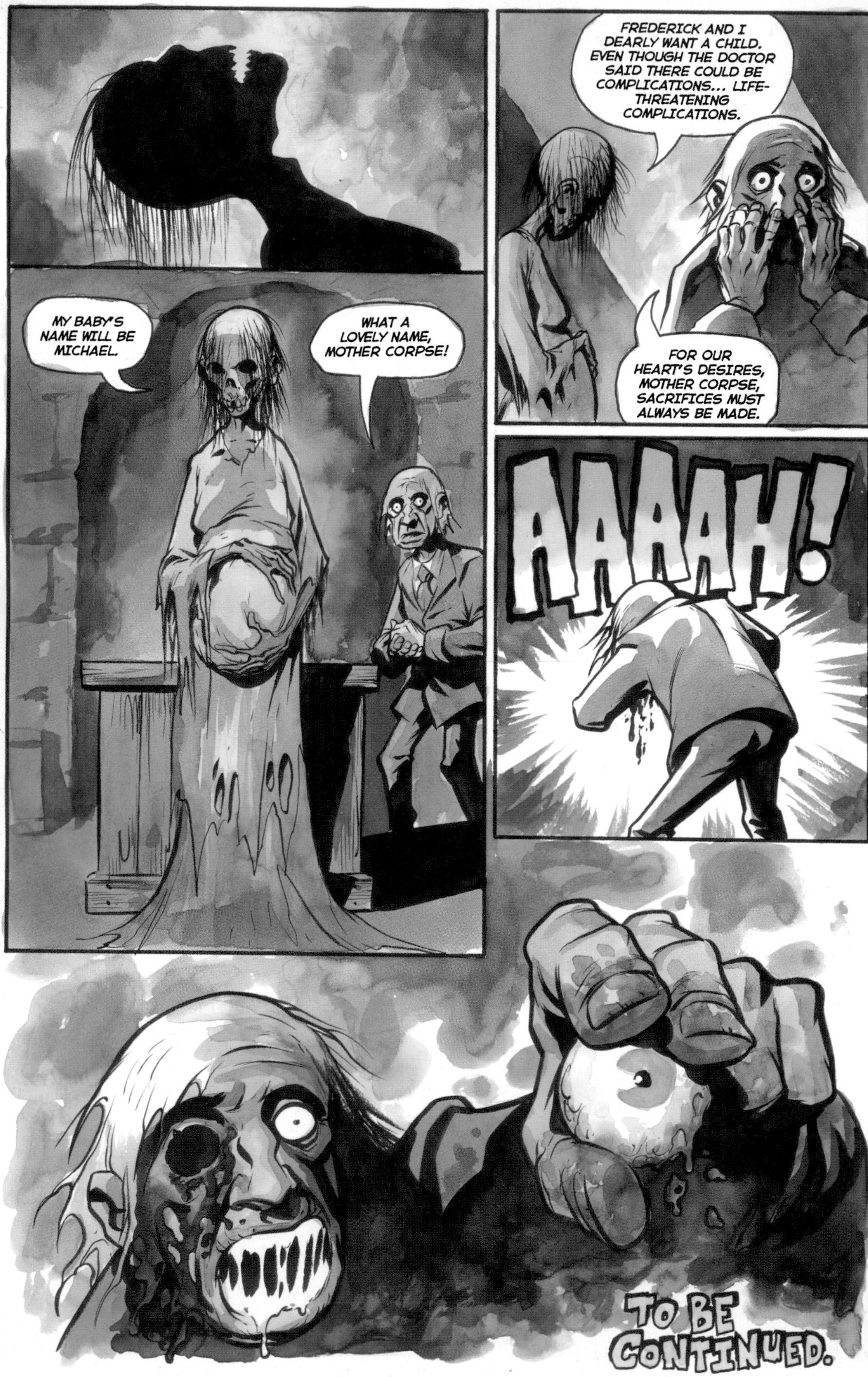
FREDERICK AND I DEARLY WANT A CHILD. EVEN THOUGH THE DOCTOR SAID THERE COULD BE COMPLICATIONS... LIFE-THREATENING COMPLICATIONS.
FOR OUR HEART'S DESIRES, MOTHER CORPSE, SACRIFICES MUST ALWAYS BE MADE.
MY BABY'S NAME WILL BE MICHAEL.
WHAT A LOVELY NAME, MOTHER CORPSE!
AAAAH!
TO BE CONTINUED.

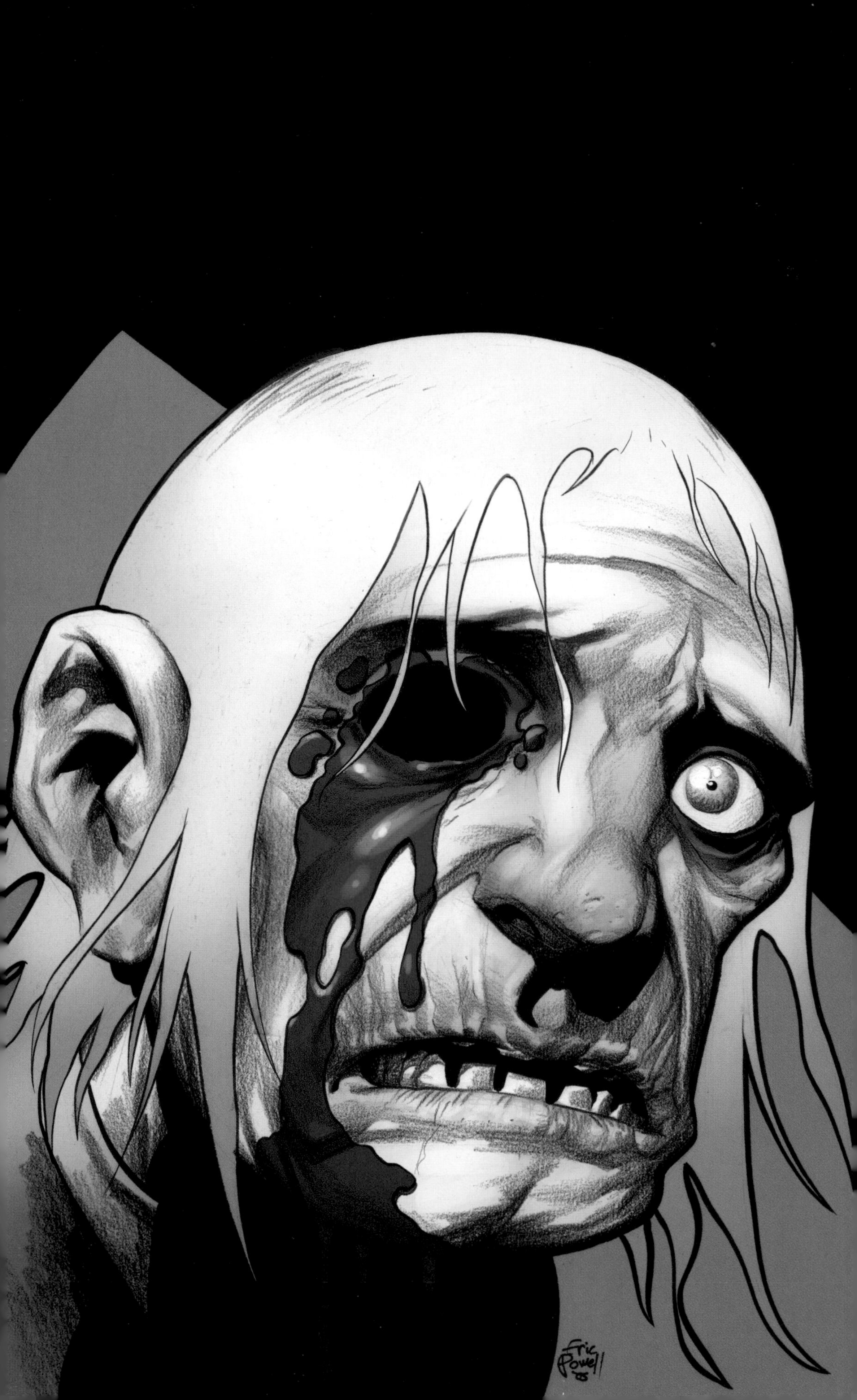
Eric Powell

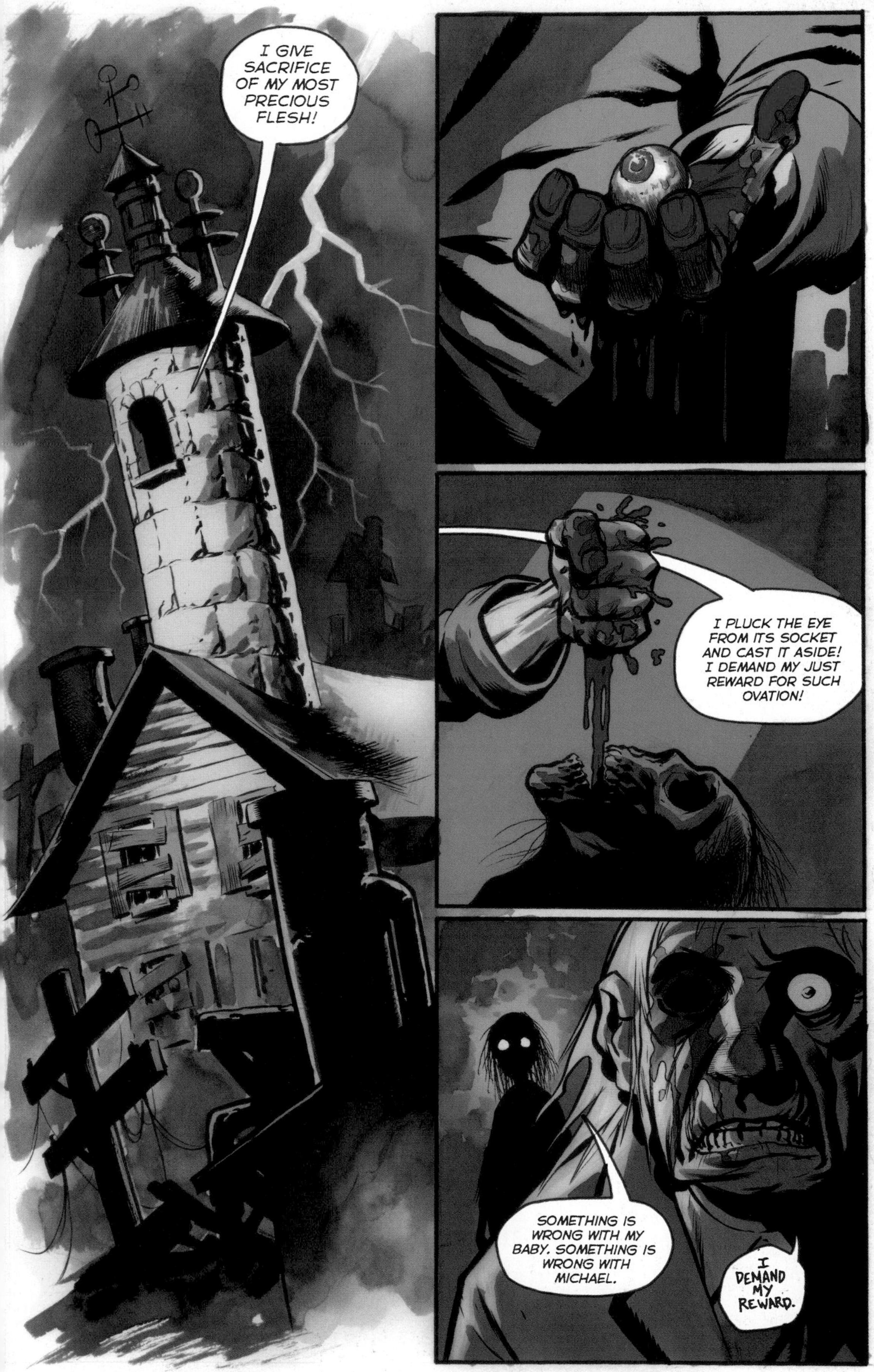
I GIVE SACRIFICE OF MY MOST PRECIOUS FLESH!
I PLUCK THE EYE FROM ITS SOCKET AND CAST IT ASIDE! I DEMAND MY JUST REWARD FOR SUCH OVATION!
SOMETHING IS WRONG WITH MY BABY. SOMETHING IS WRONG WITH MICHAEL.
I DEMAND MY REWARD.

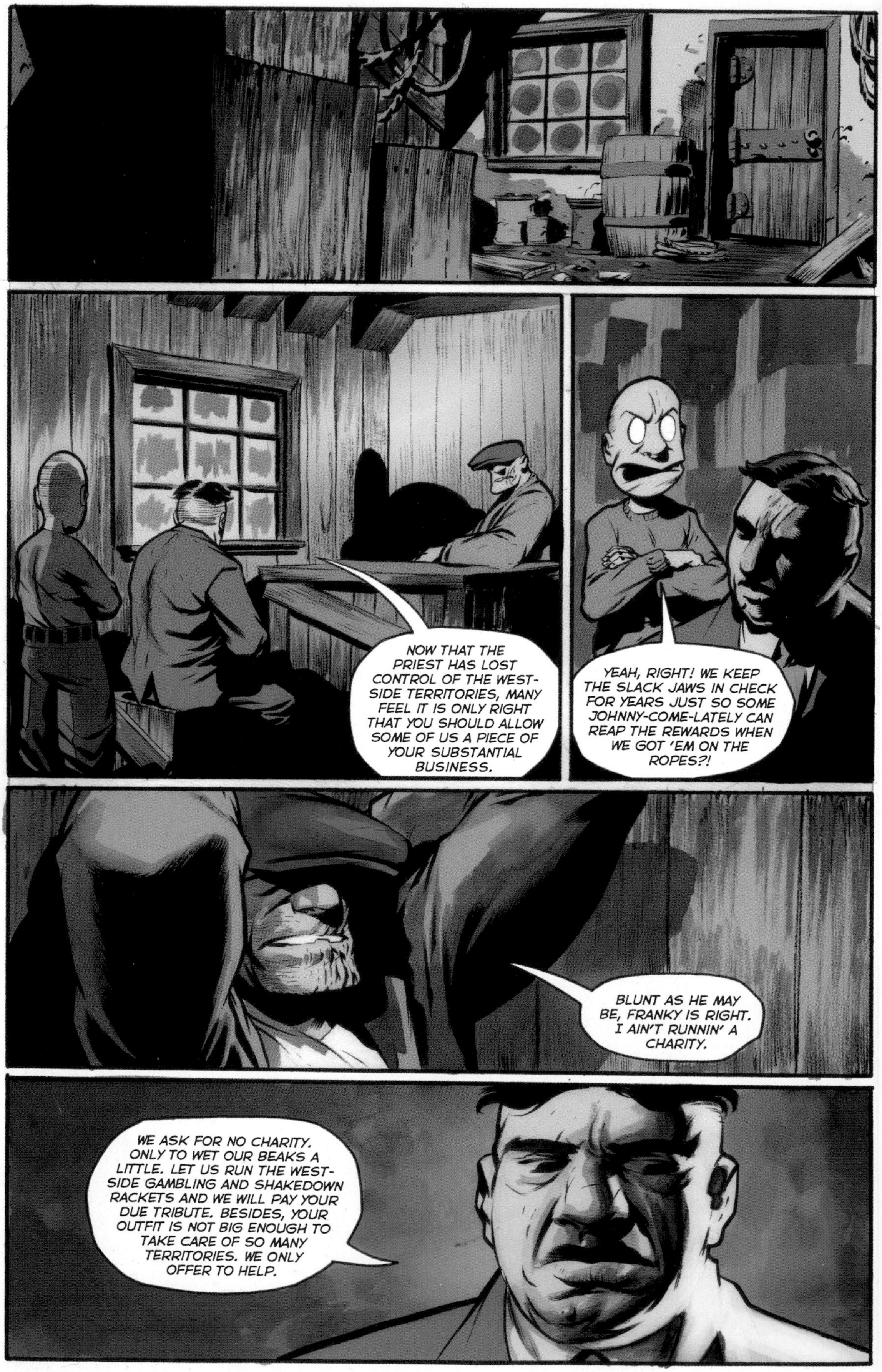
NOW THAT THE PRIEST HAS LOST CONTROL OF THE WEST-SIDE TERRITORIES, MANY FEEL IT IS ONLY RIGHT THAT YOU SHOULD ALLOW SOME OF US A PIECE OF YOUR SUBSTANTIAL BUSINESS.
YEAH, RIGHT! WE KEEP THE SLACK JAWS IN CHECK FOR YEARS JUST SO SOME JOHNNY-COME-LATELY CAN REAP THE REWARDS WHEN WE GOT 'EM ON THE ROPES?!
BLUNT AS HE MAY BE, FRANKY IS RIGHT. I AIN'T RUNNIN' A CHARITY.
WE ASK FOR NO CHARITY. ONLY TO WET OUR BEAKS A LITTLE. LET US RUN THE WEST-SIDE GAMBLING AND SHAKEDOWN RACKETS AND WE WILL PAY YOUR DUE TRIBUTE. BESIDES, YOUR OUTFIT IS NOT BIG ENOUGH TO TAKE CARE OF SO MANY TERRITORIES. WE ONLY OFFER TO HELP.

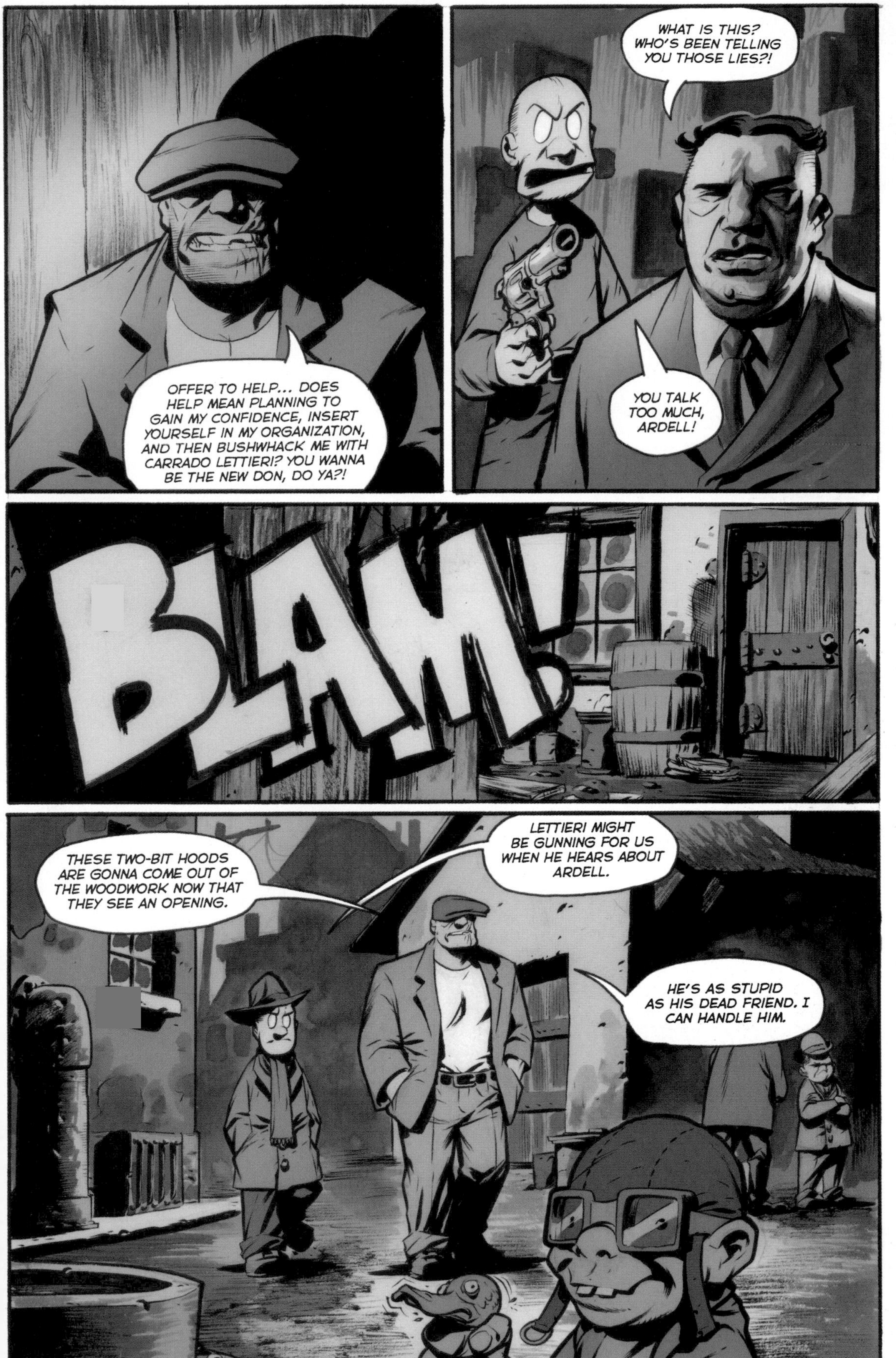
OFFER TO HELP... DOES HELP MEAN PLANNING TO GAIN MY CONFIDENCE, INSERT YOURSELF IN MY ORGANIZATION, AND THEN BUSHWHACK ME WITH CARRADO LETTIERI? YOU WANNA BE THE NEW DON, DO YA?!
WHAT IS THIS? WHO'S BEEN TELLING YOU THOSE LIES?!
YOU TALK TOO MUCH, ARDELL!
BLAM!
THESE TWO-BIT HOODS ARE GONNA COME OUT OF THE WOODWORK NOW THAT THEY SEE AN OPENING.
LETTIERI MIGHT BE GUNNING FOR US WHEN HE HEARS ABOUT ARDELL.
HE'S AS STUPID AS HIS DEAD FRIEND. I CAN HANDLE HIM.

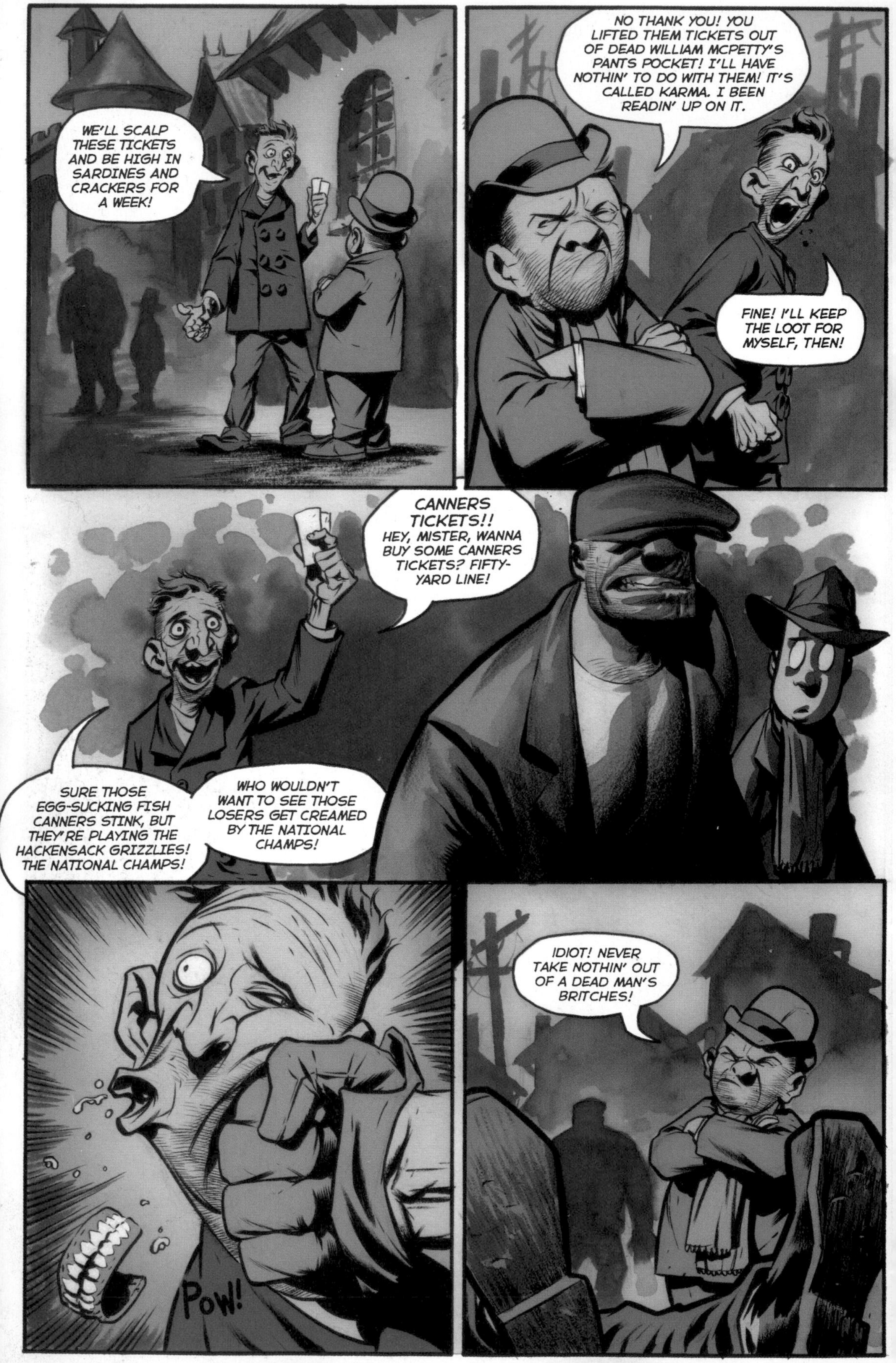
WE'LL SCALP THESE TICKETS AND BE HIGH IN SARDINES AND CRACKERS FOR A WEEK!
NO THANK YOU! YOU LIFTED THEM TICKETS OUT OF DEAD WILLIAM MCPETTY'S PANTS POCKET! I'LL HAVE NOTHIN' TO DO WITH THEM! IT'S CALLED KARMA. I BEEN READIN' UP ON IT.
FINE! I'LL KEEP THE LOOT FOR MYSELF, THEN!
CANNERS TICKETS!! HEY, MISTER, WANNA BUY SOME CANNERS TICKETS? FIFTY-YARD LINE!
SURE THOSE EGG-SUCKING FISH CANNERS STINK, BUT THEY"RE PLAYING THE HACKENSACK GRIZZLIES! THE NATIONAL CHAMPS!
WHO WOULDN'T WANT TO SEE THOSE LOSERS GET CREAMED BY THE NATIONAL CHAMPS!
POW!
IDIOT! NEVER TAKE NOTHIN' OUT OF A DEAD MAN'S BRITCHES!

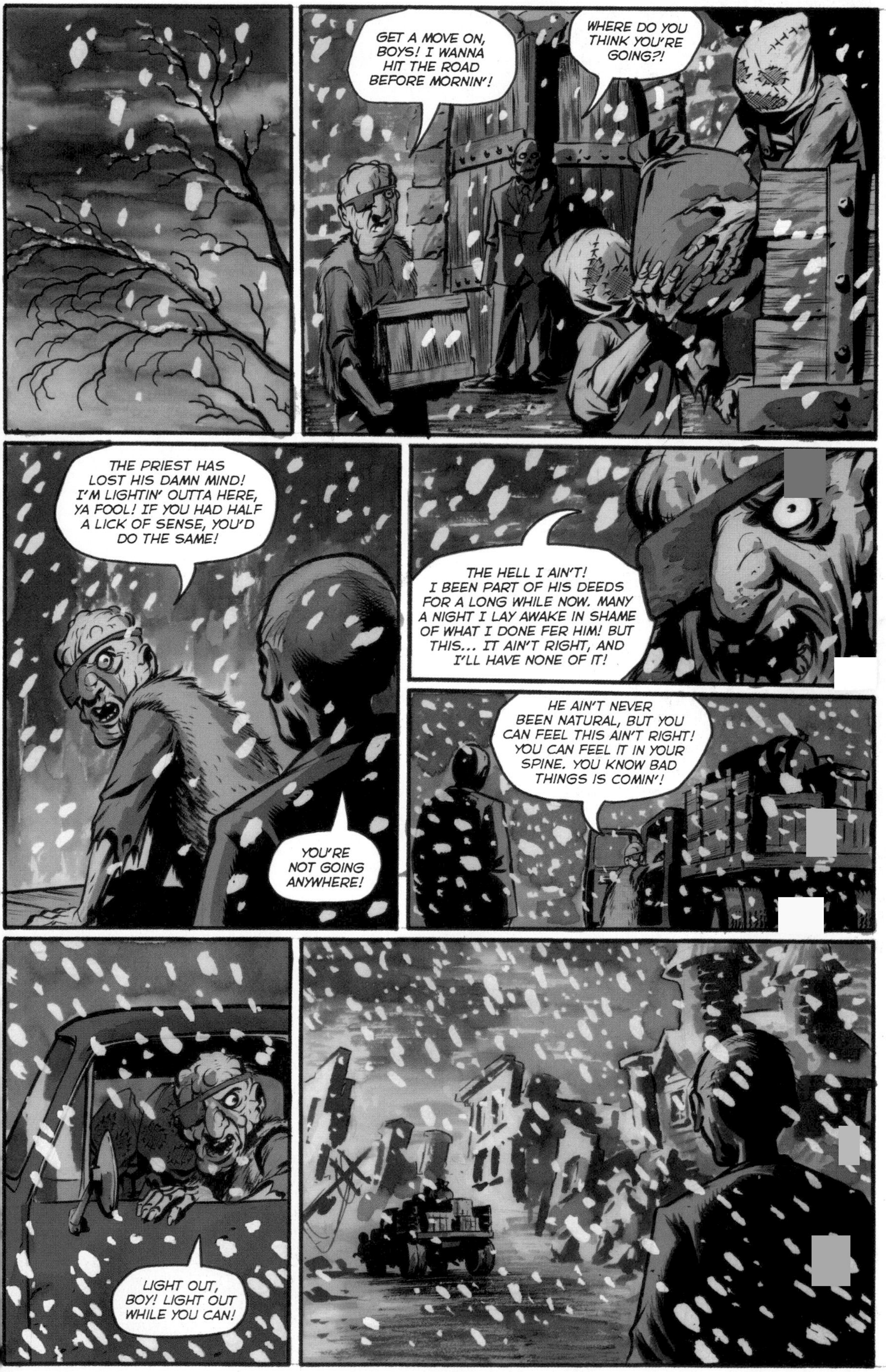
GET A MOVE ON, BOYS! I WANNA HIT THE ROAD BEFORE MORNIN'!
WHERE DO YOU THINK YOU'RE GOING?!
THE PRIEST HAS LOST HIS DAMN MIND! I'M LIGHTIN' OUTTA HERE, YA FOOL! IF YOU HAD HALF A LICK OF SENSE, YOU'D DO THE SAME!
YOU'RE NOT GOING ANYWHERE!
THE HELL I AIN'T! I BEEN PART OF HIS DEEDS FOR A LONG WHILE NOW. MANY A NIGHT I LAY AWAKE IN SHAME OF WHAT I DONE FER HIM! BUT THIS... IT AIN'T RIGHT, AND I'LL HAVE NONE OF IT!
HE AIN'T NEVER BEEN NATURAL, BUT YOU CAN FEEL THIS AIN'T RIGHT! YOU CAN FEEL IT IN YOUR SPINE. YOU KNOW BAD THINGS IS COMIN'!
LIGHT OUT, BOY! LIGHT OUT WHILE YOU CAN!

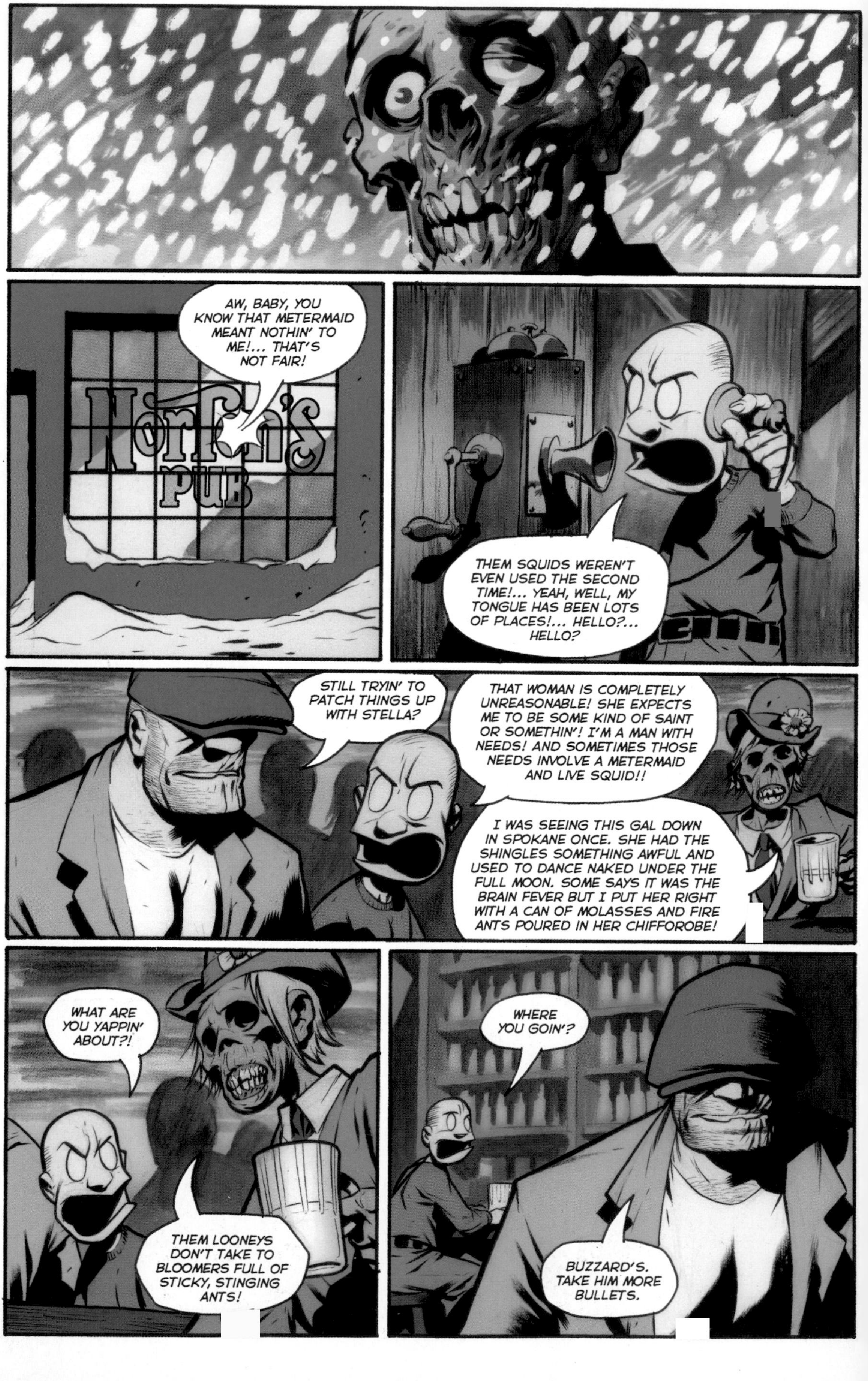

NORTON'S PUB
AW, BABY, YOU KNOW THAT METERMAID MEANT NOTHIN' TO ME!... THAT'S NOT FAIR!
THEM SQUIDS WEREN'T EVEN USED THE SECOND TIME!... YEAH, WELL, MY TONGUE HAS BEEN LOTS OF PLACES!... HELLO?... HELLO?
STILL TRYIN' TO PATCH THINGS UP WITH STELLA?
THAT WOMAN IS COMPLETELY UNREASONABLE! SHE EXPECTS ME TO BE SOME KIND OF SAINT OR SOMETHIN'! I'M A MAN WITH NEEDS! AND SOMETIMES THOSE NEEDS INVOLVE A METERMAID AND LIVE SQUID!!
I WAS SEEING THIS GAL DOWN IN SPOKANE ONCE. SHE HAD THE SHINGLES SOMETHING AWFUL AND USED TO DANCE NAKED UNDER THE FULL MOON. SOME SAYS IT WAS THE BRAIN FEVER BUT I PUT HER RIGHT WITH A CAN OF MOLASSES AND FIRE ANTS POURED IN HER CHIFFOROBE!
WHAT ARE YOU YAPPIN' ABOUT?!
THEM LOONEYS DON'T TAKE TO BLOOMERS FULL OF STICKY, STINGING ANTS!
WHERE YOU GOIN'?
BUZZARD'S. TAKE HIM MORE BULLETS.

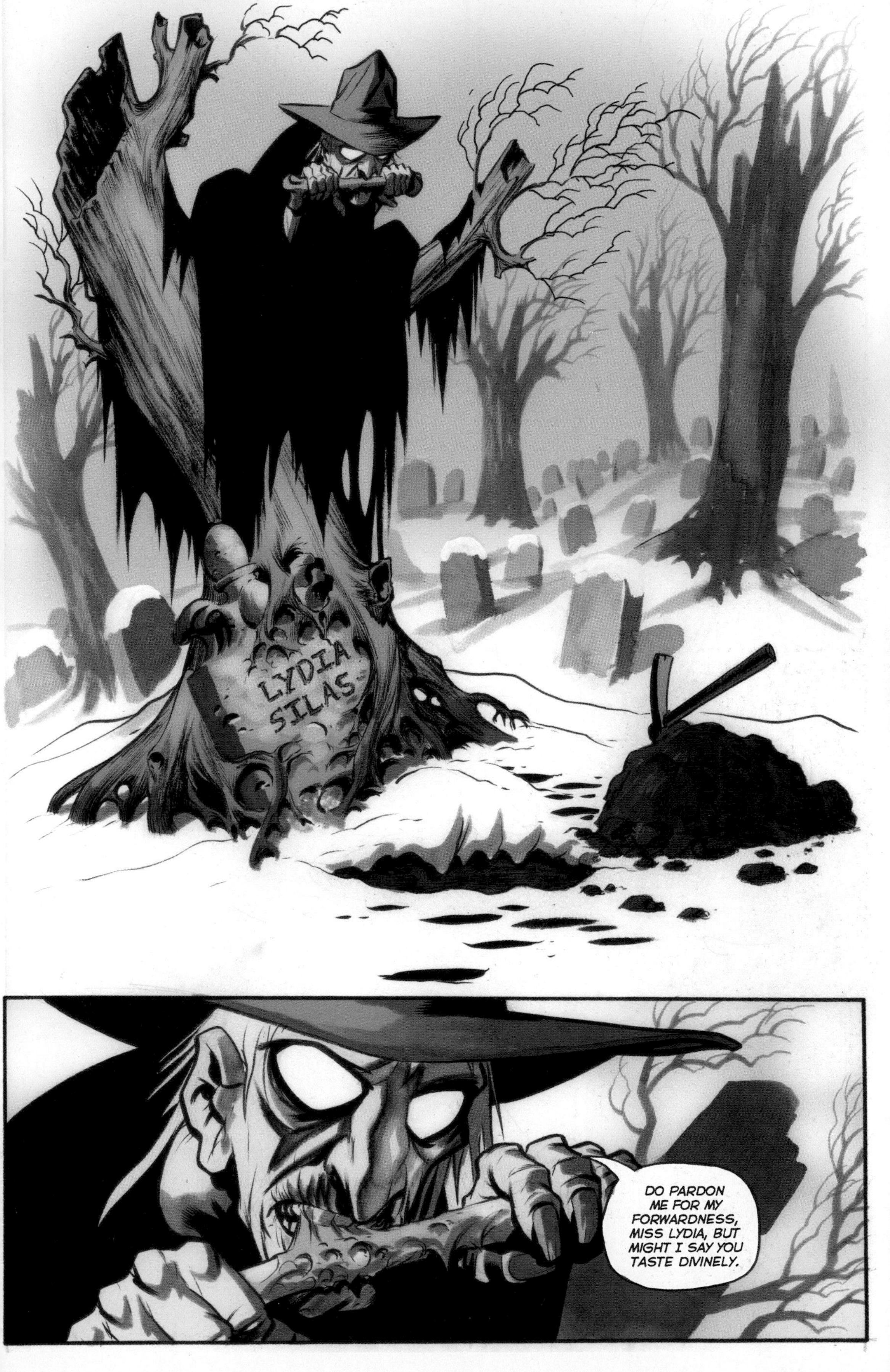
LYDIA SILAS
DO PARDON ME FOR MY FORWARDNESS, MISS LYDIA, BUT MIGHT I SAY YOU TASTE DIVINELY.

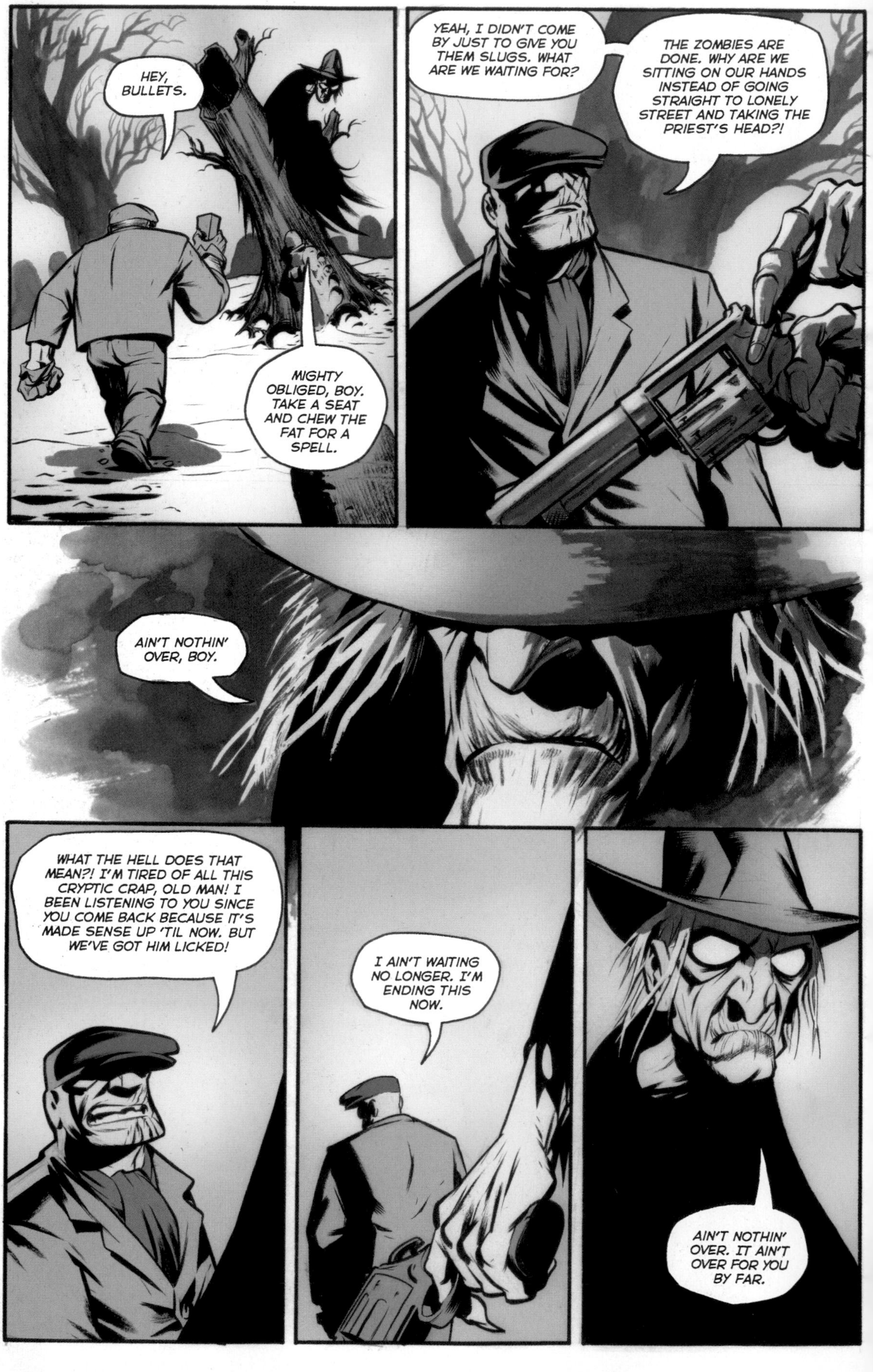
HEY, BULLETS.
MIGHTY OBLIGED, BOY. TAKE A SEAT AND CHEW THE FAT FOR A SPELL.
YEAH, I DIDN'T COME BY JUST TO GIVE YOU THEM SLUGS. WHAT ARE WE WAITING FOR?
THE ZOMBIES ARE DONE. WHY ARE WE SITTING ON OUR HANDS INSTEAD OF GOING STRAIGHT TO LONELY STREET AND TAKING THE PRIEST'S HEAD?!
AIN'T NOTHIN' OVER, BOY.
WHAT THE HELL DOES THAT MEAN?! I'M TIRED OF ALL THIS CRYPTIC CRAP, OLD MAN! I BEEN LISTENING TO YOU SINCE YOU COME BACK BECAUSE IT'S MADE SENSE UP 'TIL NOW. BUT WE'VE GOT HIM LICKED!
I AIN'T WAITING NO LONGER. I'M ENDING THIS NOW.
AIN'T NOTHIN' OVER. IT AIN'T OVER FOR YOU BY FAR.

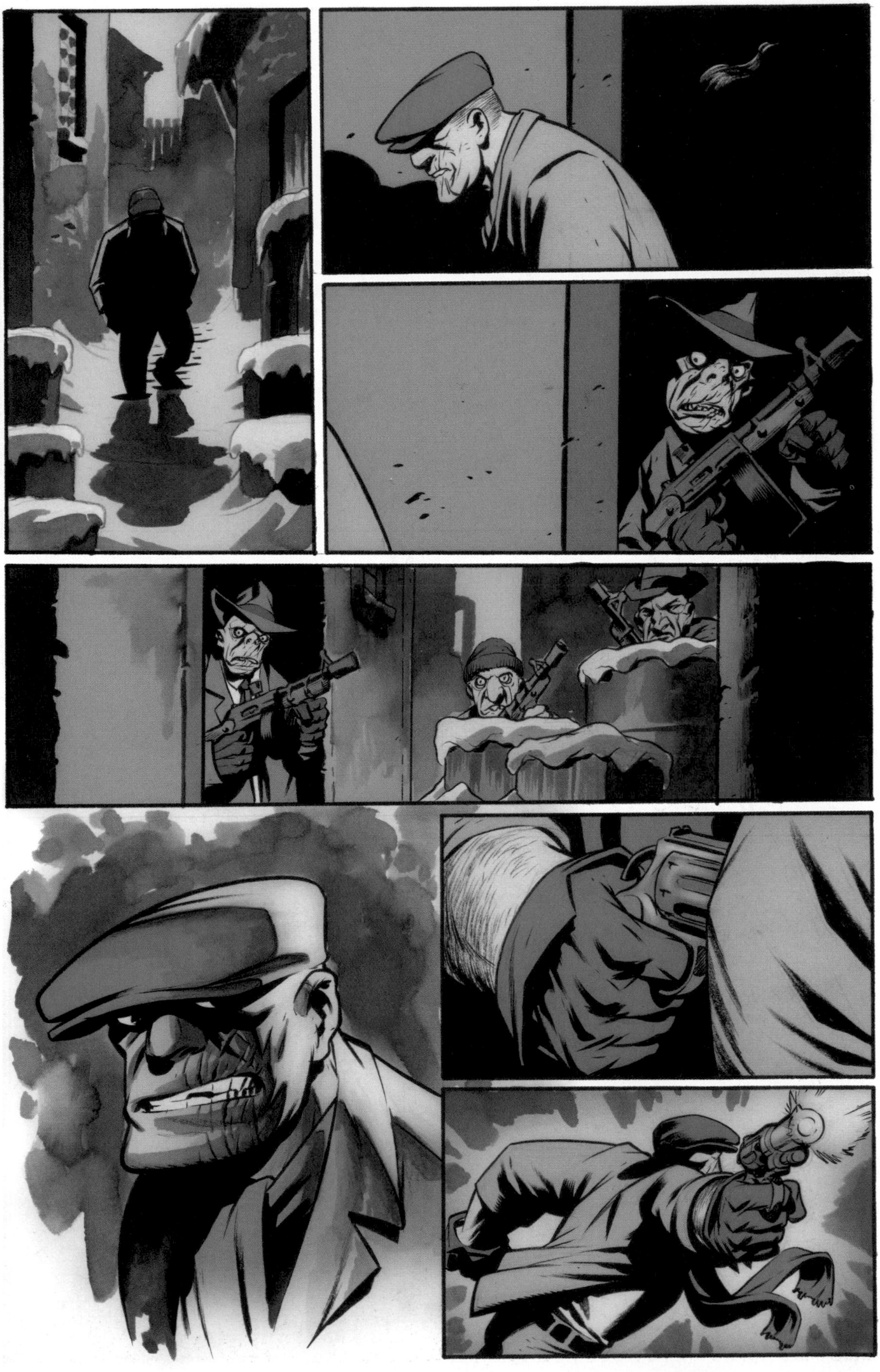

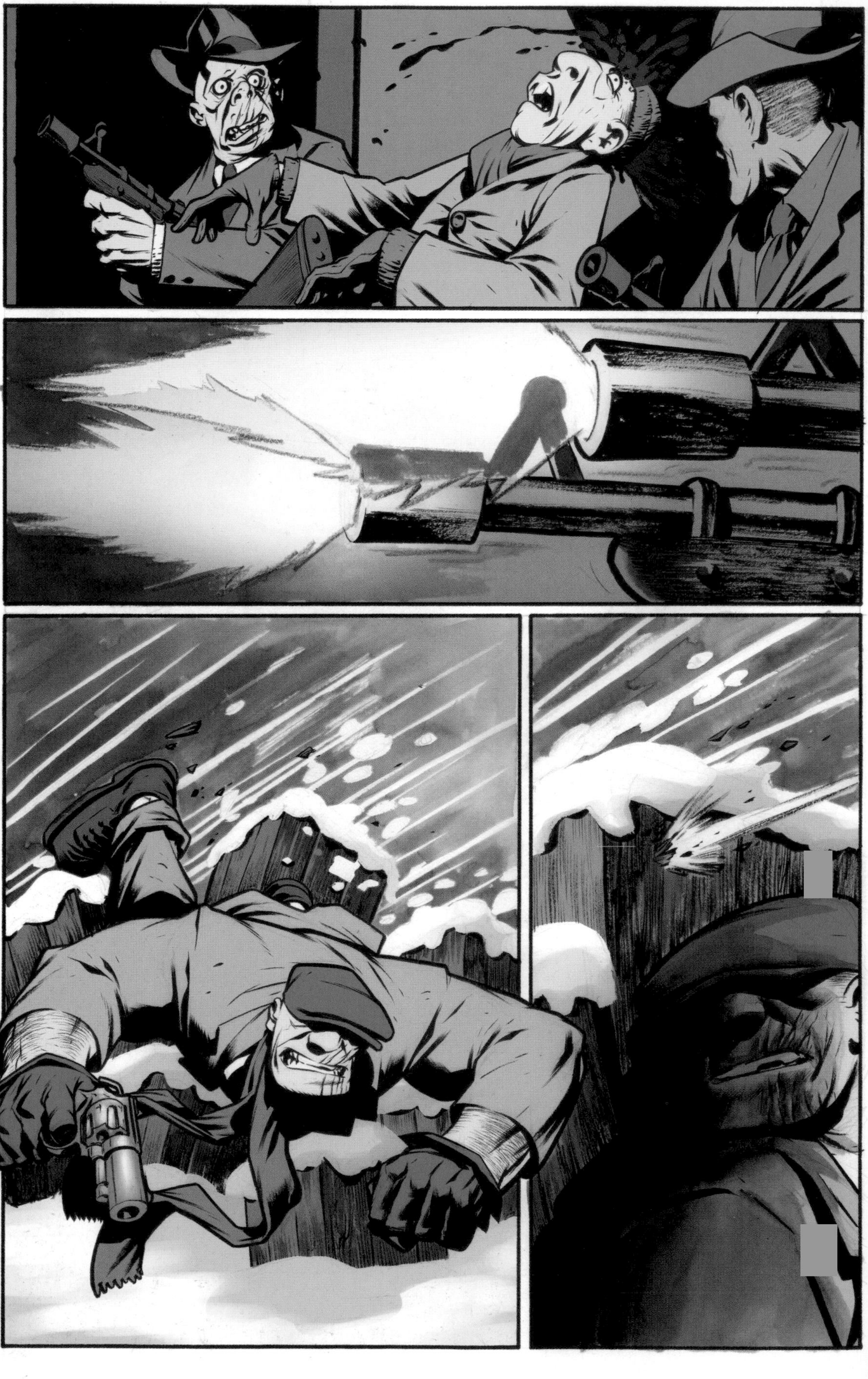

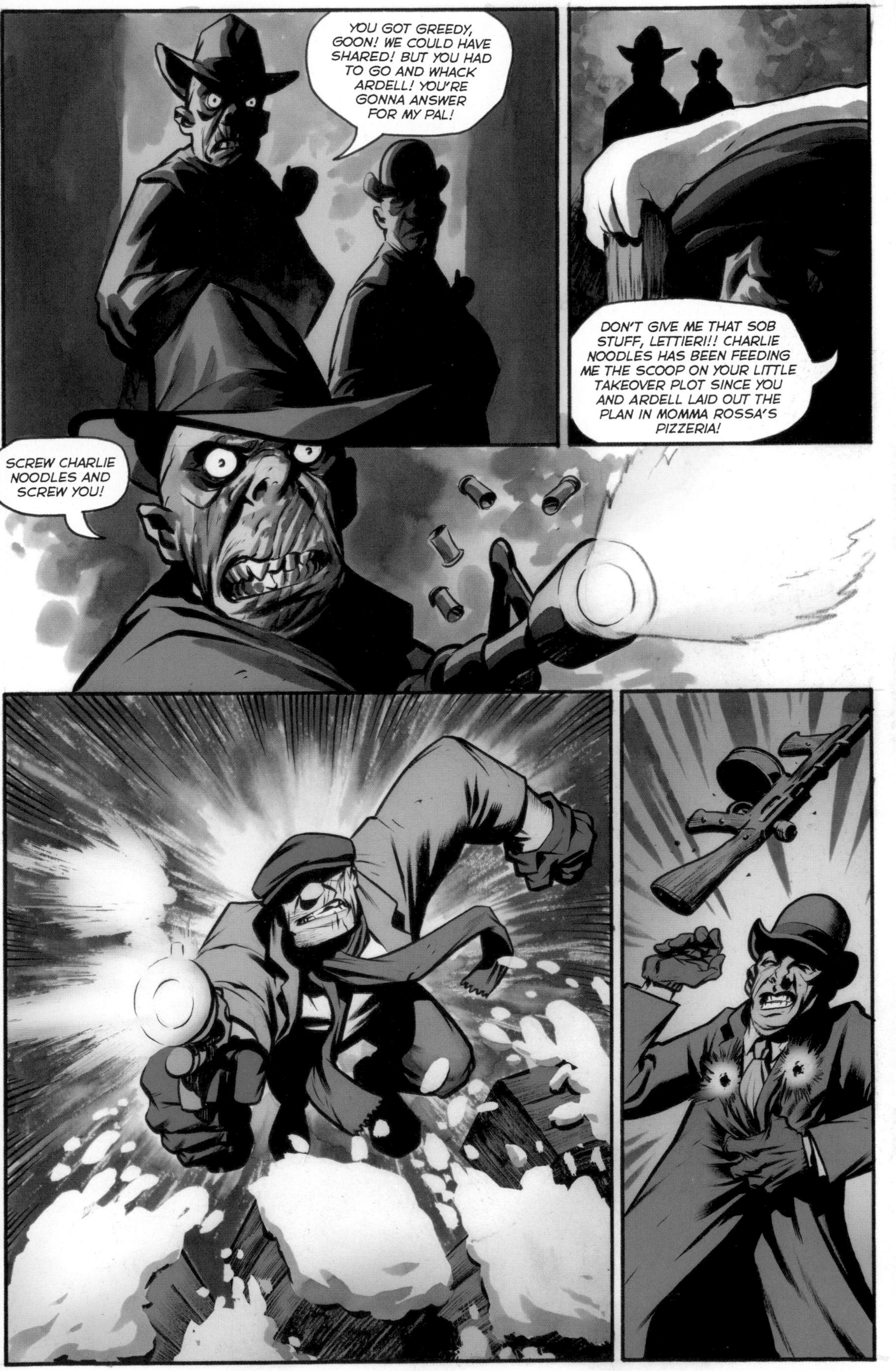
YOU GOT GREEDY, GOON! WE COULD HAVE SHARED! BUT YOU HAD TO GO AND WHACK ARDELL! YOU'RE GONNA ANSWER FOR MY PAL!
DON'T GIVE ME THAT SOB STUFF, LETTIERI!! CHARLIE NOODLES HAS BEEN FEEDING ME THE SCOOP ON YOUR LITTLE TAKEOVER PLOT SINCE YOU AND ARDELL LAID OUT THE PLAN IN MOMMA ROSSA'S PIZZERIA!
SCREW CHARLIE NOODLES AND SCREW YOU!

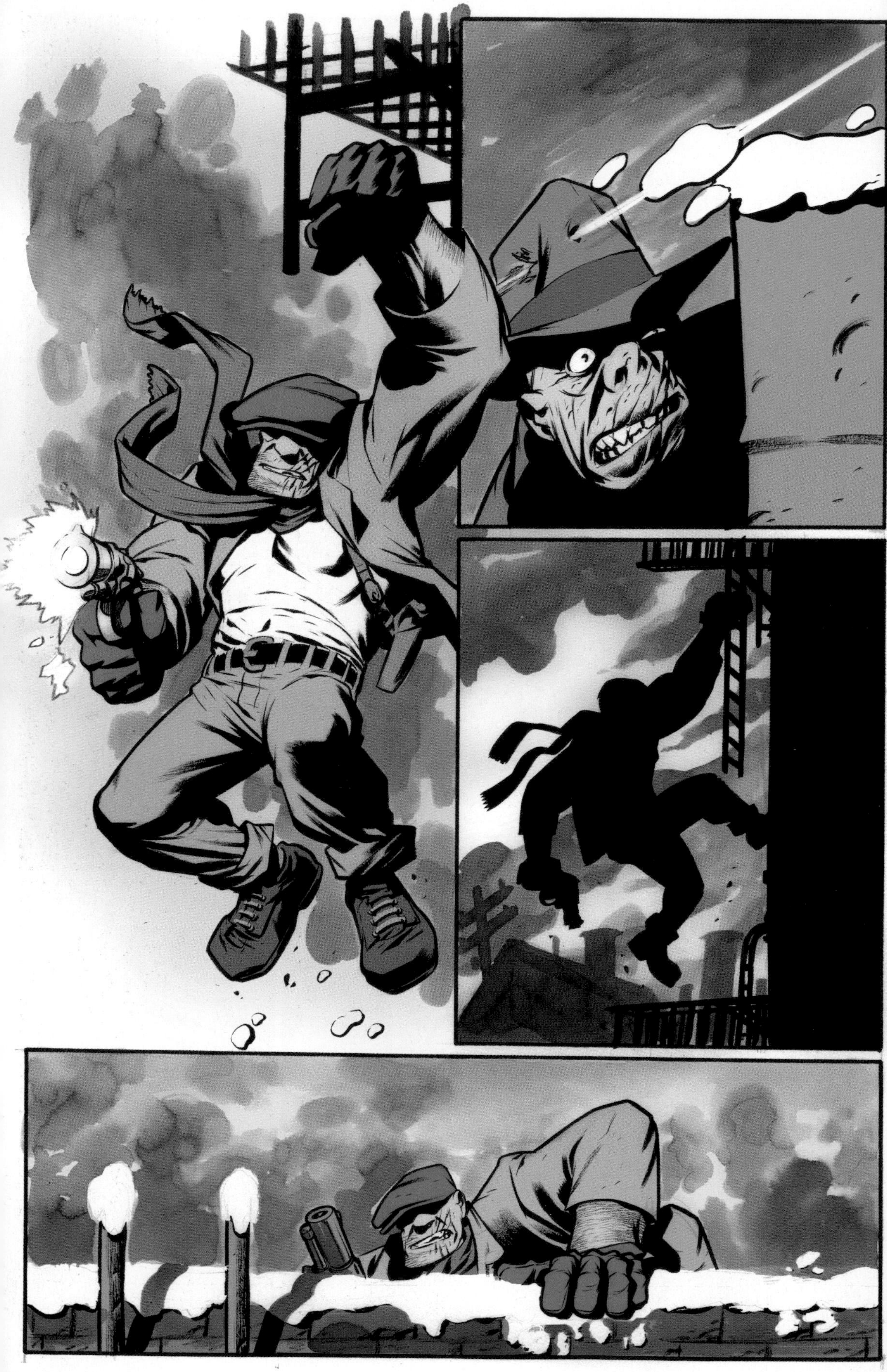

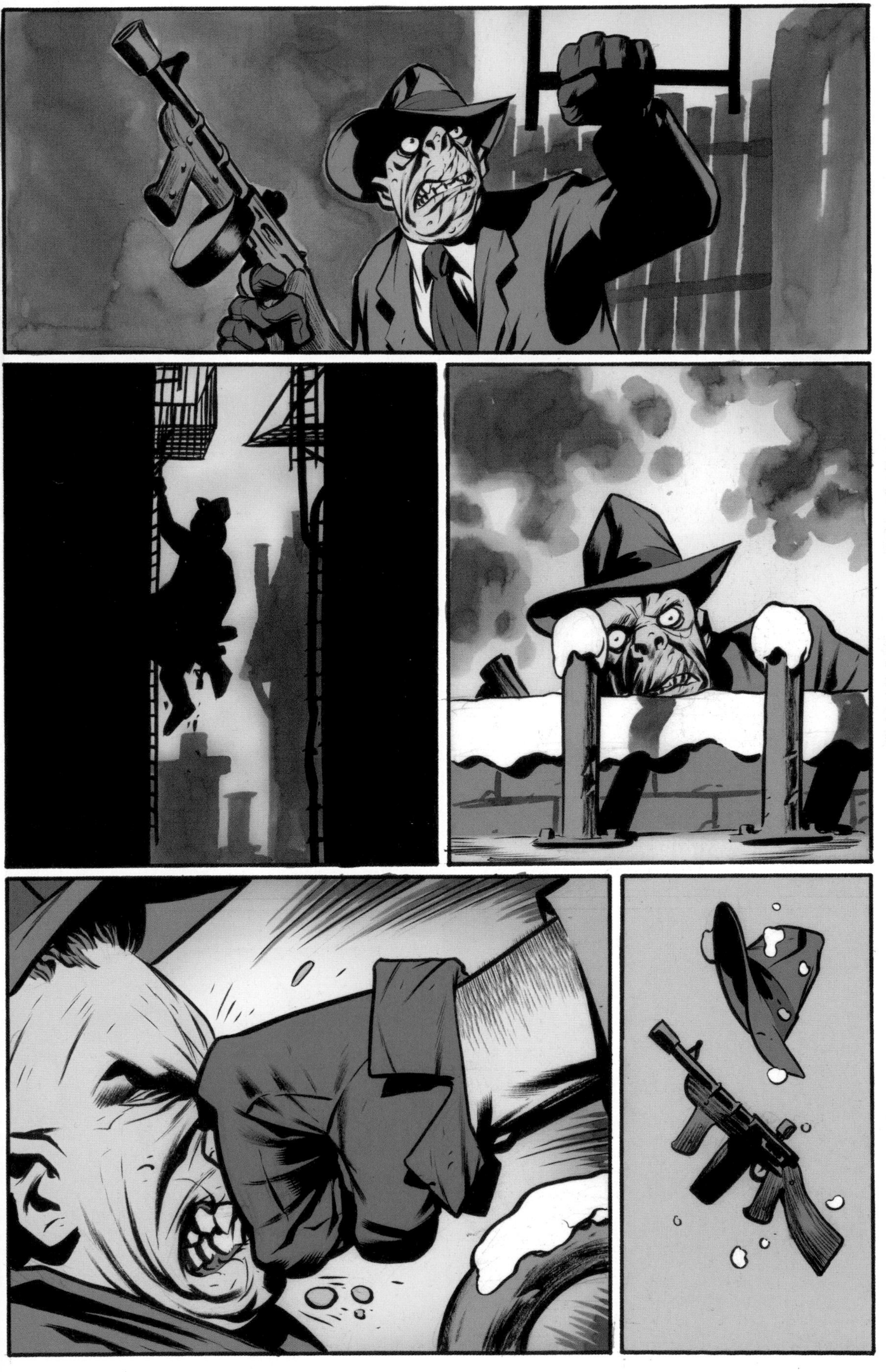

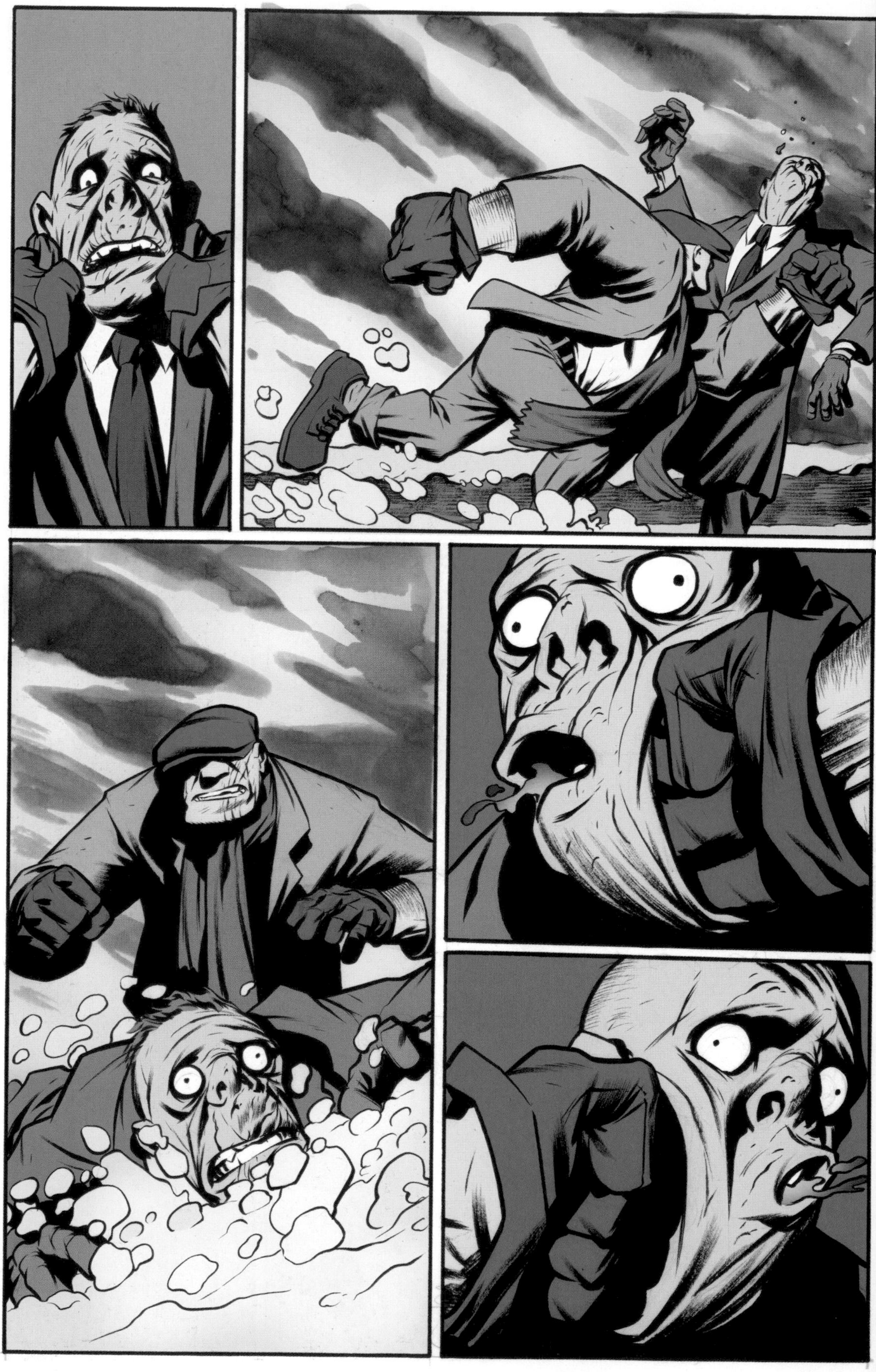

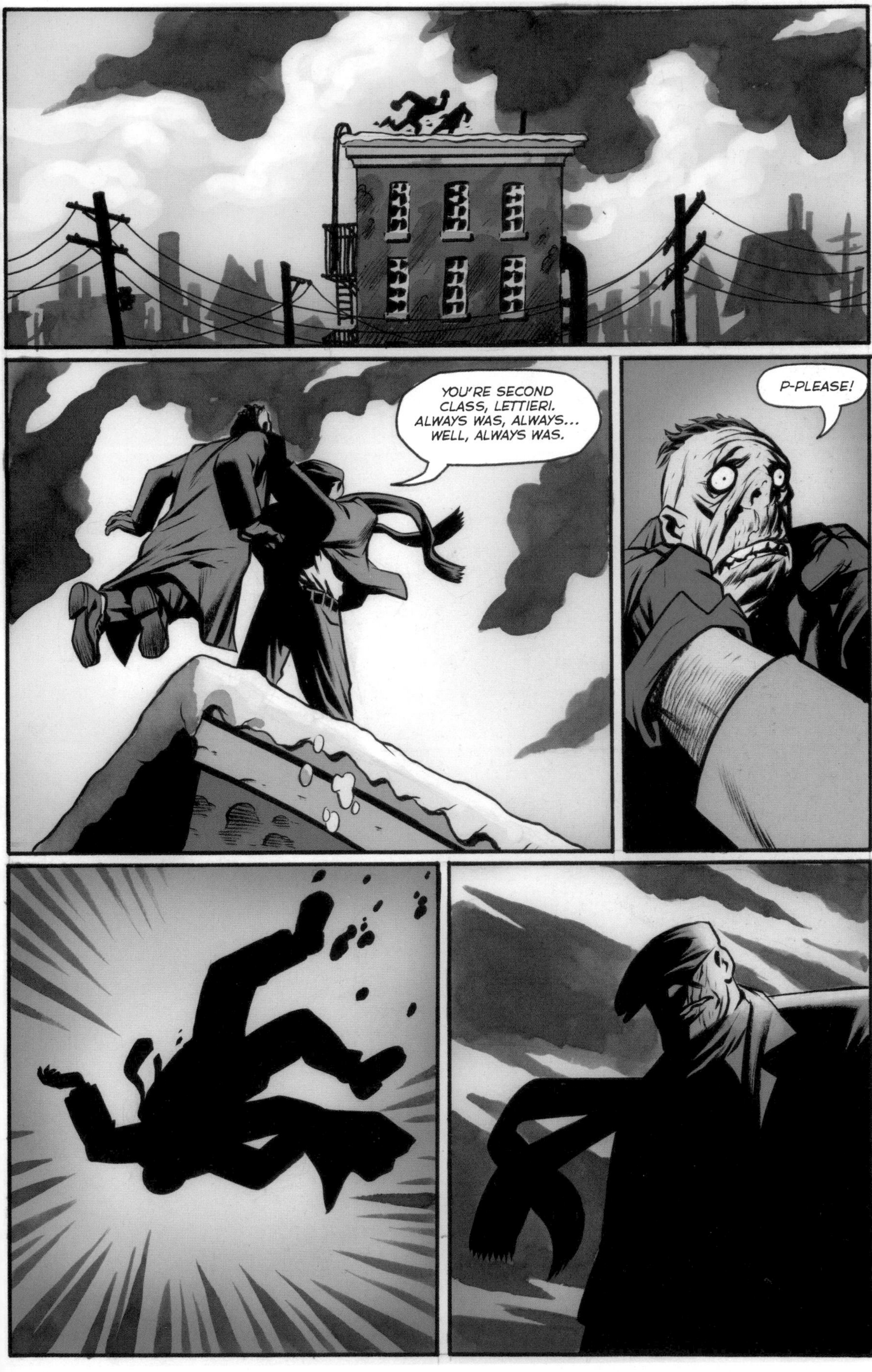
YOU'RE SECOND CLASS, LETTIERI. ALWAYS WAS, ALWAYS... WELL, ALWAYS WAS.
P-PLEASE!

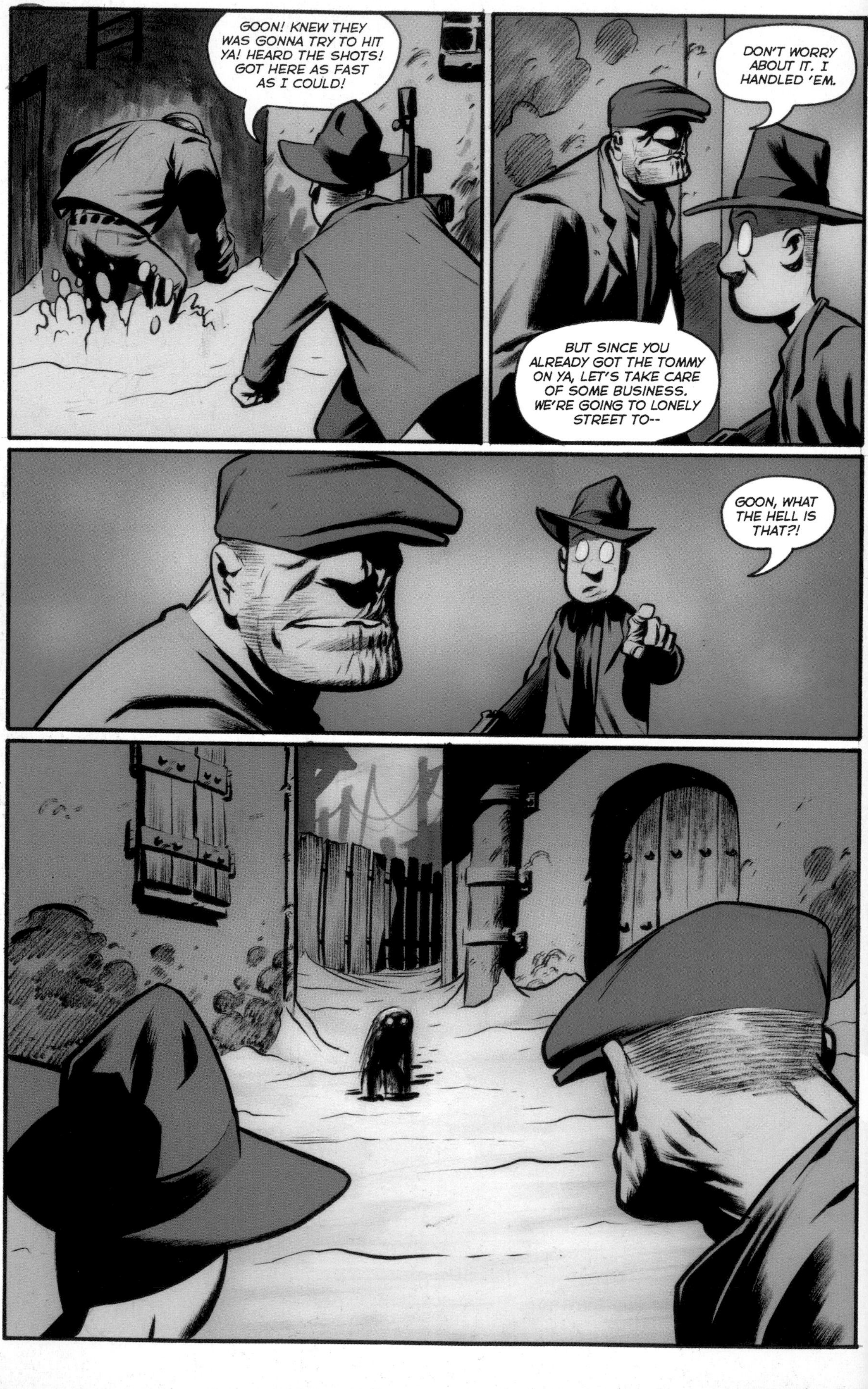
GOON! KNEW THEY WAS GONNA TRY TO HIT YA! HEARD THE SHOTS! GOT HERE AS FAST AS I COULD!
DON'T WORRY ABOUT IT. I HANDLED 'EM.
BUT SINCE YOU ALREADY GOT THE TOMMY ON YA, LET'S TAKE CARE OF SOME BUSINESS. WE'RE GOING TO LONELY STREET TO--
GOON, WHAT THE HELL IS THAT?!

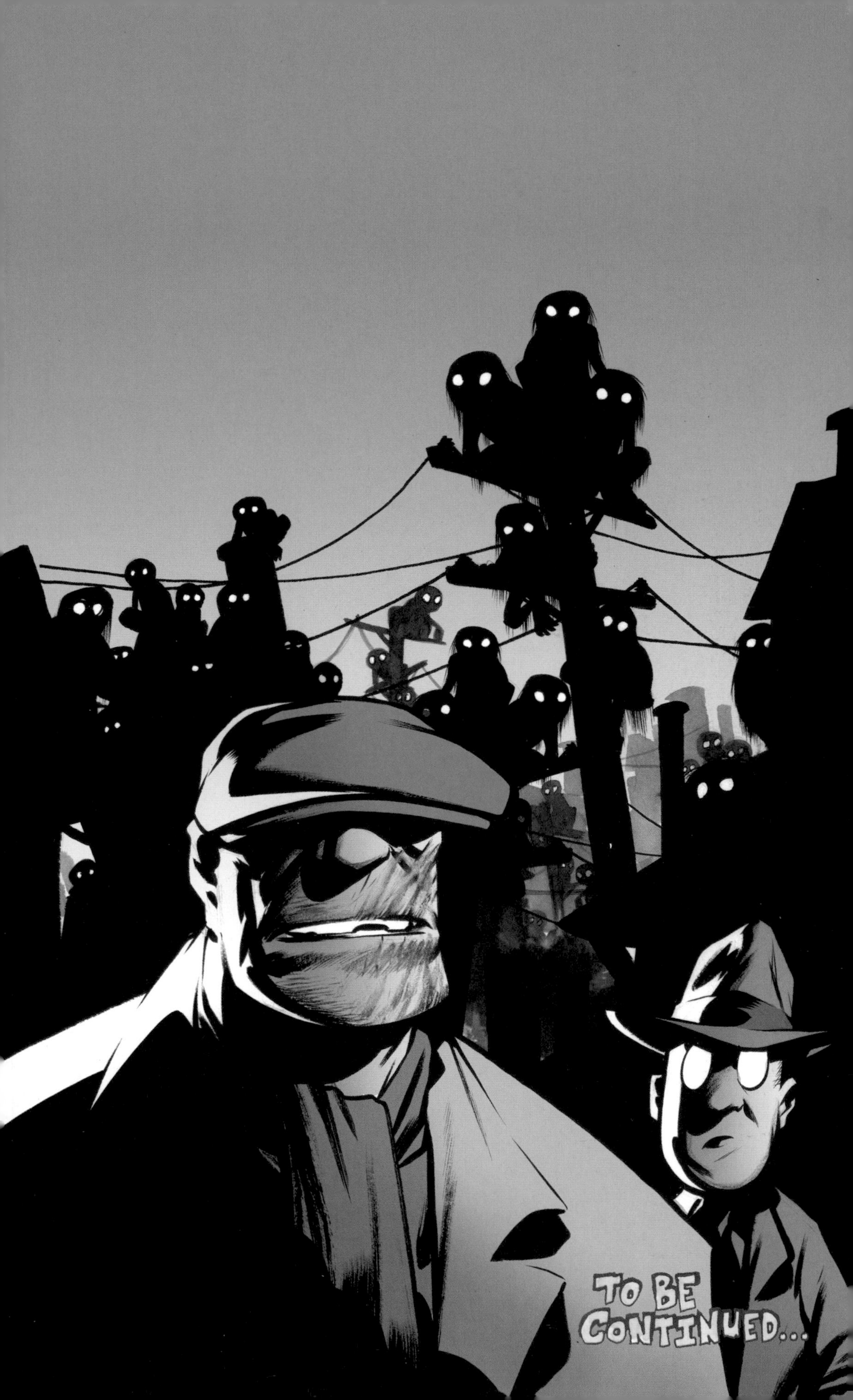
TO BE CONTINUED...

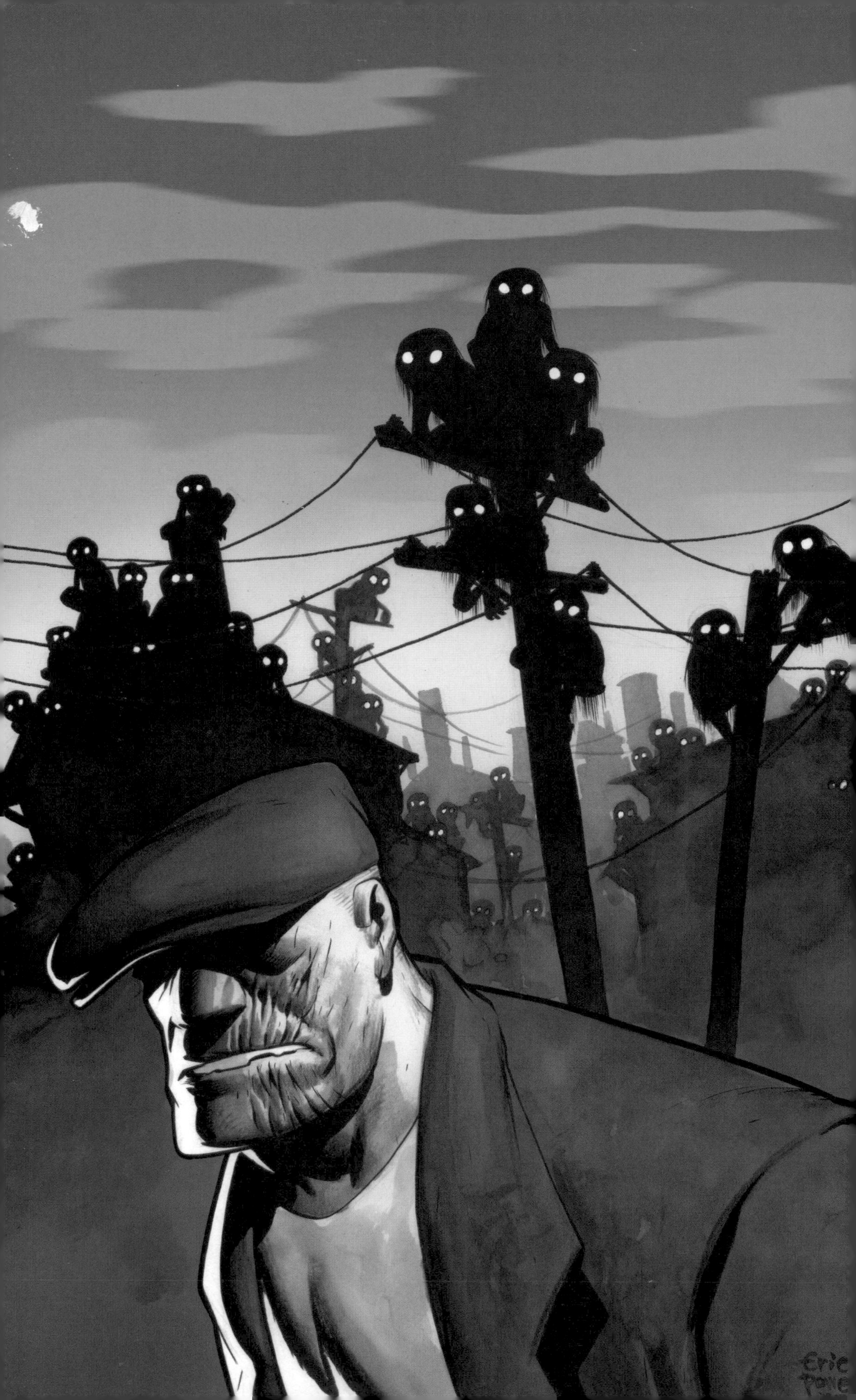

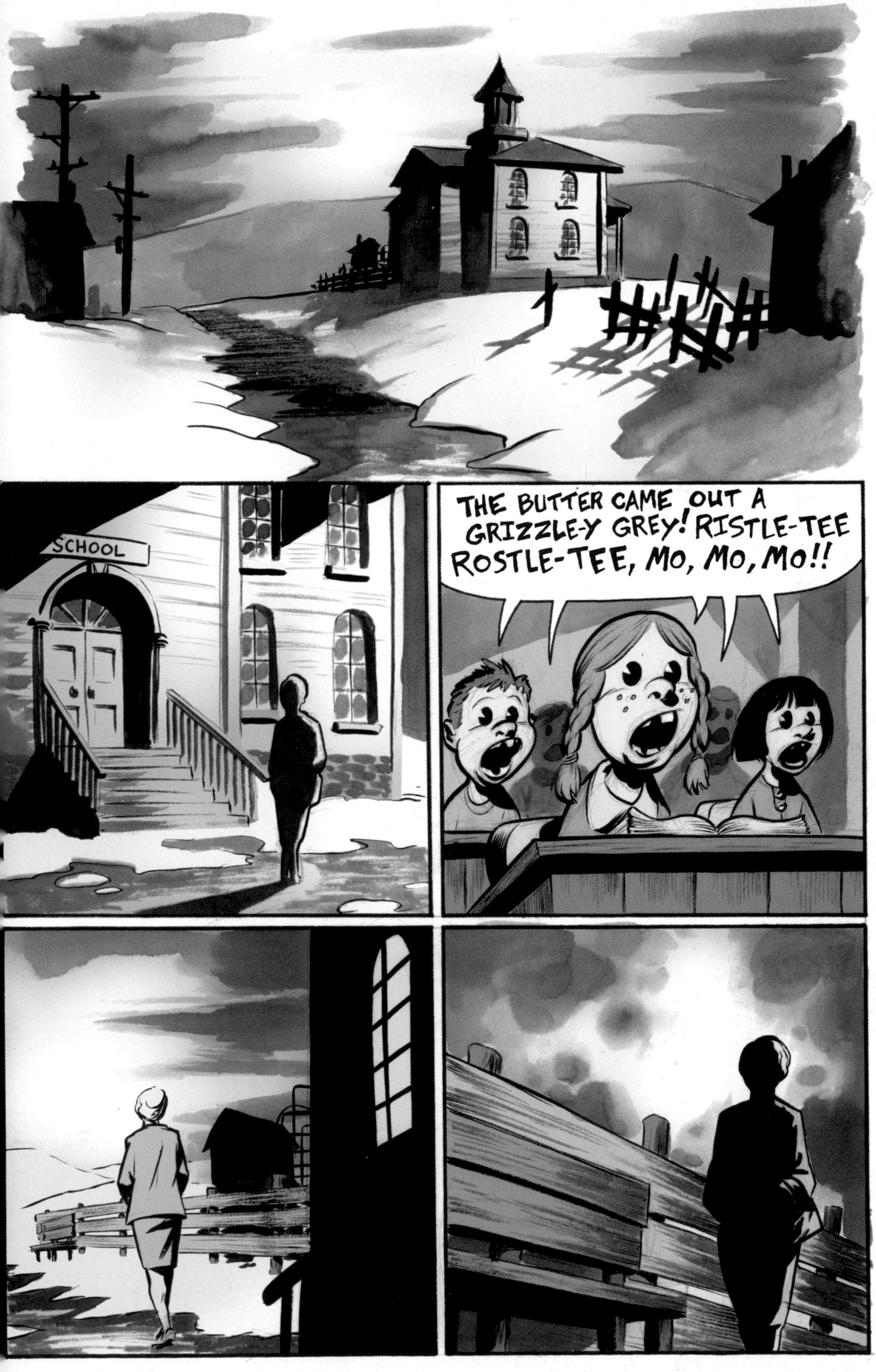
SCHOOL
THE BUTTER CAME OUT A GRIZZLE-Y GREY! RISTLE-TEE ROSTLE-TEE, MO, MO, MO!!

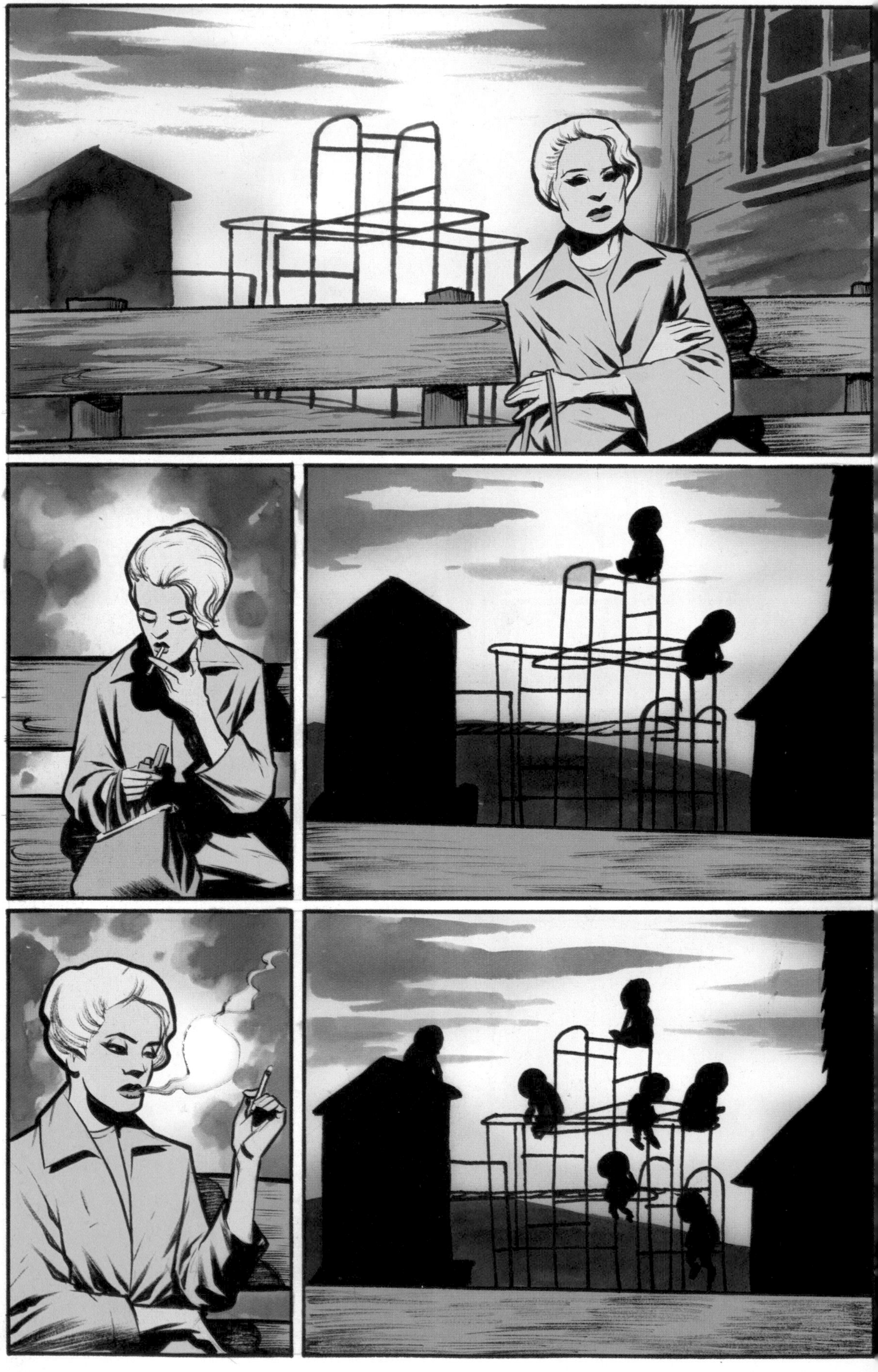

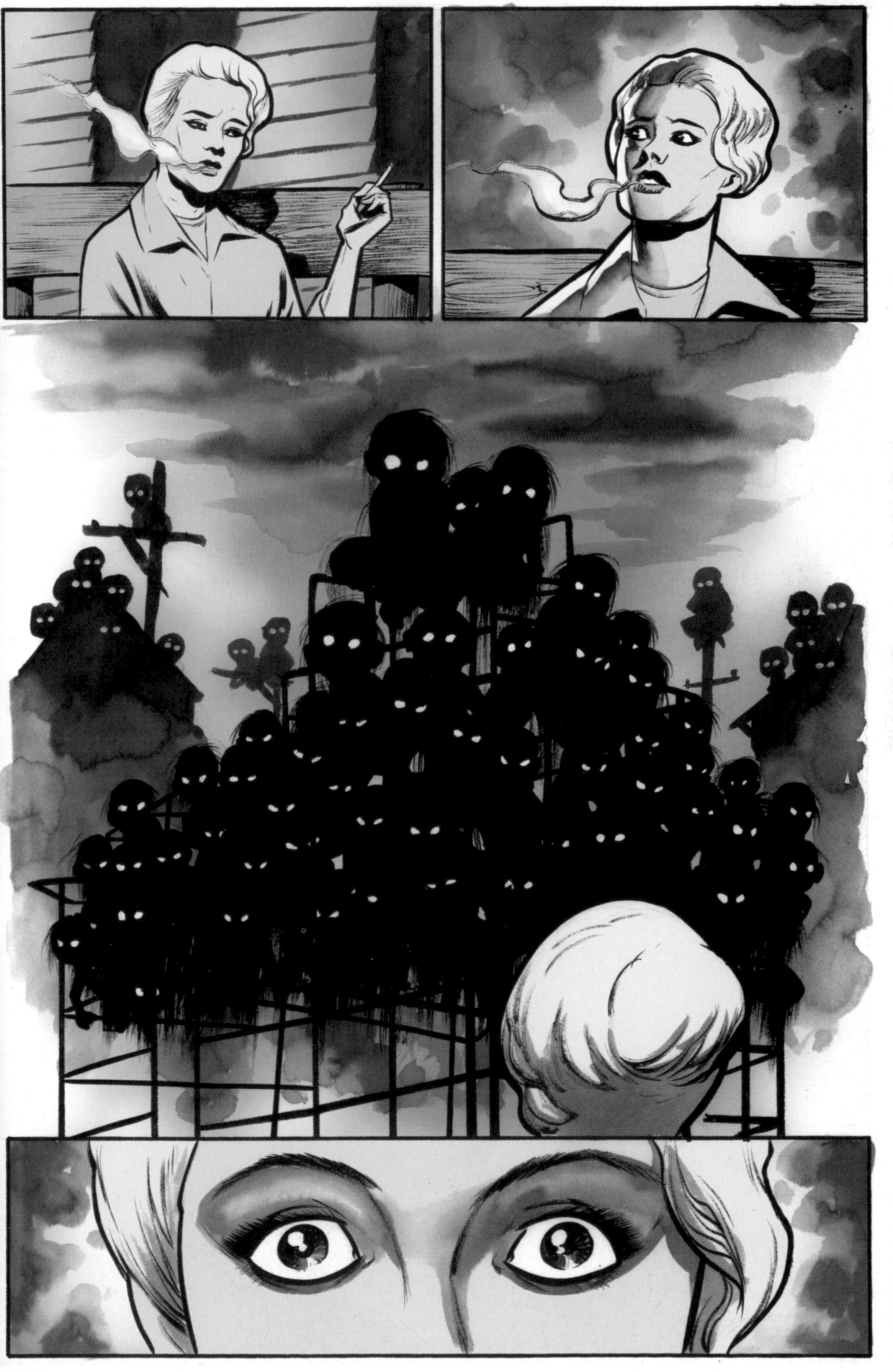

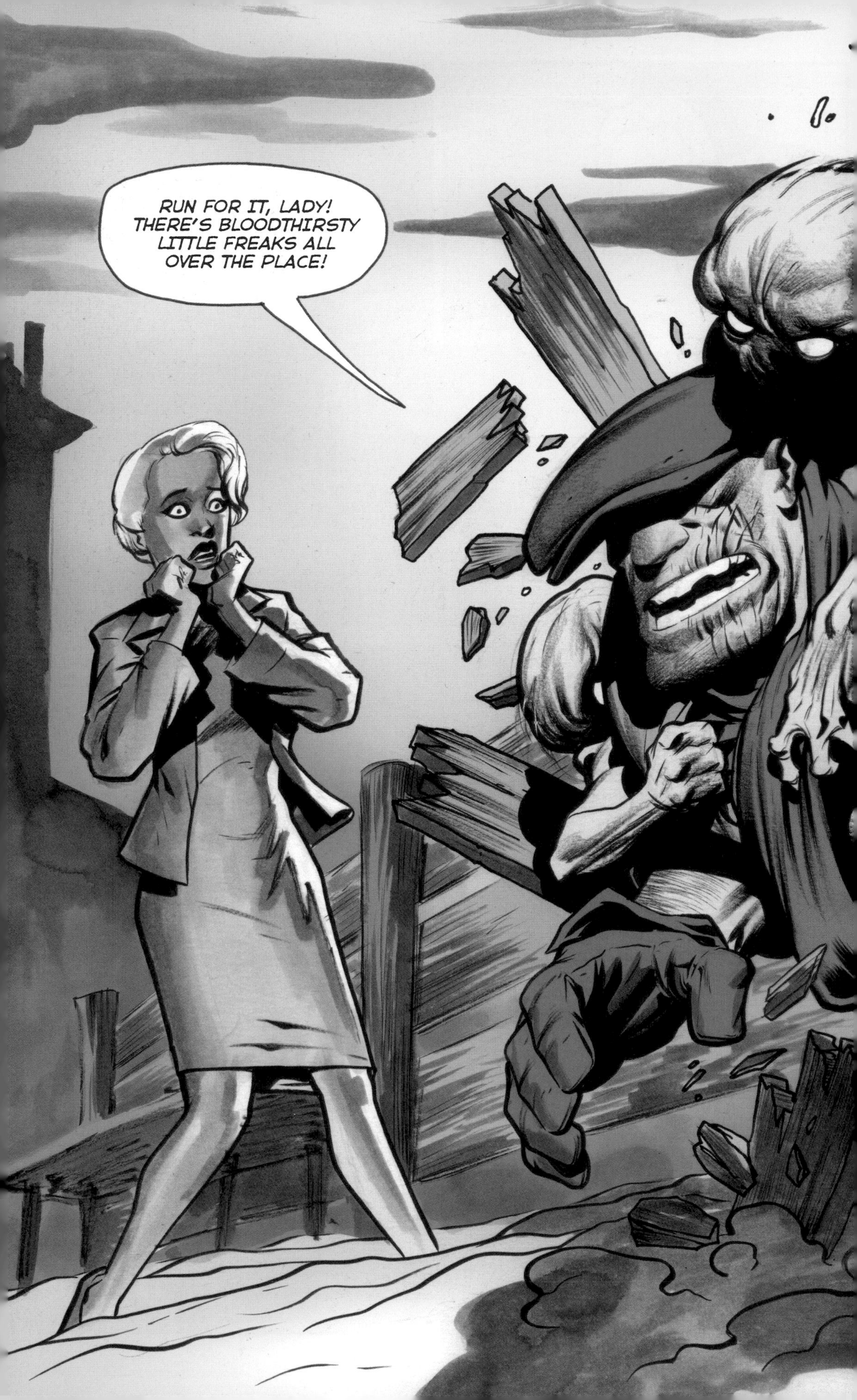
RUN FOR IT, LADY! THERE'S BLOODTHIRSTY LITTLE FREAKS ALL OVER THE PLACE!

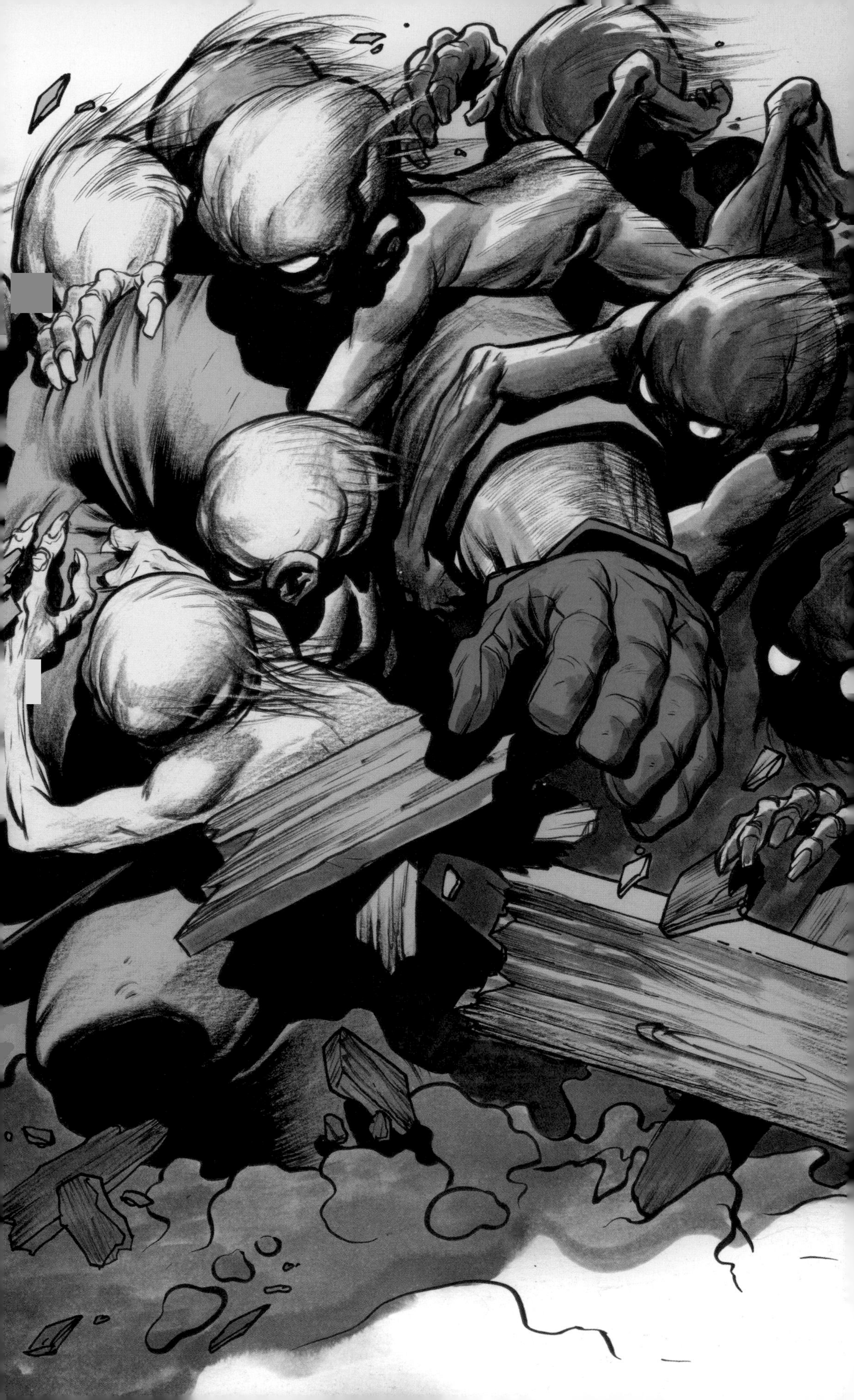

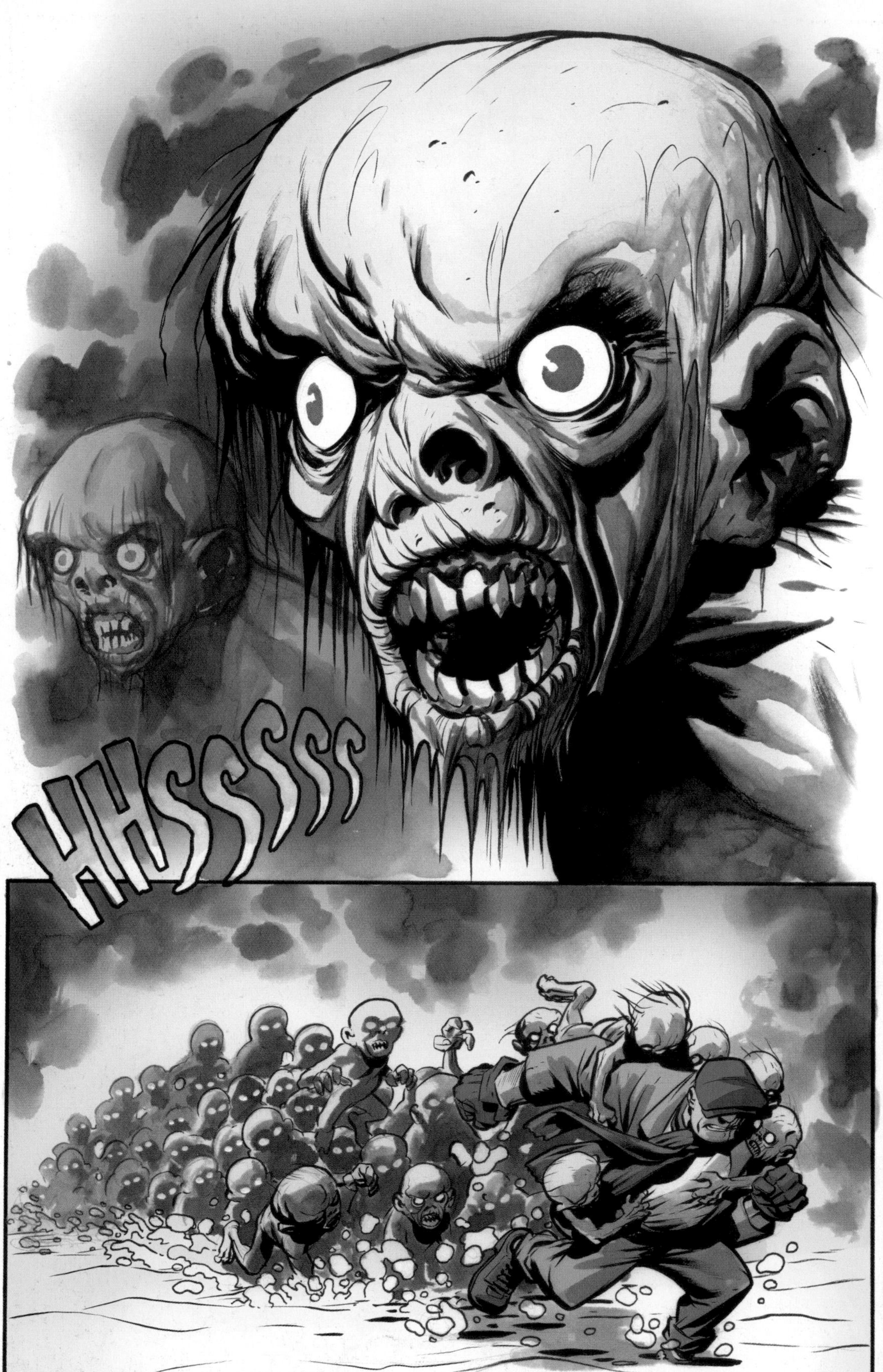
HHSSSSS

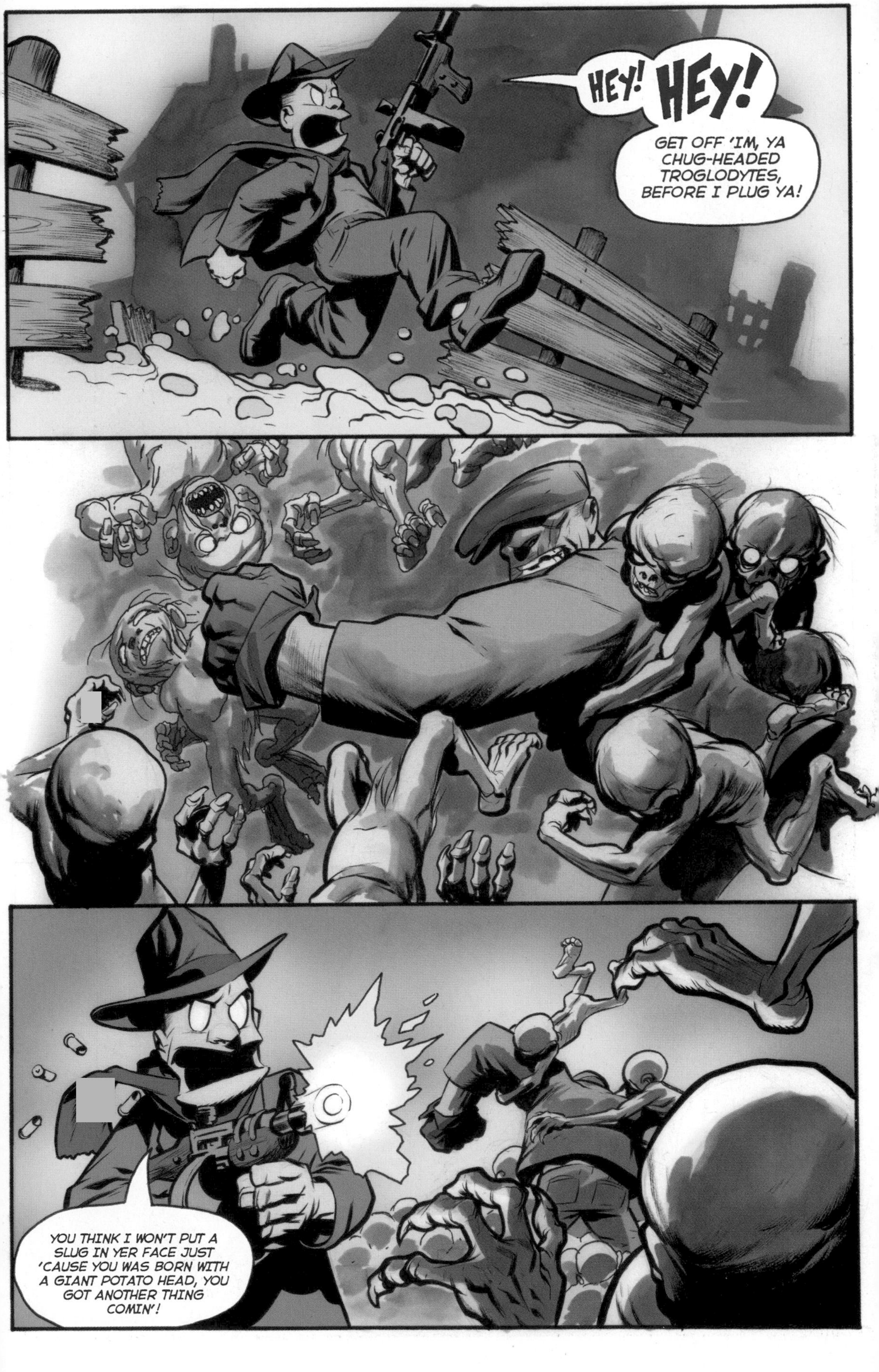
HEY! HEY!
GET OFF 'IM, YA CHUG-HEADED TROGLODYTES, BEFORE I PLUG YA!
YOU THINK I WON'T PUT A SLUG IN YER FACE JUST 'CAUSE YOU WAS BORN WITH A GIANT POTATO HEAD, YOU GOT ANOTHER THING COMIN'!

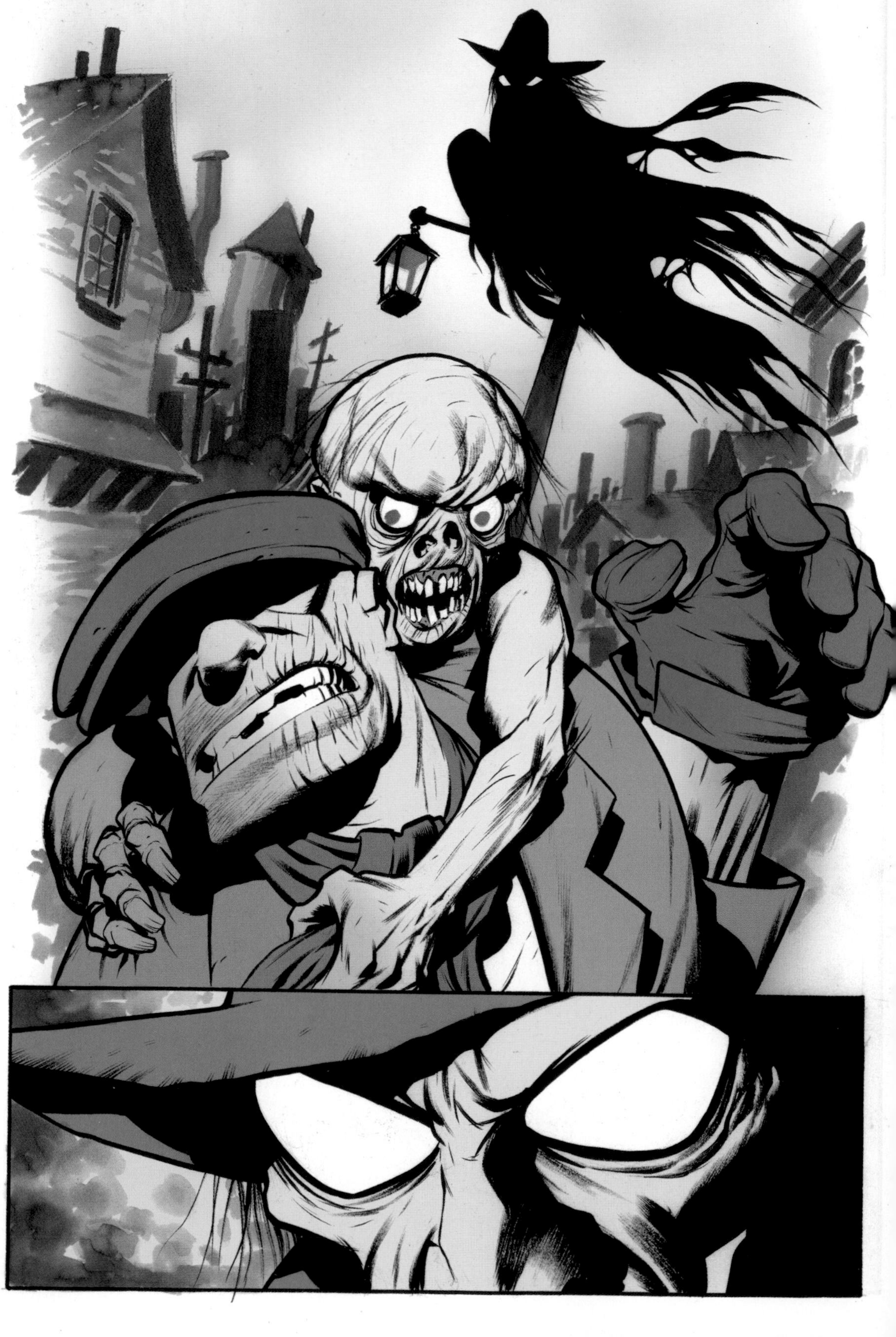

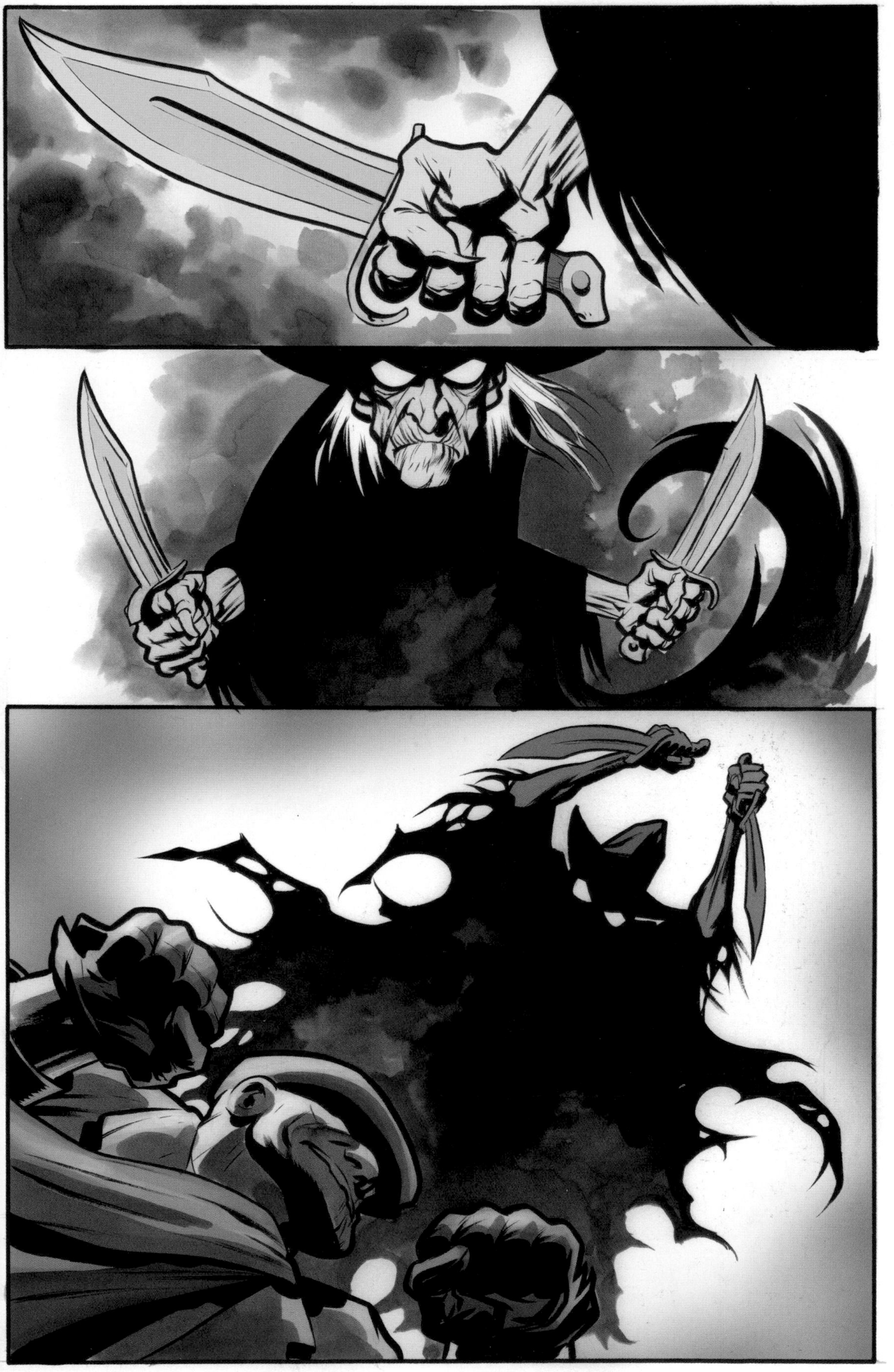

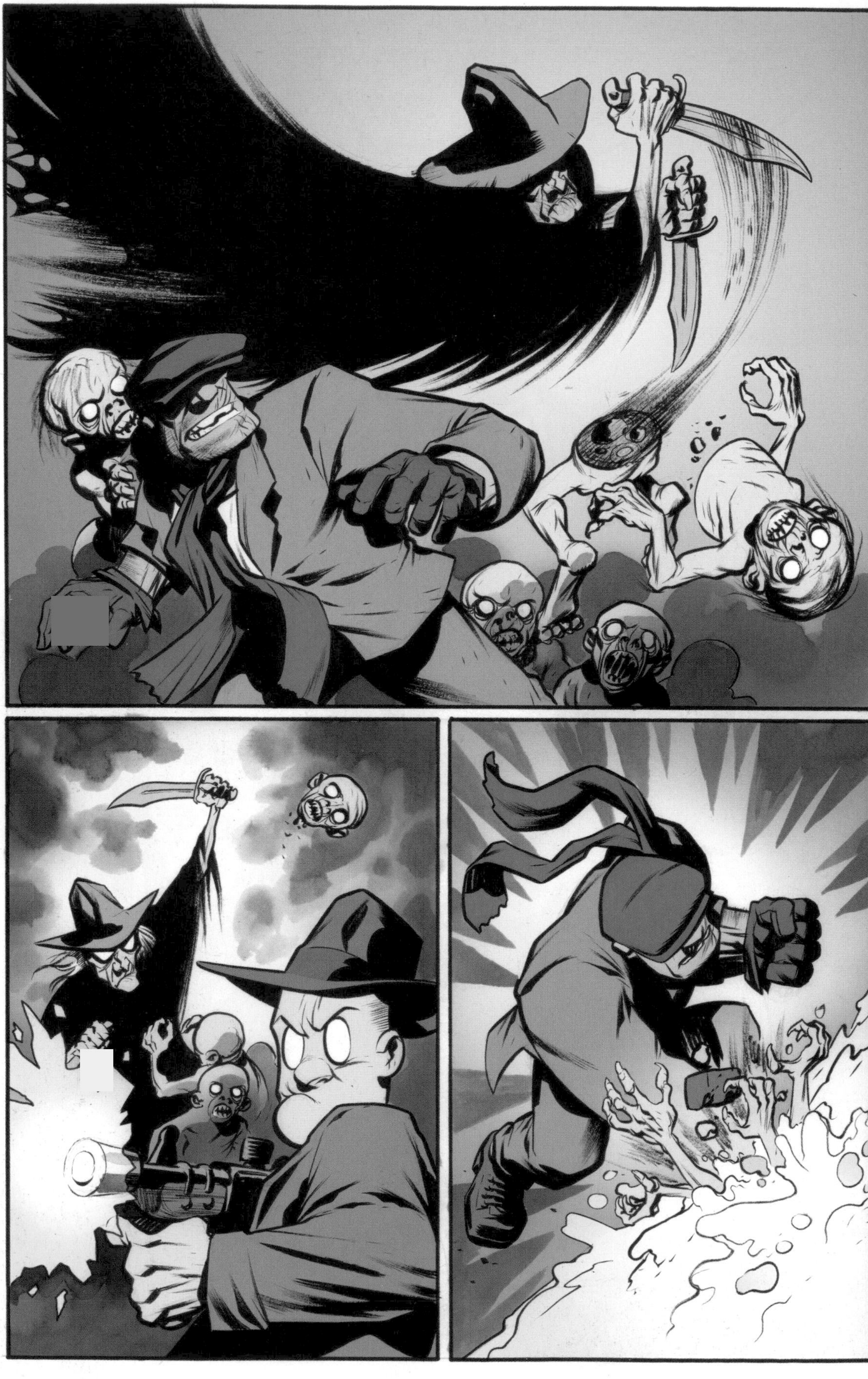

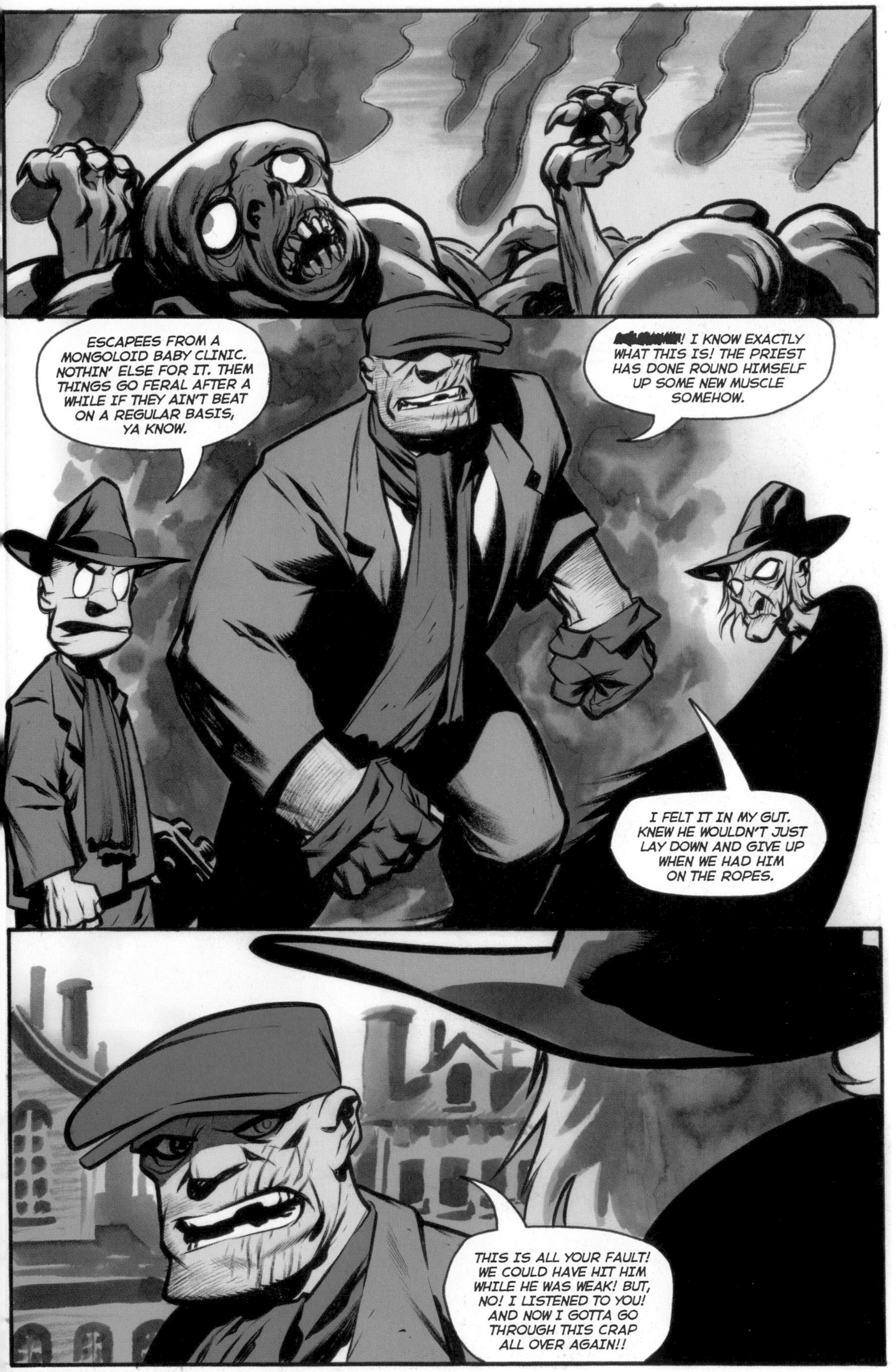
ESCAPEES FROM A MONGOLOID BABY CLINIC. NOTHIN' ELSE FOR IT. THEM THINGS GO FERAL AFTER A WHILE IF THEY AIN'T BEAT ON A REGULAR BASIS, YA KNOW.
[redacted]! I KNOW EXACTLY WHAT THIS IS! THE PRIEST HAS DONE ROUND HIMSELF UP SOME NEW MUSCLE SOMEHOW.
I FELT IT IN MY GUT. KNEW HE WOULDN'T JUST LAY DOWN AND GIVE UP WHEN WE HAD HIM ON THE ROPES.
THIS IS ALL YOUR FAULT! WE COULD HAVE HIT HIM WHILE HE WAS WEAK! BUT, NO! I LISTENED TO YOU! AND NOW I GOTTA GO THROUGH THIS CRAP ALL OVER AGAIN!!

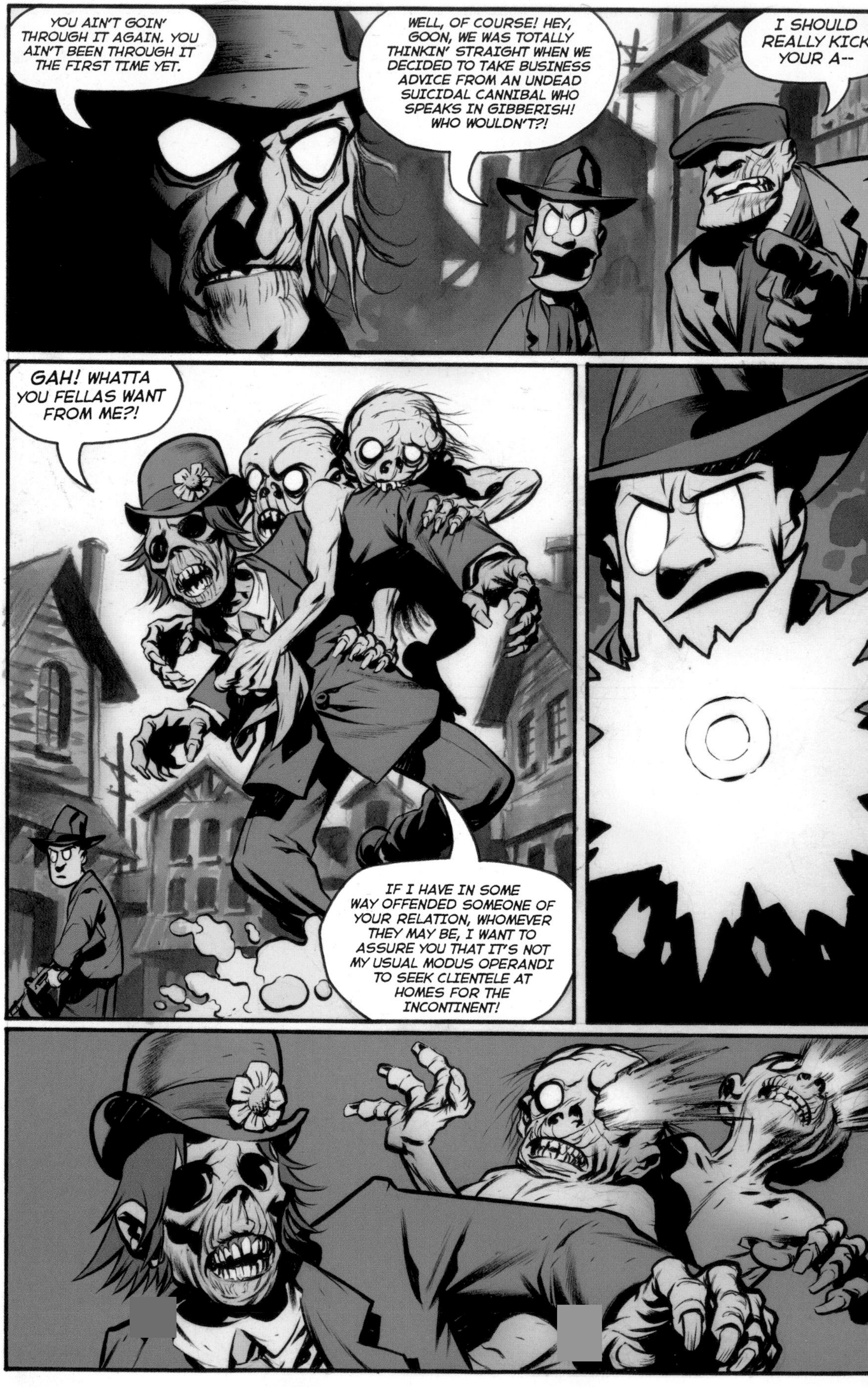
YOU AIN'T GOIN' THROUGH IT AGAIN. YOU AIN'T BEEN THROUGH IT THE FIRST TIME YET.
WELL, OF COURSE! HEY, GOON, WE WAS TOTALLY THINKIN' STRAIGHT WHEN WE DECIDED TO TAKE BUSINESS ADVICE FROM AN UNDEAD SUICIDAL CANNIBAL WHO SPEAKS IN GIBBERISH! WHO WOULDN'T?!
I SHOULD REALLY KICK YOUR A--
GAH! WHATTA YOU FELLAS WANT FROM ME?!
IF I HAVE IN SOME WAY OFFENDED SOMEONE OF YOUR RELATION, WHOMEVER THEY MAY BE, I WANT TO ASSURE YOU THAT IT'S NOT MY USUAL MODUS OPERANDI TO SEEK CLIENTELE AT HOMES FOR THE INCONTINENT!

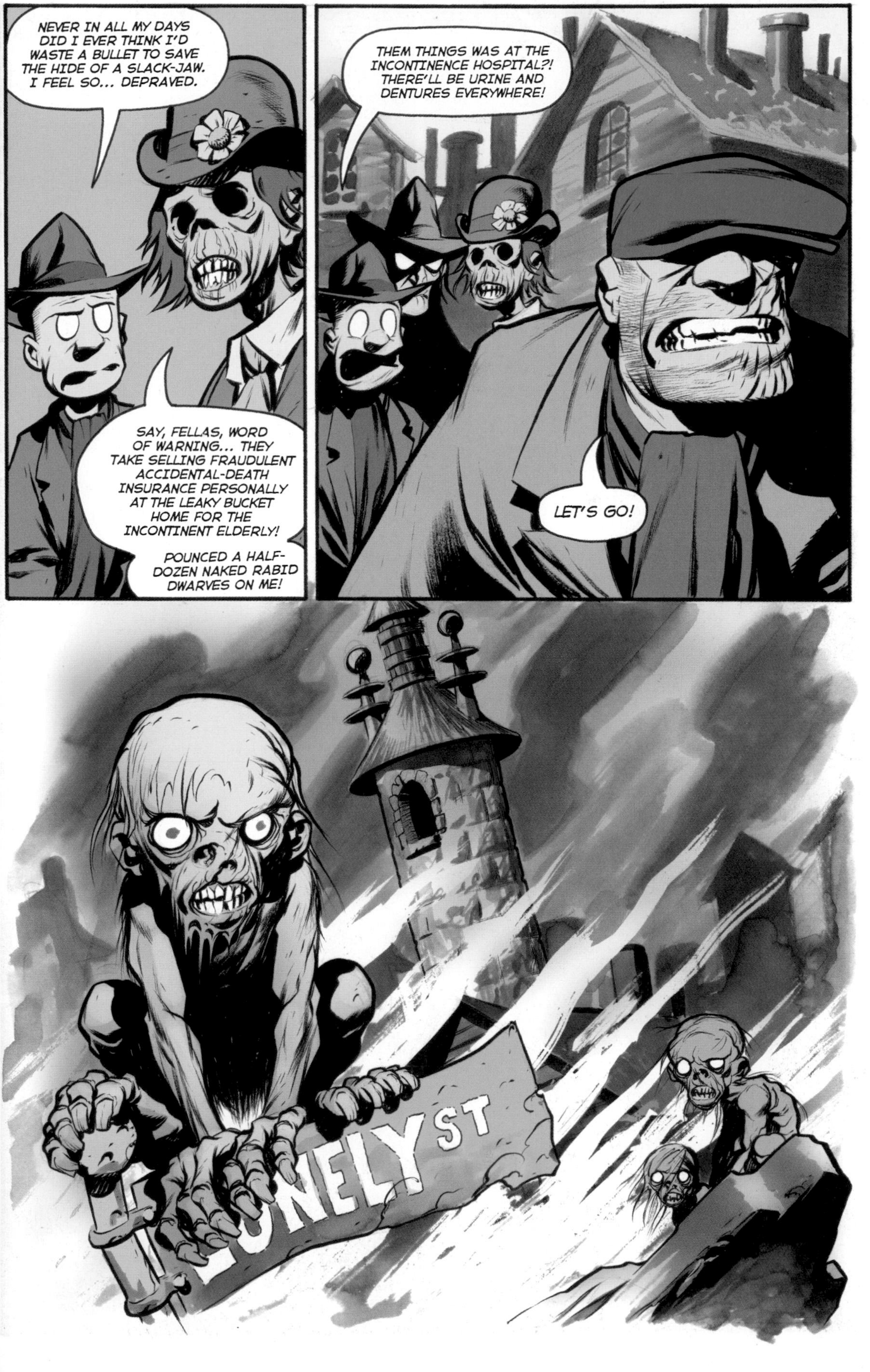
NEVER IN ALL MY DAYS DID I EVER THINK I'D WASTE A BULLET TO SAVE THE HIDE OF A SLACK-JAW. I FEEL SO... DEPRAVED.
SAY, FELLAS, WORD OF WARNING... THEY TAKE SELLING FRAUDULENT ACCIDENTAL-DEATH INSURANCE PERSONALLY AT THE LEAKY BUCKET HOME FOR THE INCONTINENT ELDERLY!
POUNCED A HALF-DOZEN NAKED RABID DWARVES ON ME!
THEM THINGS WAS AT THE INCONTINENCE HOSPITAL?! THERE'LL BE URINE AND DENTURES EVERYWHERE!
LET'S GO!
LONELY ST

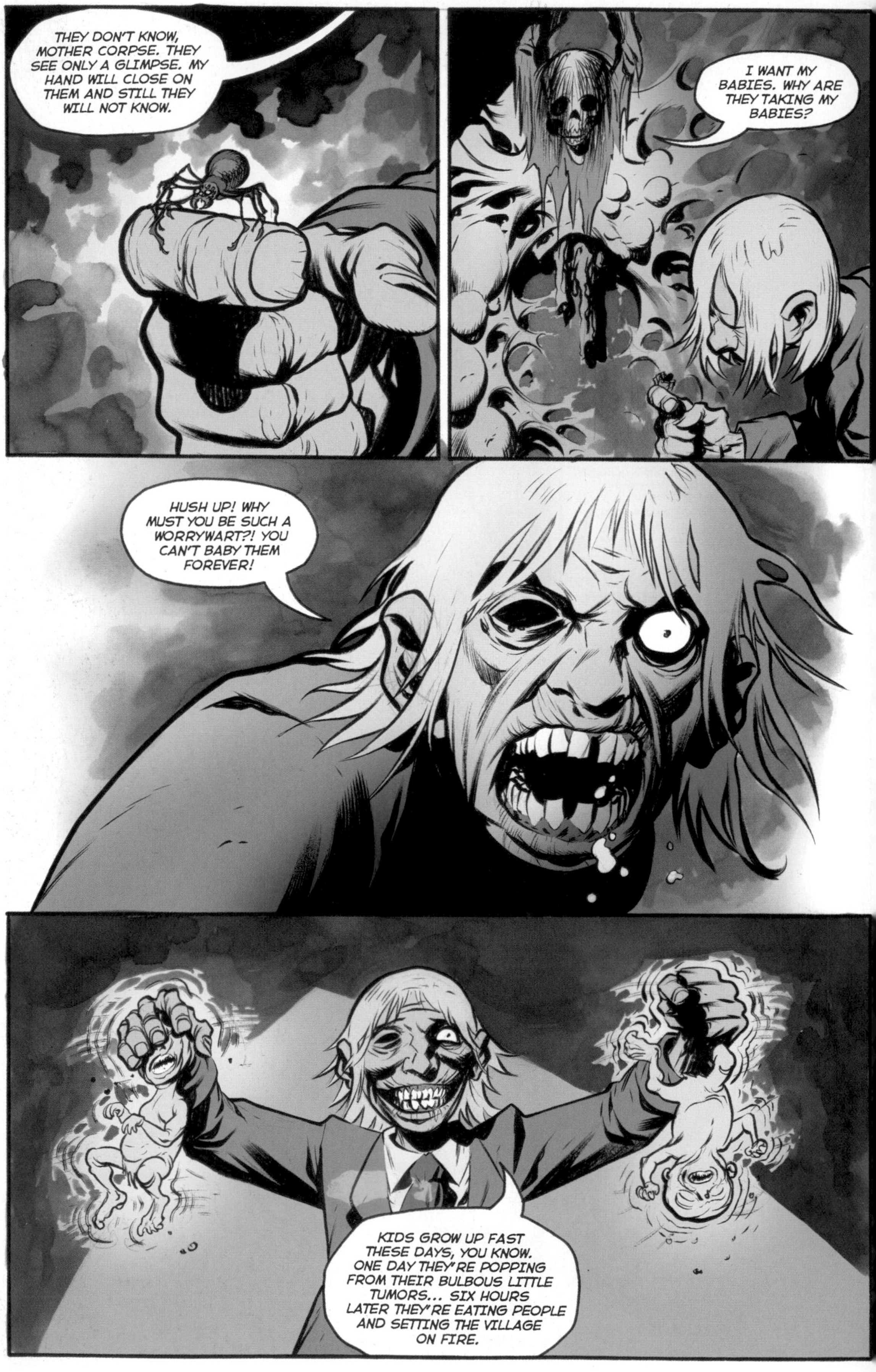
THEY DON'T KNOW, MOTHER CORPSE. THEY SEE ONLY A GLIMPSE. MY HAND WILL CLOSE ON THEM AND STILL THEY WILL NOT KNOW.
I WANT MY BABIES. WHY ARE THEY TAKING MY BABIES?
HUSH UP! WHY MUST YOU BE SUCH A WORRYWART?! YOU CAN'T BABY THEM FOREVER!
KIDS GROW UP FAST THESE DAYS, YOU KNOW. ONE DAY THEY'RE POPPING FROM THEIR BULBOUS LITTLE TUMORS... SIX HOURS LATER THEY'RE EATING PEOPLE AND SETTING THE VILLAGE ON FIRE.

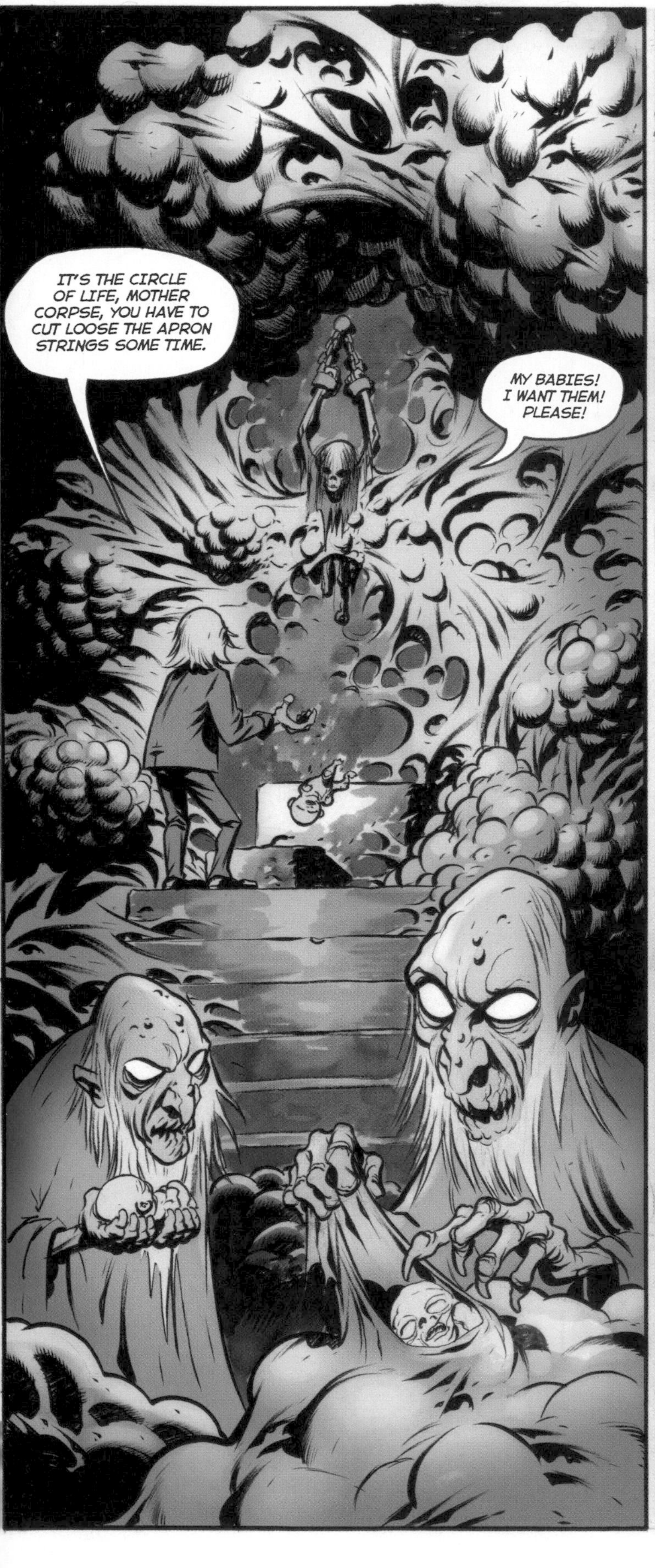
IT'S THE CIRCLE OF LIFE, MOTHER CORPSE, YOU HAVE TO CUT LOOSE THE APRON STRINGS SOME TIME.
MY BABIES! I WANT THEM! PLEASE!

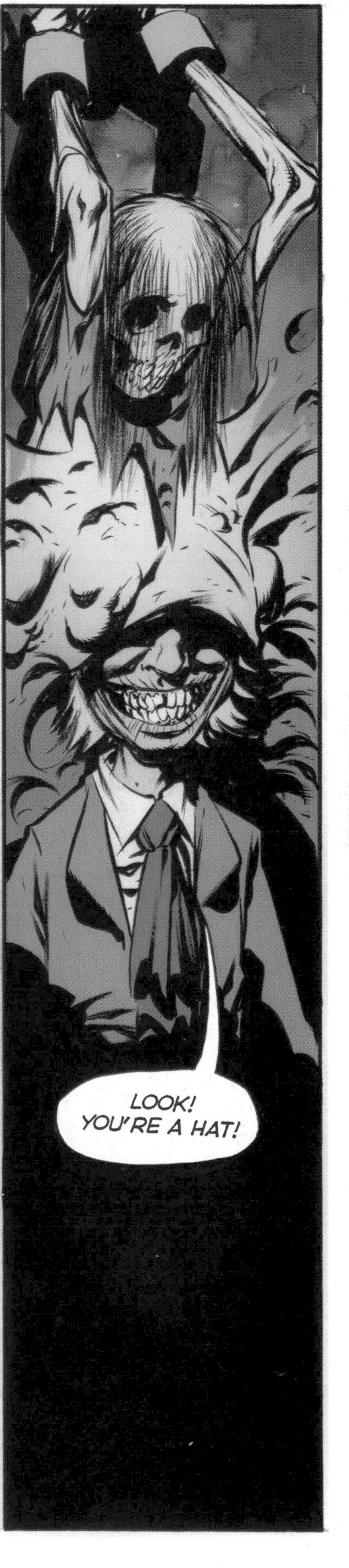
LOOK! YOU'RE A HAT!

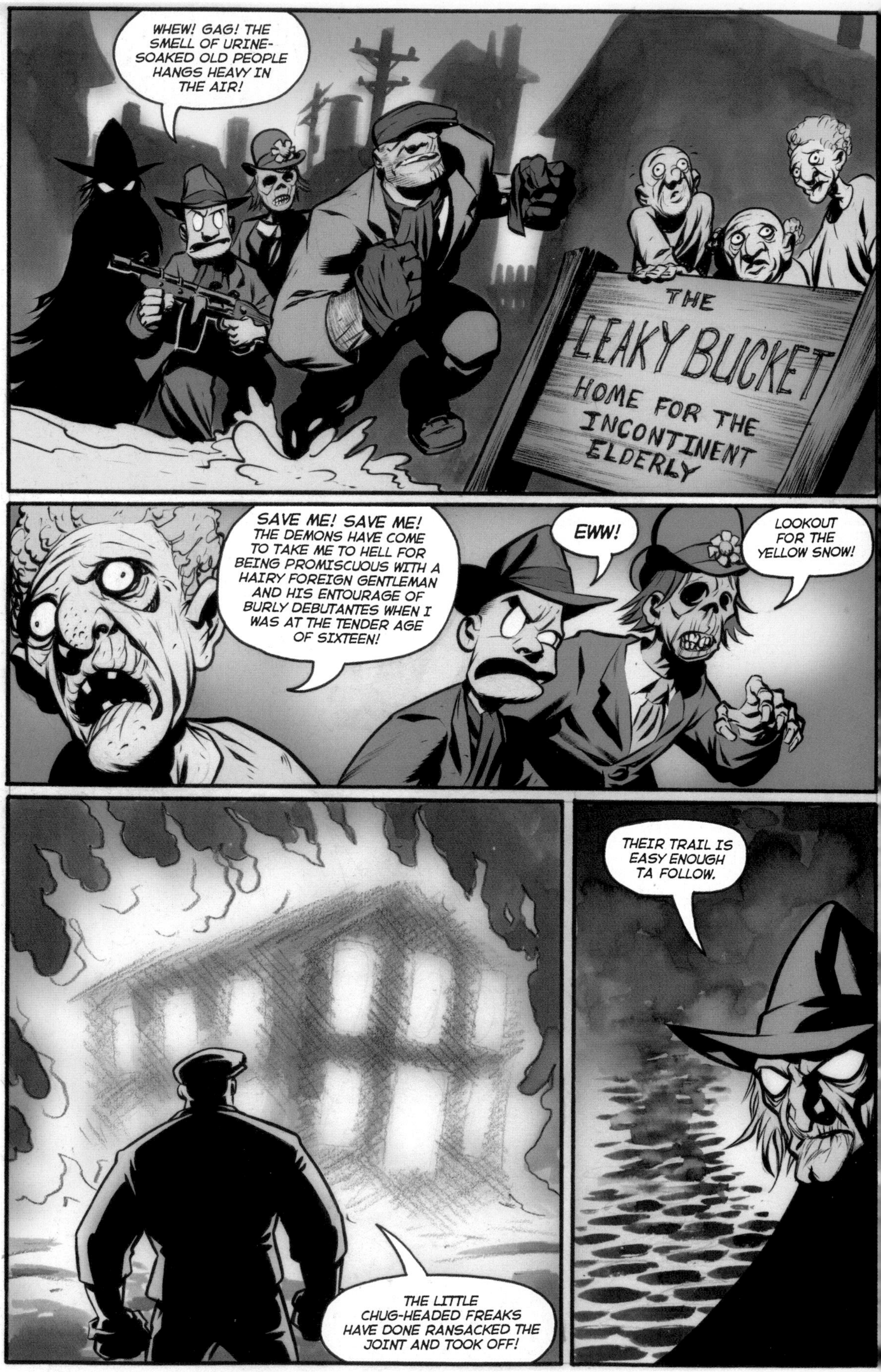
WHEW! GAG! THE SMELL OF URINE-SOAKED OLD PEOPLE HANGS HEAVY IN THE AIR!
THE LEAKY BUCKET HOME FOR THE INCONTINENT ELDERLY
SAVE ME! SAVE ME! THE DEMONS HAVE COME TO TAKE ME TO HELL FOR BEING PROMISCUOUS WITH A HAIRY FOREIGN GENTLEMAN AND HIS ENTOURAGE OF BURLY DEBUTANTES WHEN I WAS AT THE TENDER AGE OF SIXTEEN!
EWW!
LOOKOUT FOR THE YELLOW SNOW!
THE LITTLE CHUG-HEADED FREAKS HAVE DONE RANSACKED THE JOINT AND TOOK OFF!
THEIR TRAIL IS EASY ENOUGH TA FOLLOW.

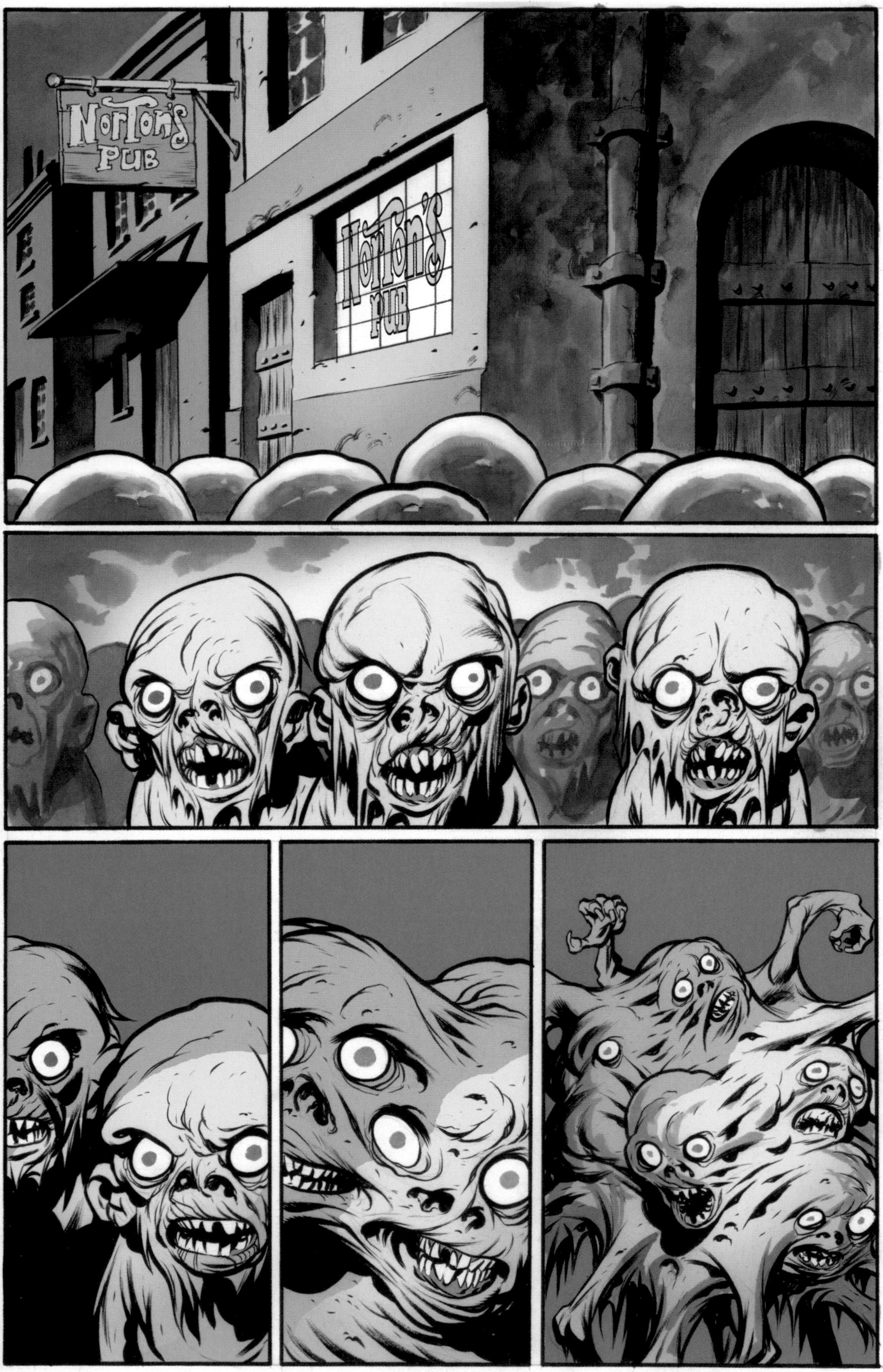
Norton's
PUB
Norton's
PUB

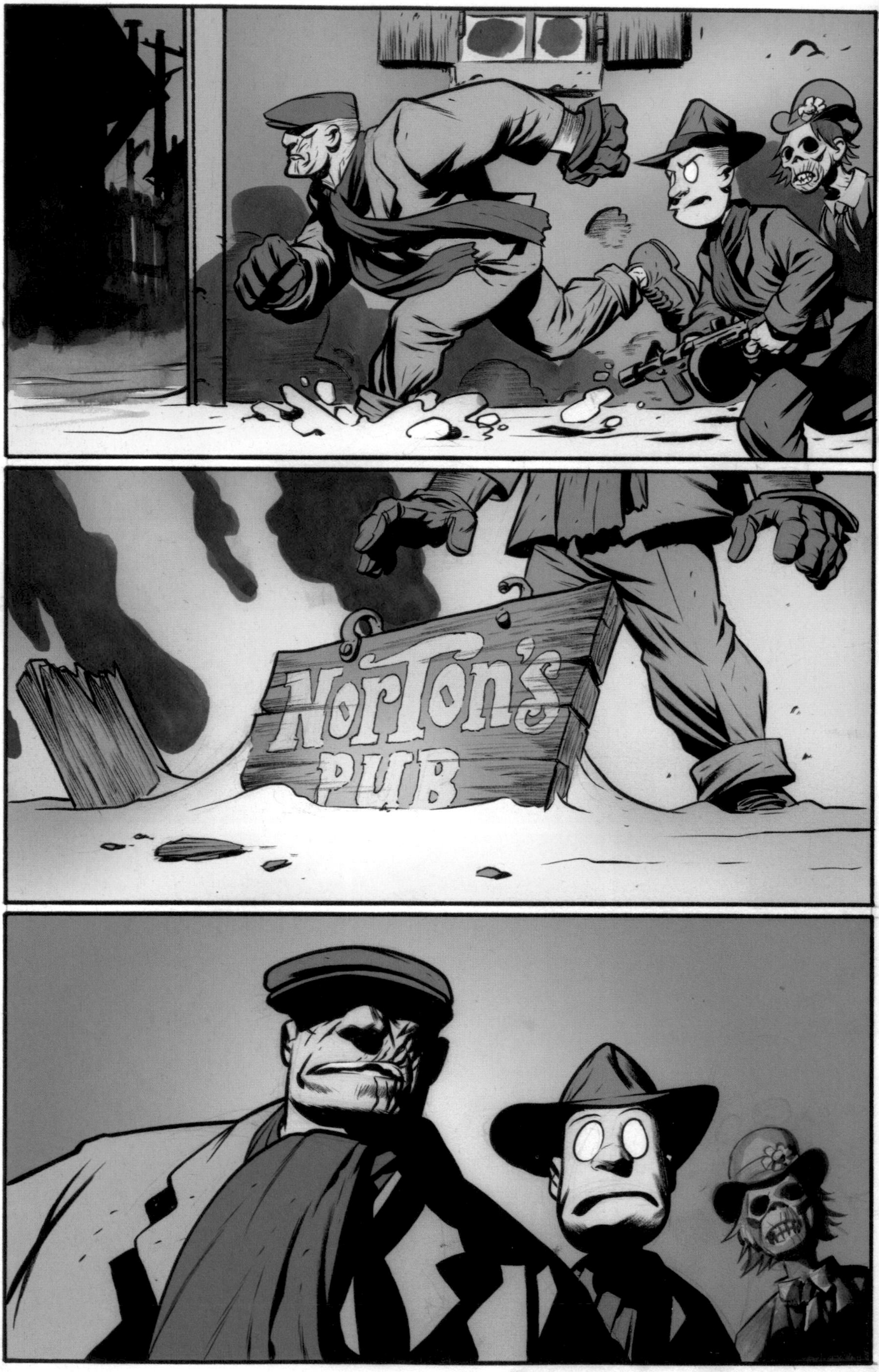
Norton's
PUB

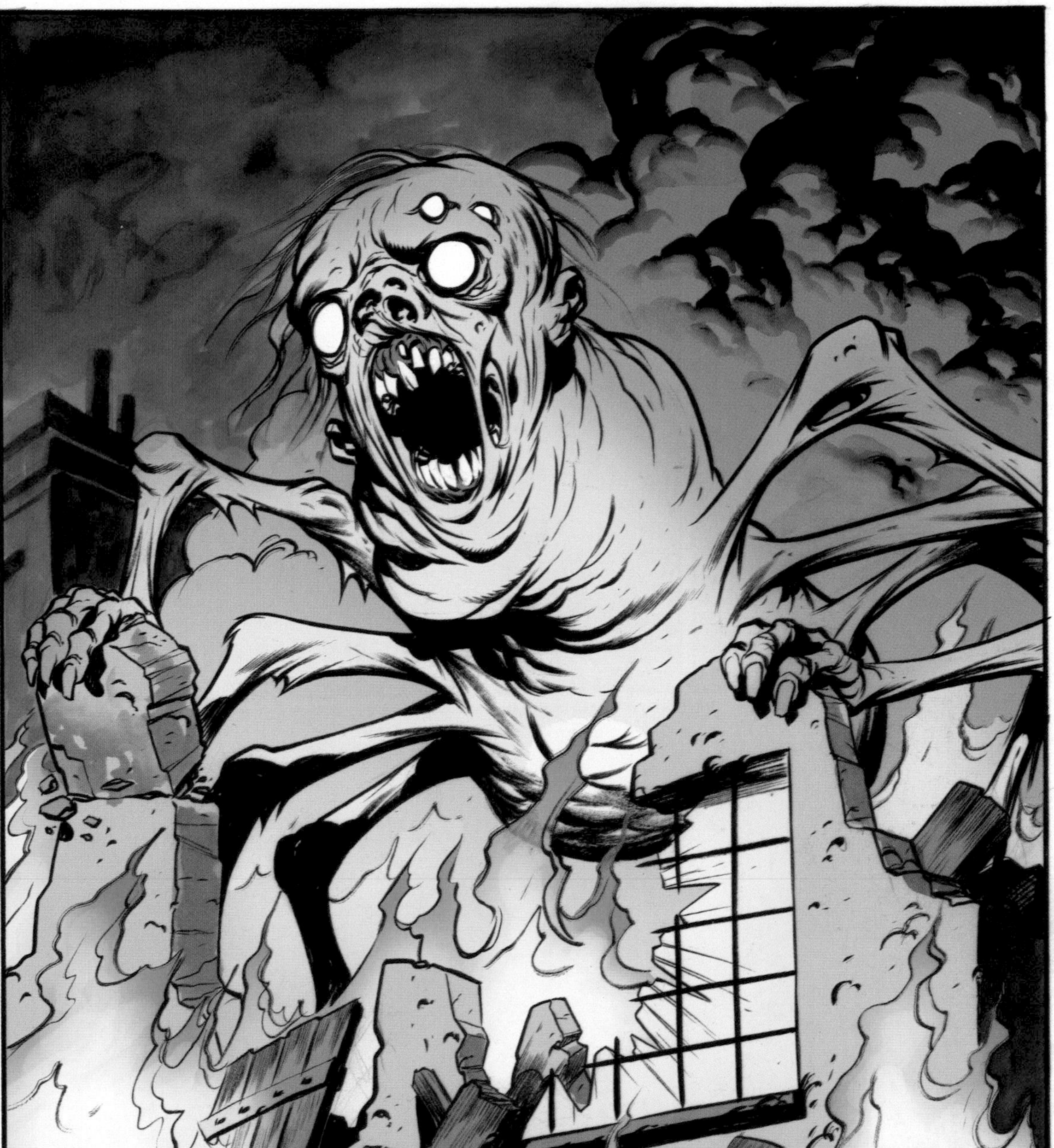

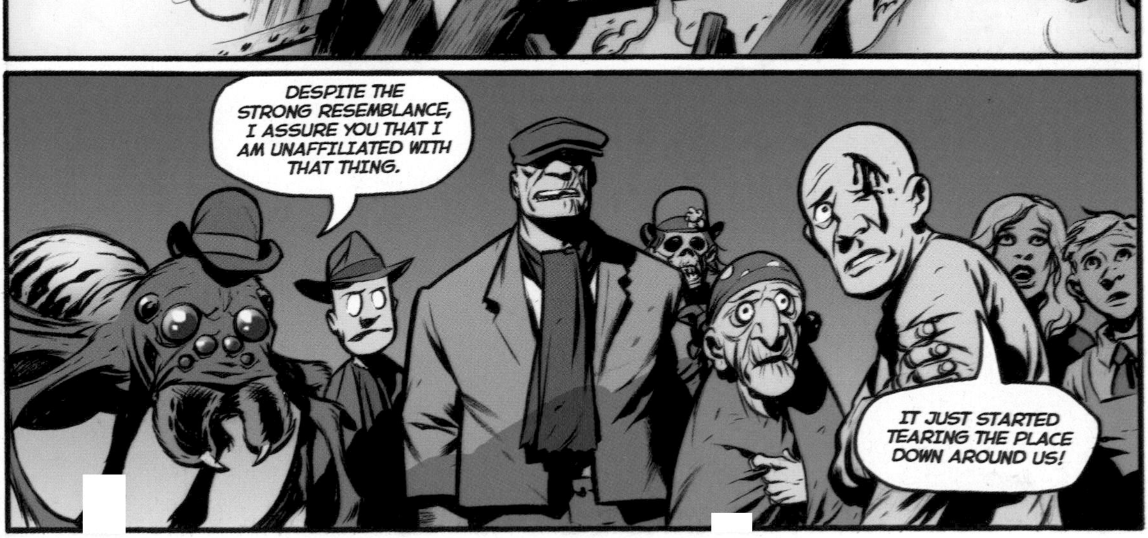
DESPITE THE STRONG RESEMBLANCE, I ASSURE YOU THAT I AM UNAFFILIATED WITH THAT THING.
IT JUST STARTED TEARING THE PLACE DOWN AROUND US!

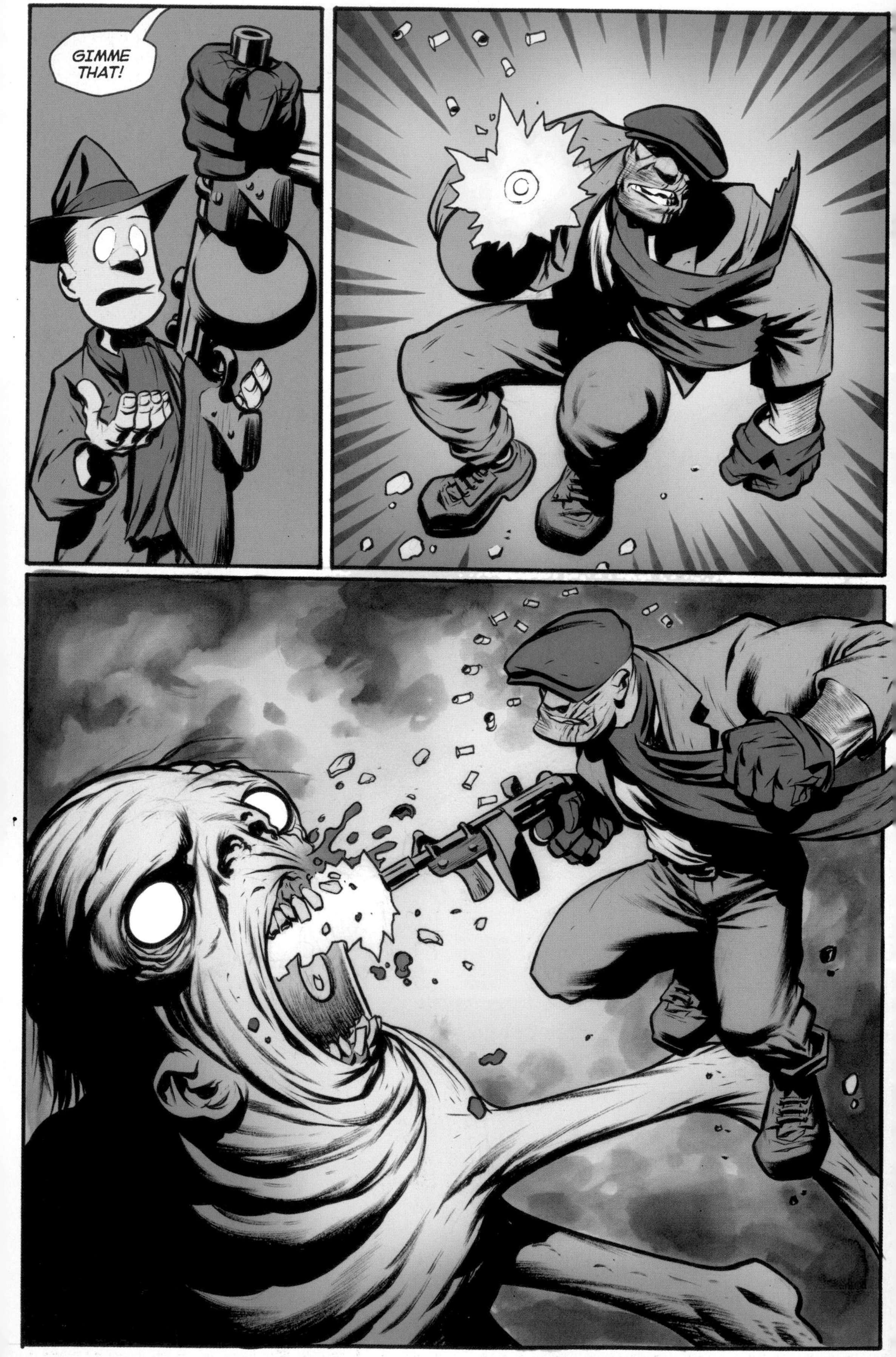
GIMME THAT!

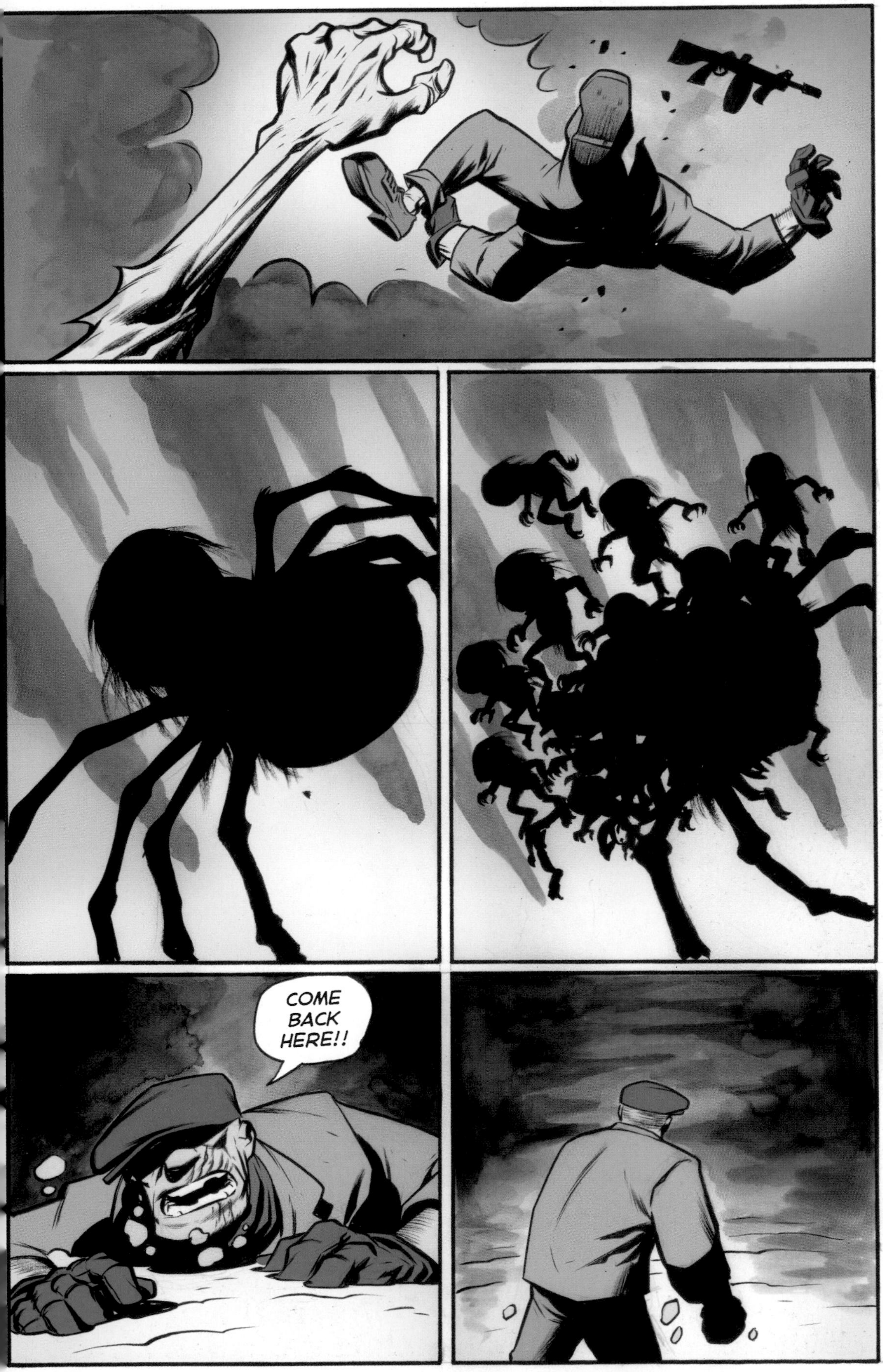
COME BACK HERE!!

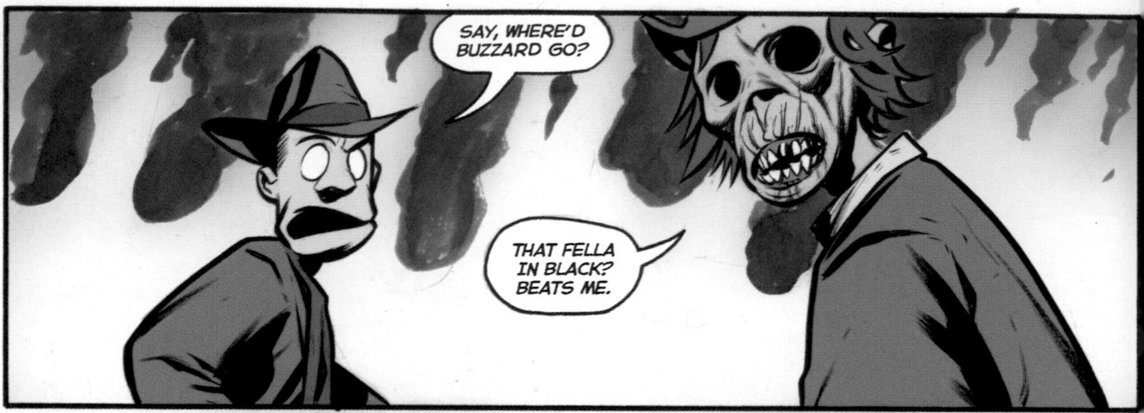
SAY, WHERE'D BUZZARD GO?
THAT FELLA IN BLACK? BEATS ME.

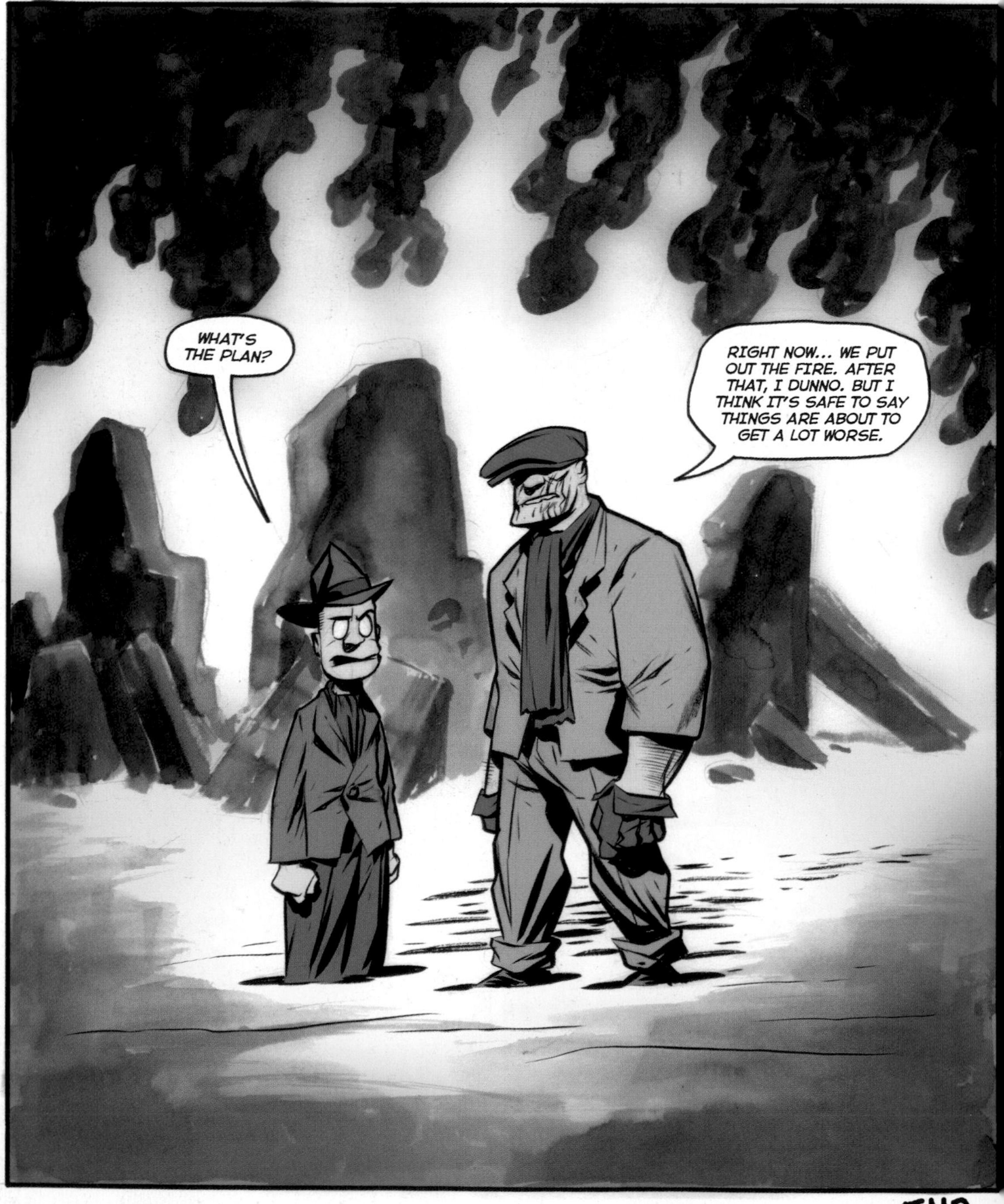
WHAT'S THE PLAN?
RIGHT NOW... WE PUT OUT THE FIRE. AFTER THAT, I DUNNO. BUT I THINK IT'S SAFE TO SAY THINGS ARE ABOUT TO GET A LOT WORSE.

END.

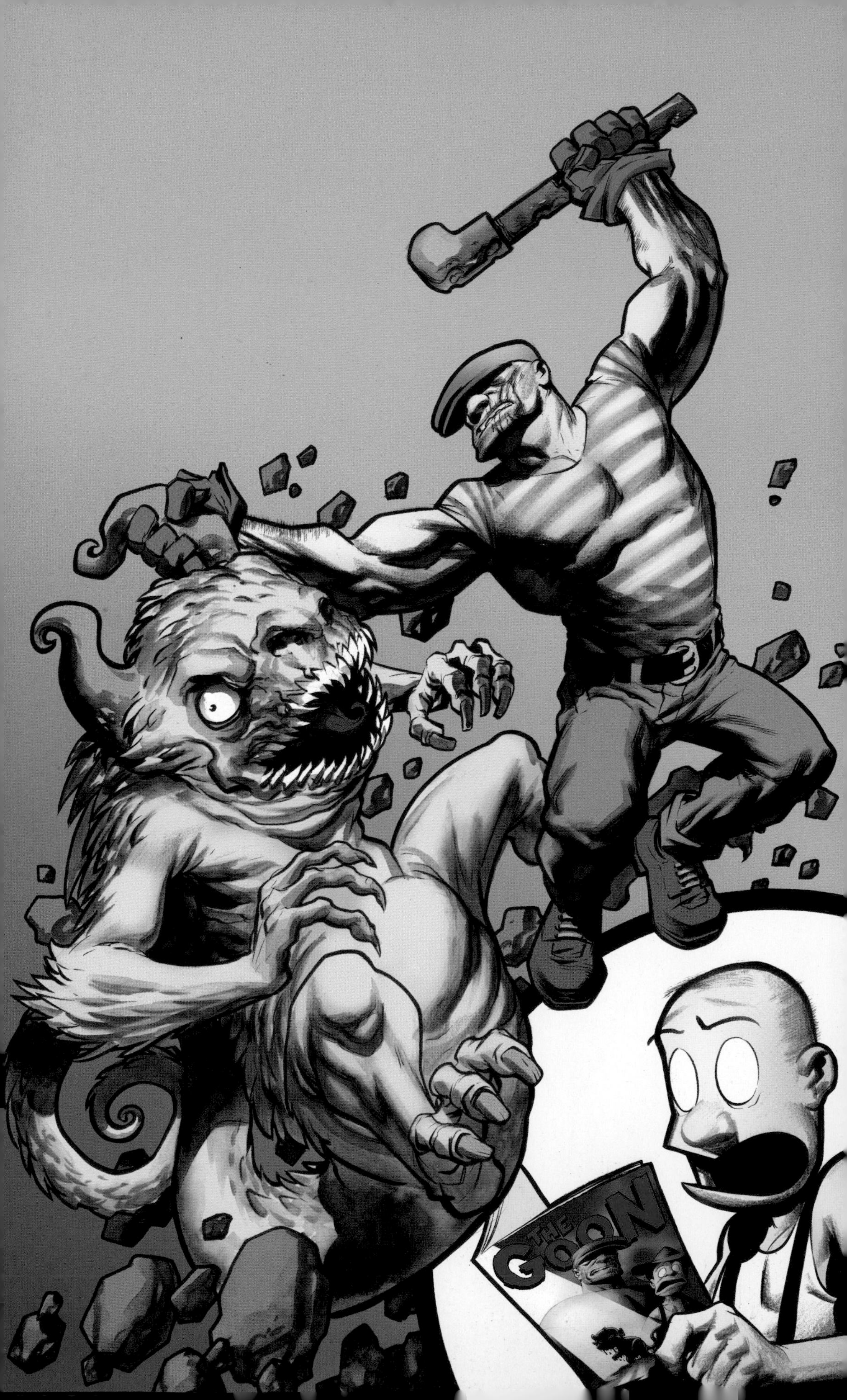
THE GOON

it was the funniest comic I had written yet. But it was not an all-ages story. I thought it would be fine to have just one issue of *The Goon* labeled as a "NOT FOR MINORS" comic. We even planned on having a giant warning printed on a blank cover that would conceal the actual cover. I thought all this was a riot.

Supportive as ever, Dark Horse feared a backlash that might hurt the momentum of the comic but did not try to keep me from doing the story and backed me 100 percent. However, word of the outrageousness of this comic got out and a grass-roots movement was started to try to keep retailers from carrying it by a right-wing bible thumper in Alabama named Margaret Snodgrass. She, in her almighty wisdom, claimed that the comic was morally reprehensible and contacted area retailers telling them that even allowing the comic to be stocked on their shelves could lead to their ever-lasting damnation. Sadly enough, some listened to her and threatened to stop carrying *The Goon* altogether because of this single issue. Fearing for my livelihood, I decided to hold off on the issue. But let me say this . . . "SATAN'S SODOMY BABY" WILL BE RELEASED! You may have won the battle, but you'll never win the war, Snodgrass!! My story of demonic homosexual assault on the unsuspecting buttocks of a backwoods rube and the progeny of said union cannot be withheld forever!! It's time to fight back, readers! Go to your local comics retailer and demand "SATAN'S SODOMY BABY"!

Those readers and retailers wishing to voice their concerns about the outlandish treatment of "Satan's Sodomy Baby" can contact us at goonmail@aol.com.

Thank you for your thoughts and prayers,

Eric Powell

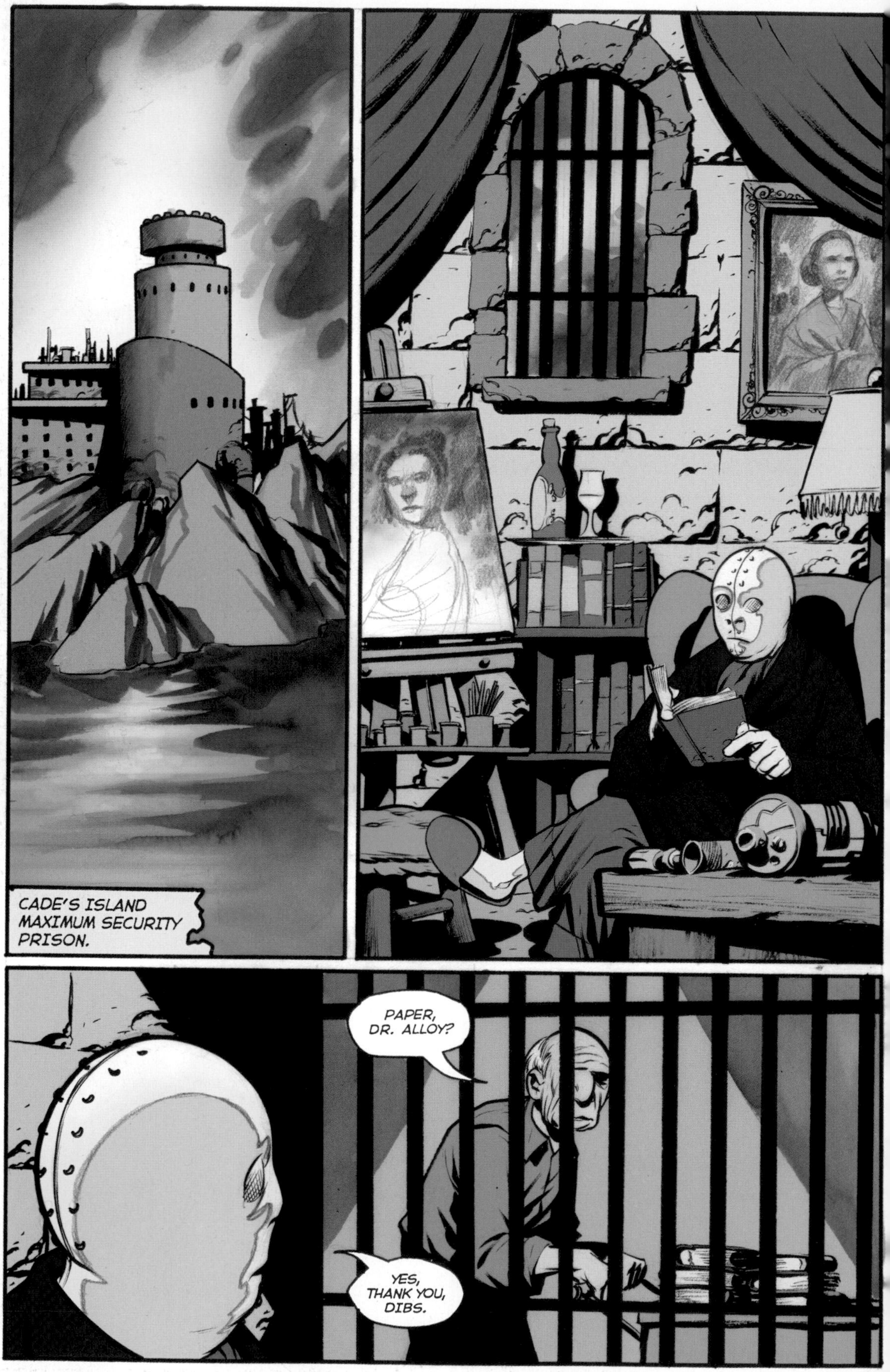
CADE'S ISLAND MAXIMUM SECURITY PRISON.
PAPER, DR. ALLOY?
YES, THANK YOU, DIBS.

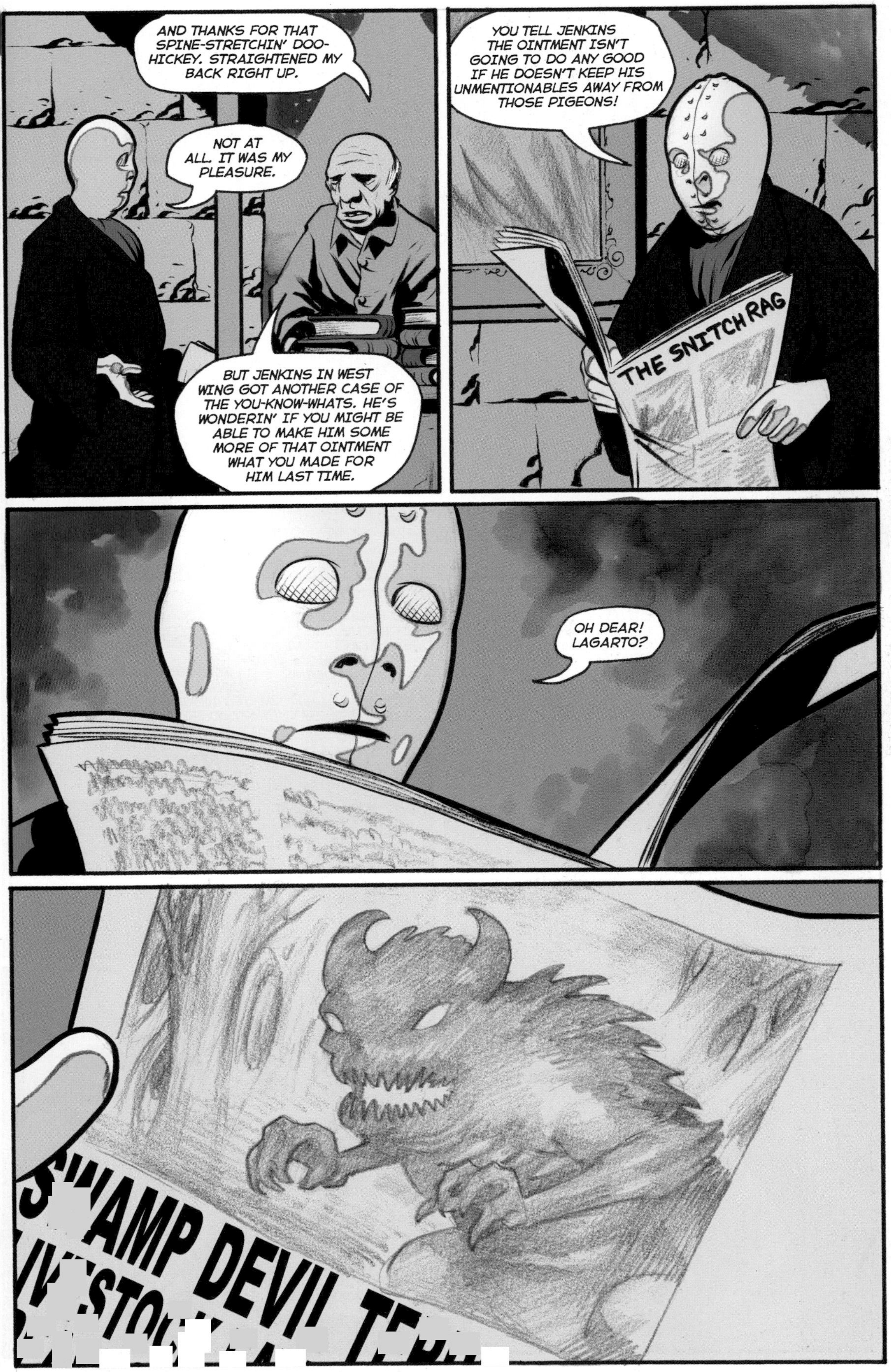
AND THANKS FOR THAT SPINE-STRETCHIN' DOO-HICKEY. STRAIGHTENED MY BACK RIGHT UP.
NOT AT ALL. IT WAS MY PLEASURE.
BUT JENKINS IN WEST WING GOT ANOTHER CASE OF THE YOU-KNOW-WHATS. HE'S WONDERIN' IF YOU MIGHT BE ABLE TO MAKE HIM SOME MORE OF THAT OINTMENT WHAT YOU MADE FOR HIM LAST TIME.
YOU TELL JENKINS THE OINTMENT ISN'T GOING TO DO ANY GOOD IF HE DOESN'T KEEP HIS UNMENTIONABLES AWAY FROM THOSE PIGEONS!
THE SNITCH RAG
OH DEAR! LAGARTO?

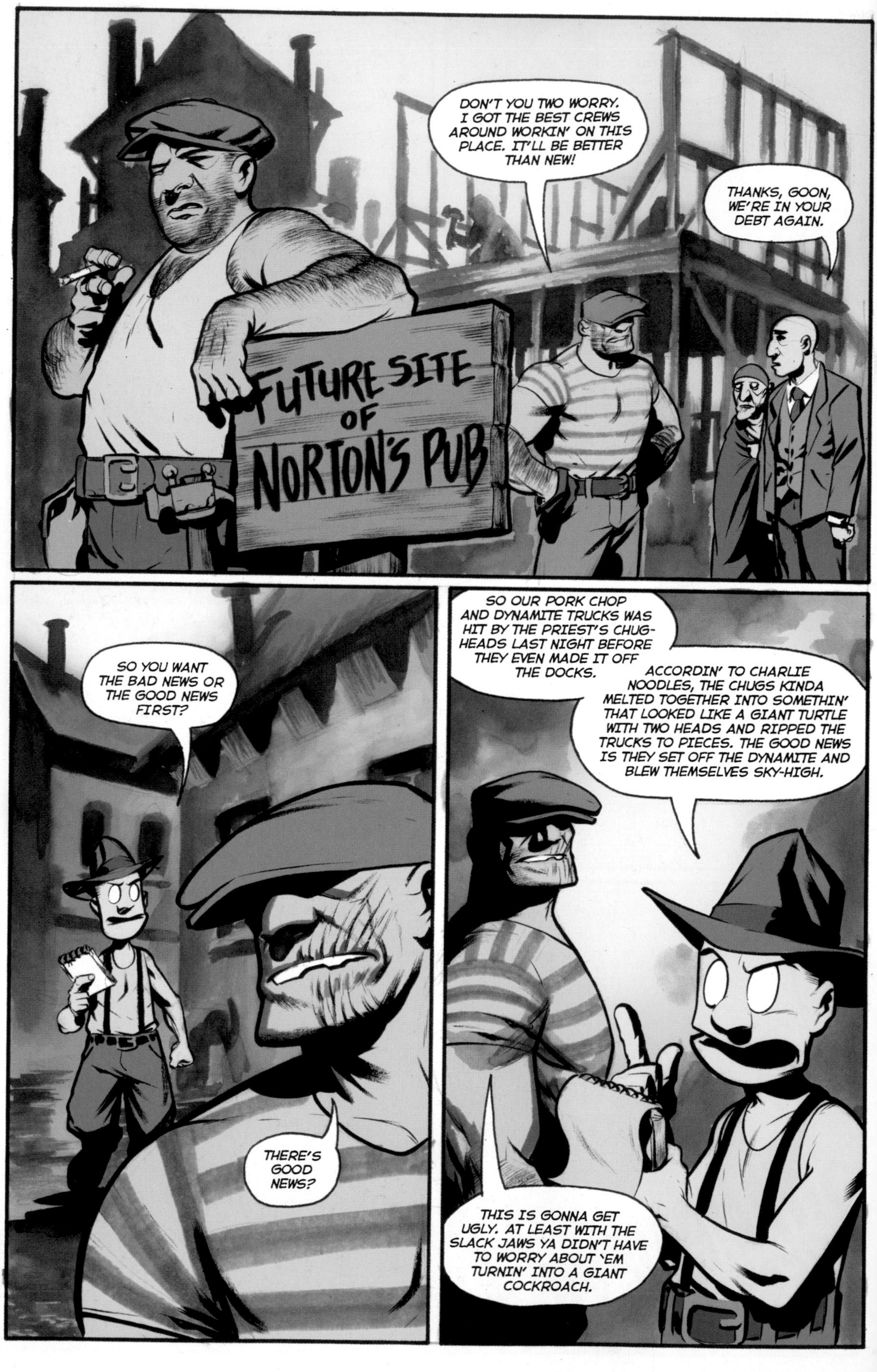
FUTURE SITE OF NORTON'S PUB
DON'T YOU TWO WORRY. I GOT THE BEST CREWS AROUND WORKIN' ON THIS PLACE. IT'LL BE BETTER THAN NEW!
THANKS, GOON, WE'RE IN YOUR DEBT AGAIN.
SO YOU WANT THE BAD NEWS OR THE GOOD NEWS FIRST?
THERE'S GOOD NEWS?
SO OUR PORK CHOP AND DYNAMITE TRUCKS WAS HIT BY THE PRIEST'S CHUG-HEADS LAST NIGHT BEFORE THEY EVEN MADE IT OFF THE DOCKS.
ACCORDIN' TO CHARLIE NOODLES, THE CHUGS KINDA MELTED TOGETHER INTO SOMETHIN' THAT LOOKED LIKE A GIANT TURTLE WITH TWO HEADS AND RIPPED THE TRUCKS TO PIECES. THE GOOD NEWS IS THEY SET OFF THE DYNAMITE AND BLEW THEMSELVES SKY-HIGH.
THIS IS GONNA GET UGLY. AT LEAST WITH THE SLACK JAWS YA DIDN'T HAVE TO WORRY ABOUT 'EM TURNIN' INTO A GIANT COCKROACH.

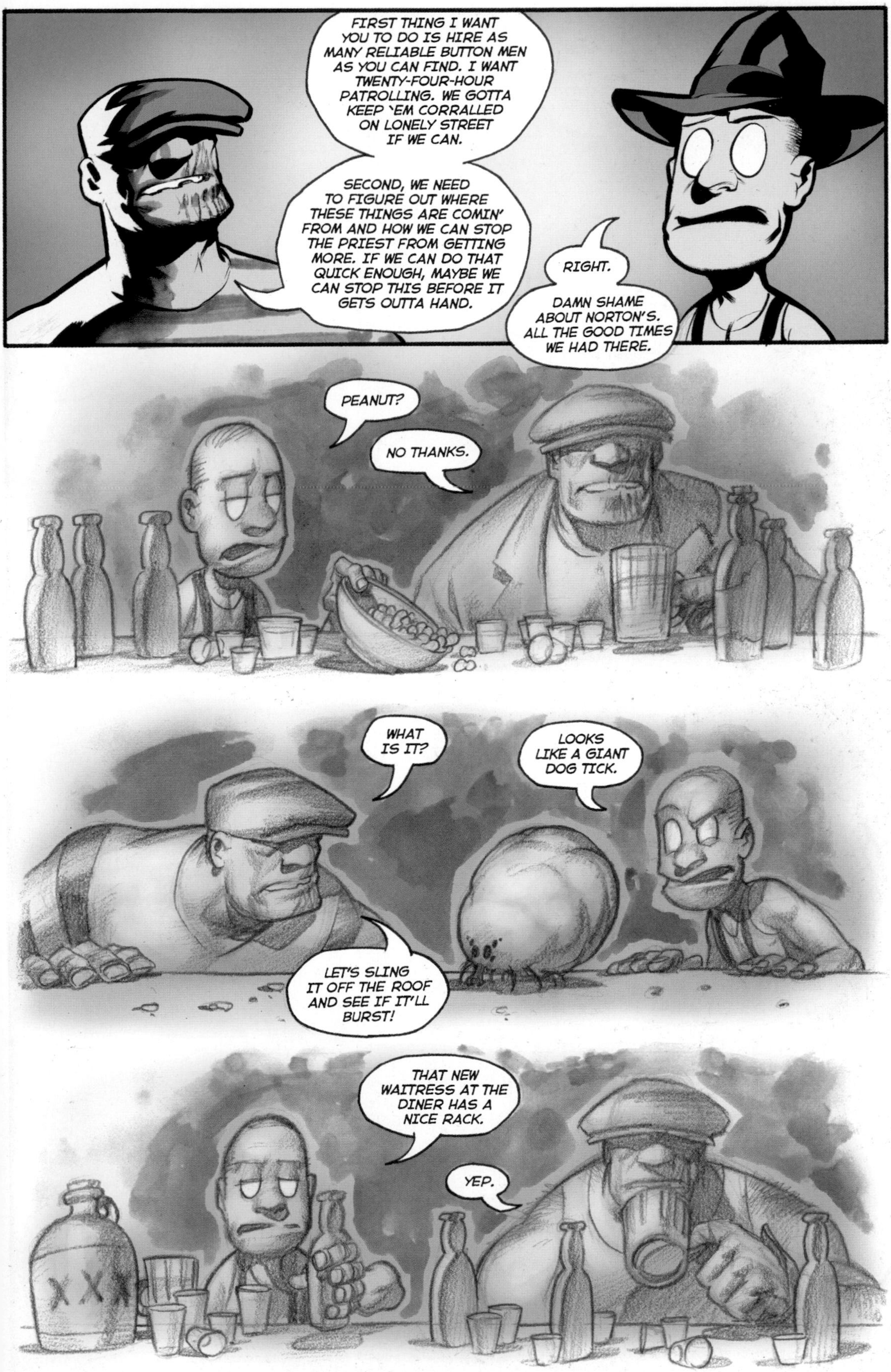
FIRST THING I WANT YOU TO DO IS HIRE AS MANY RELIABLE BUTTON MEN AS YOU CAN FIND. I WANT TWENTY-FOUR-HOUR PATROLLING. WE GOTTA KEEP 'EM CORRALLED ON LONELY STREET IF WE CAN.
SECOND, WE NEED TO FIGURE OUT WHERE THESE THINGS ARE COMIN' FROM AND HOW WE CAN STOP THE PRIEST FROM GETTING MORE. IF WE CAN DO THAT QUICK ENOUGH, MAYBE WE CAN STOP THIS BEFORE IT GETS OUTTA HAND.
RIGHT.
DAMN SHAME ABOUT NORTON'S. ALL THE GOOD TIMES WE HAD THERE.
PEANUT?
NO THANKS.
WHAT IS IT?
LOOKS LIKE A GIANT DOG TICK.
LET'S SLING IT OFF THE ROOF AND SEE IF IT'LL BURST!
THAT NEW WAITRESS AT THE DINER HAS A NICE RACK.
YEP.

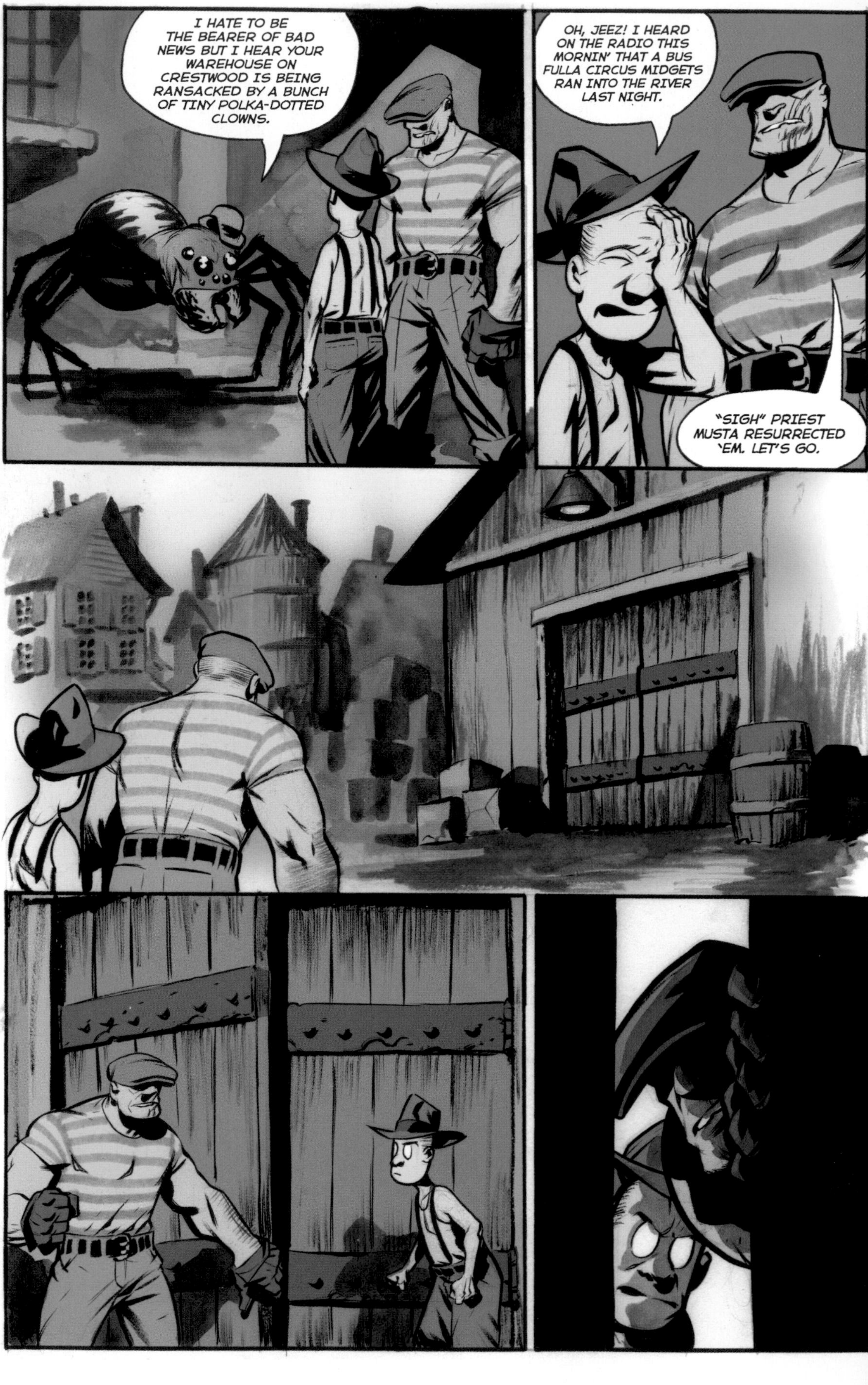
I HATE TO BE THE BEARER OF BAD NEWS BUT I HEAR YOUR WAREHOUSE ON CRESTWOOD IS BEING RANSACKED BY A BUNCH OF TINY POLKA-DOTTED CLOWNS.
OH, JEEZ! I HEARD ON THE RADIO THIS MORNIN' THAT A BUS FULLA CIRCUS MIDGETS RAN INTO THE RIVER LAST NIGHT.
"SIGH" PRIEST MUSTA RESURRECTED 'EM. LET'S GO.

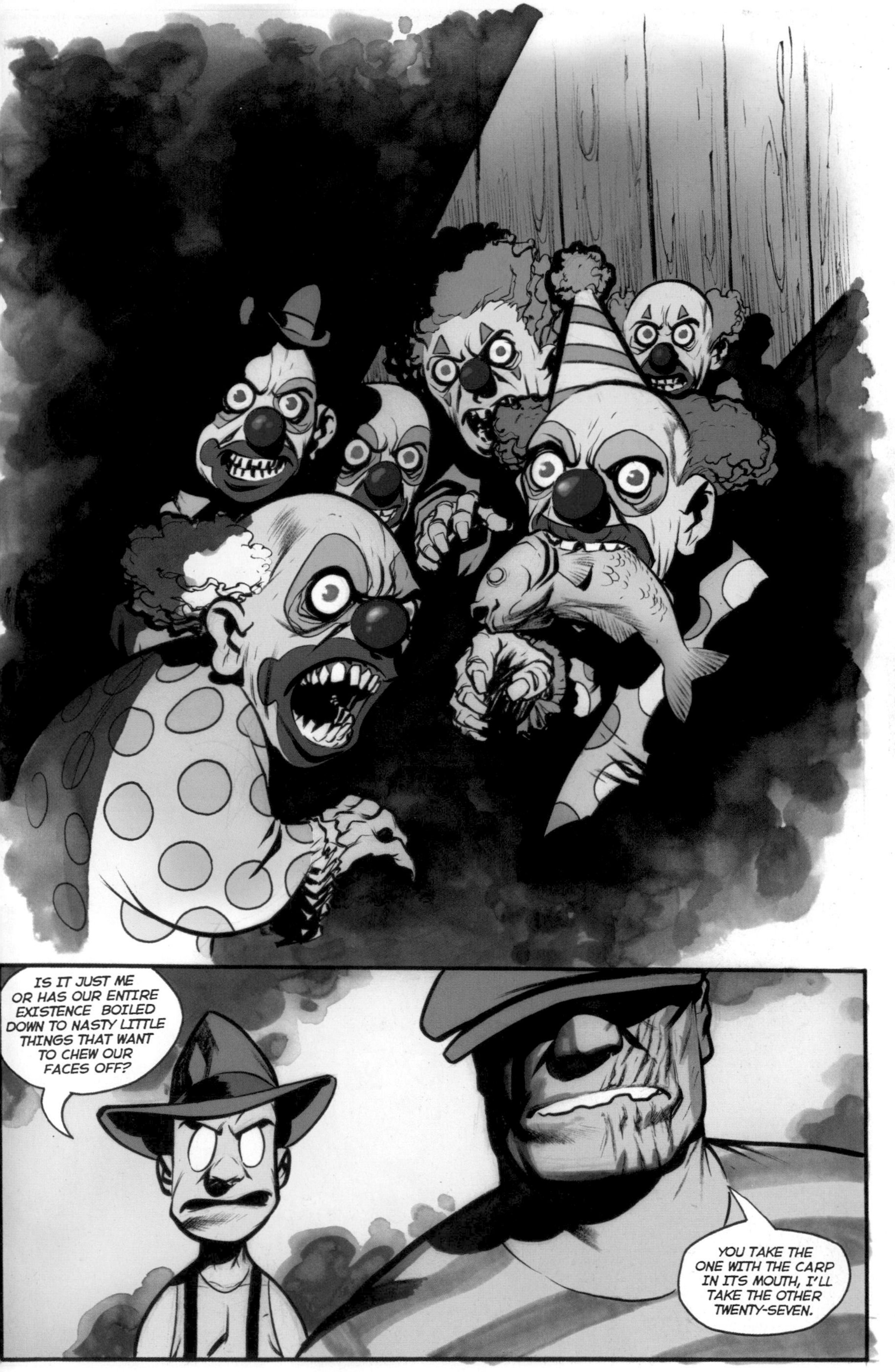
IS IT JUST ME OR HAS OUR ENTIRE EXISTENCE BOILED DOWN TO NASTY LITTLE THINGS THAT WANT TO CHEW OUR FACES OFF?
YOU TAKE THE ONE WITH THE CARP IN ITS MOUTH, I'LL TAKE THE OTHER TWENTY-SEVEN.

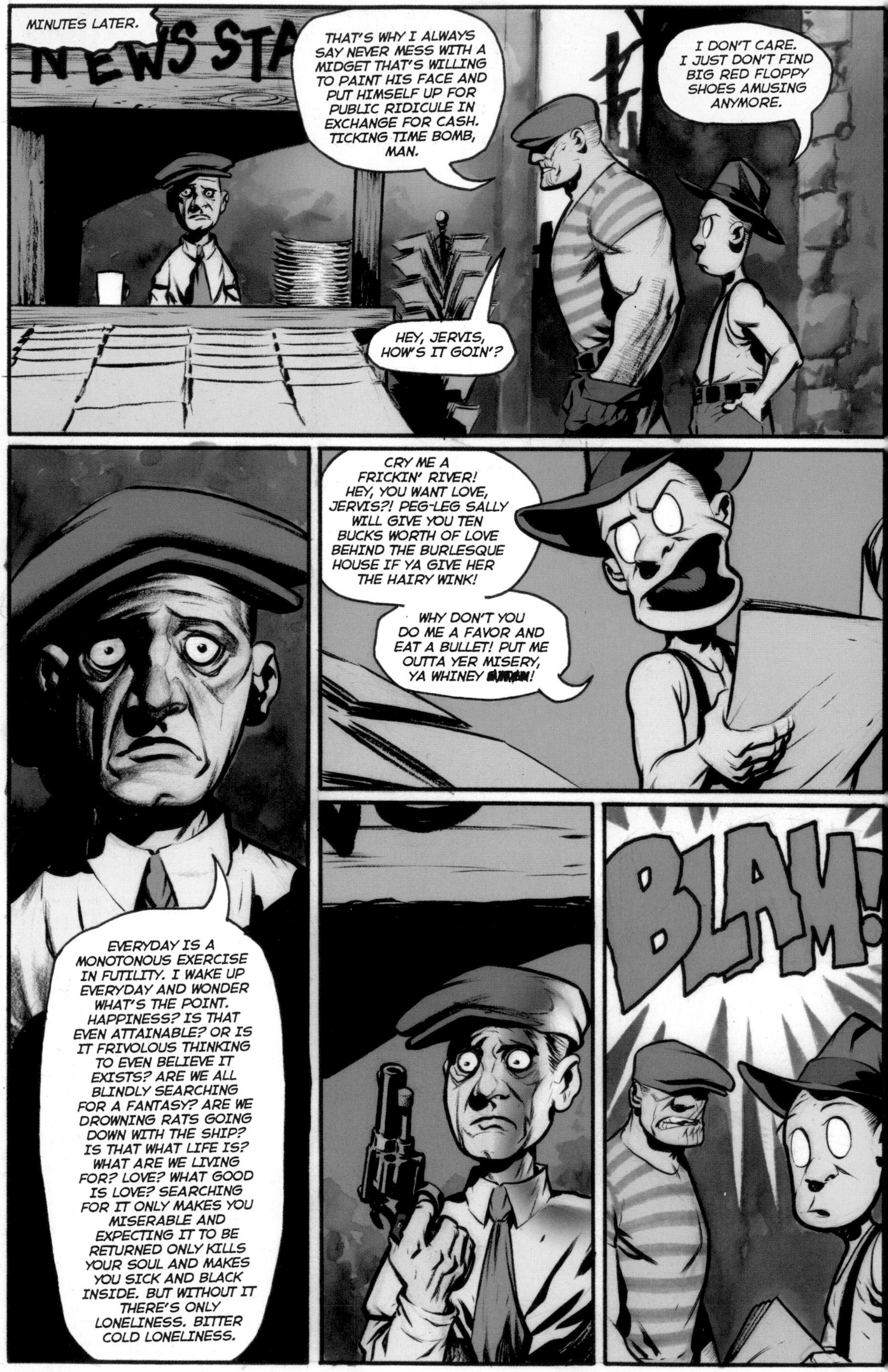
MINUTES LATER.
NEWS STA
THAT'S WHY I ALWAYS SAY NEVER MESS WITH A MIDGET THAT'S WILLING TO PAINT HIS FACE AND PUT HIMSELF UP FOR PUBLIC RIDICULE IN EXCHANGE FOR CASH. TICKING TIME BOMB, MAN.
I DON'T CARE. I JUST DON'T FIND BIG RED FLOPPY SHOES AMUSING ANYMORE.
HEY, JERVIS, HOW'S IT GOIN'?
EVERYDAY IS A MONOTONOUS EXERCISE IN FUTILITY. I WAKE UP EVERYDAY AND WONDER WHAT'S THE POINT. HAPPINESS? IS THAT EVEN ATTAINABLE? OR IS IT FRIVOLOUS THINKING TO EVEN BELIEVE IT EXISTS? ARE WE ALL BLINDLY SEARCHING FOR A FANTASY? ARE WE DROWNING RATS GOING DOWN WITH THE SHIP? IS THAT WHAT LIFE IS? WHAT ARE WE LIVING FOR? LOVE? WHAT GOOD IS LOVE? SEARCHING FOR IT ONLY MAKES YOU MISERABLE AND EXPECTING IT TO BE RETURNED ONLY KILLS YOUR SOUL AND MAKES YOU SICK AND BLACK INSIDE. BUT WITHOUT IT THERE'S ONLY LONELINESS. BITTER COLD LONELINESS.
CRY ME A FRICKIN' RIVER! HEY, YOU WANT LOVE, JERVIS?! PEG-LEG SALLY WILL GIVE YOU TEN BUCKS WORTH OF LOVE BEHIND THE BURLESQUE HOUSE IF YA GIVE HER THE HAIRY WINK!
WHY DON'T YOU DO ME A FAVOR AND EAT A BULLET! PUT ME OUTTA YER MISERY, YA WHINEY [redacted]!
BLAM!

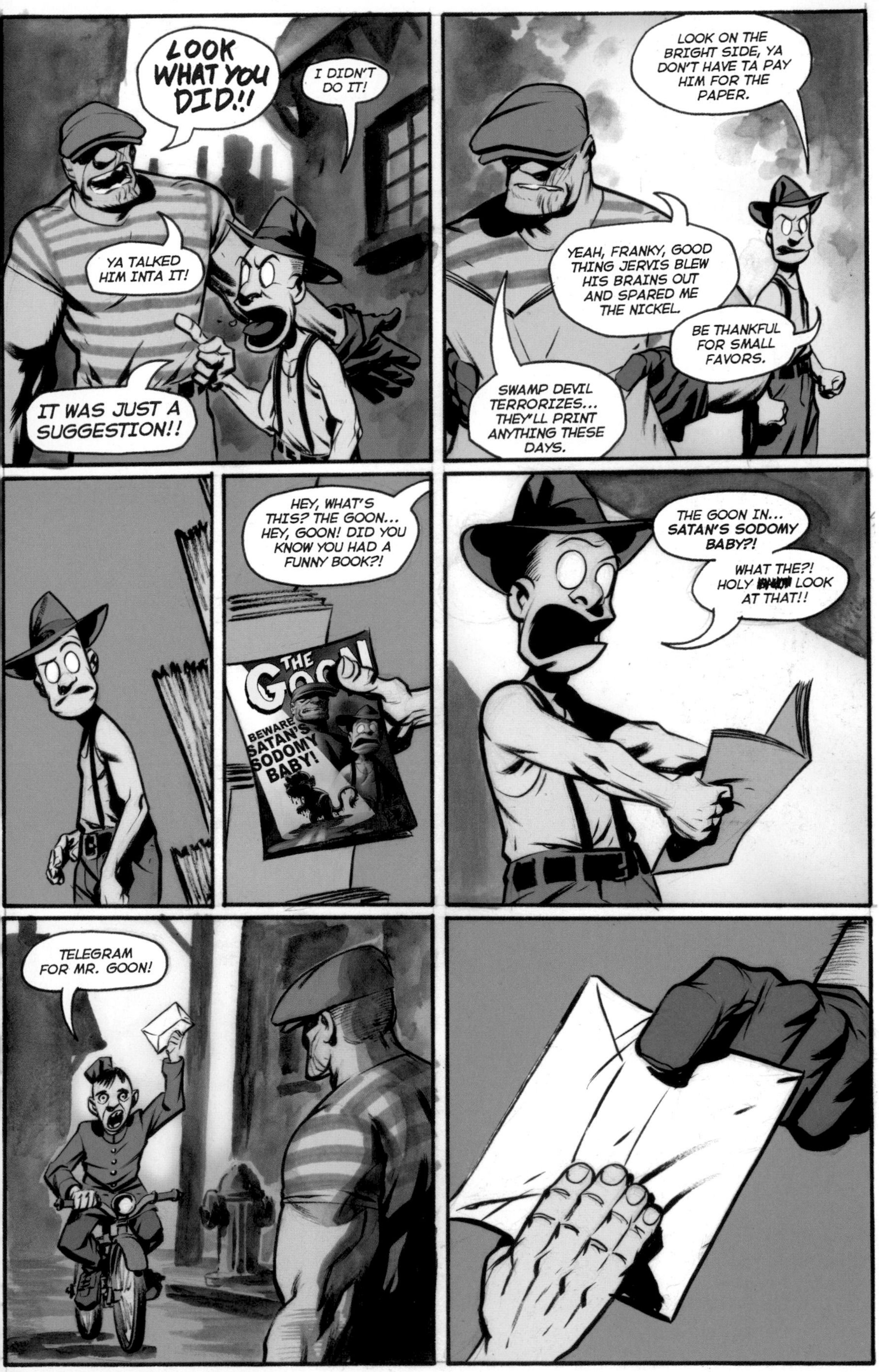
LOOK WHAT YOU DID!!
I DIDN'T DO IT!
YA TALKED HIM INTA IT!
IT WAS JUST A SUGGESTION!!
LOOK ON THE BRIGHT SIDE, YA DON'T HAVE TA PAY HIM FOR THE PAPER.
YEAH, FRANKY, GOOD THING JERVIS BLEW HIS BRAINS OUT AND SPARED ME THE NICKEL.
BE THANKFUL FOR SMALL FAVORS.
SWAMP DEVIL TERRORIZES... THEY'LL PRINT ANYTHING THESE DAYS.
HEY, WHAT'S THIS? THE GOON... HEY, GOON! DID YOU KNOW YOU HAD A FUNNY BOOK?!
THE GOON
BEWARE SATAN'S SODOMY BABY!
THE GOON IN... SATAN'S SODOMY BABY?!
WHAT THE?! HOLY [redacted] LOOK AT THAT!!
TELEGRAM FOR MR. GOON!

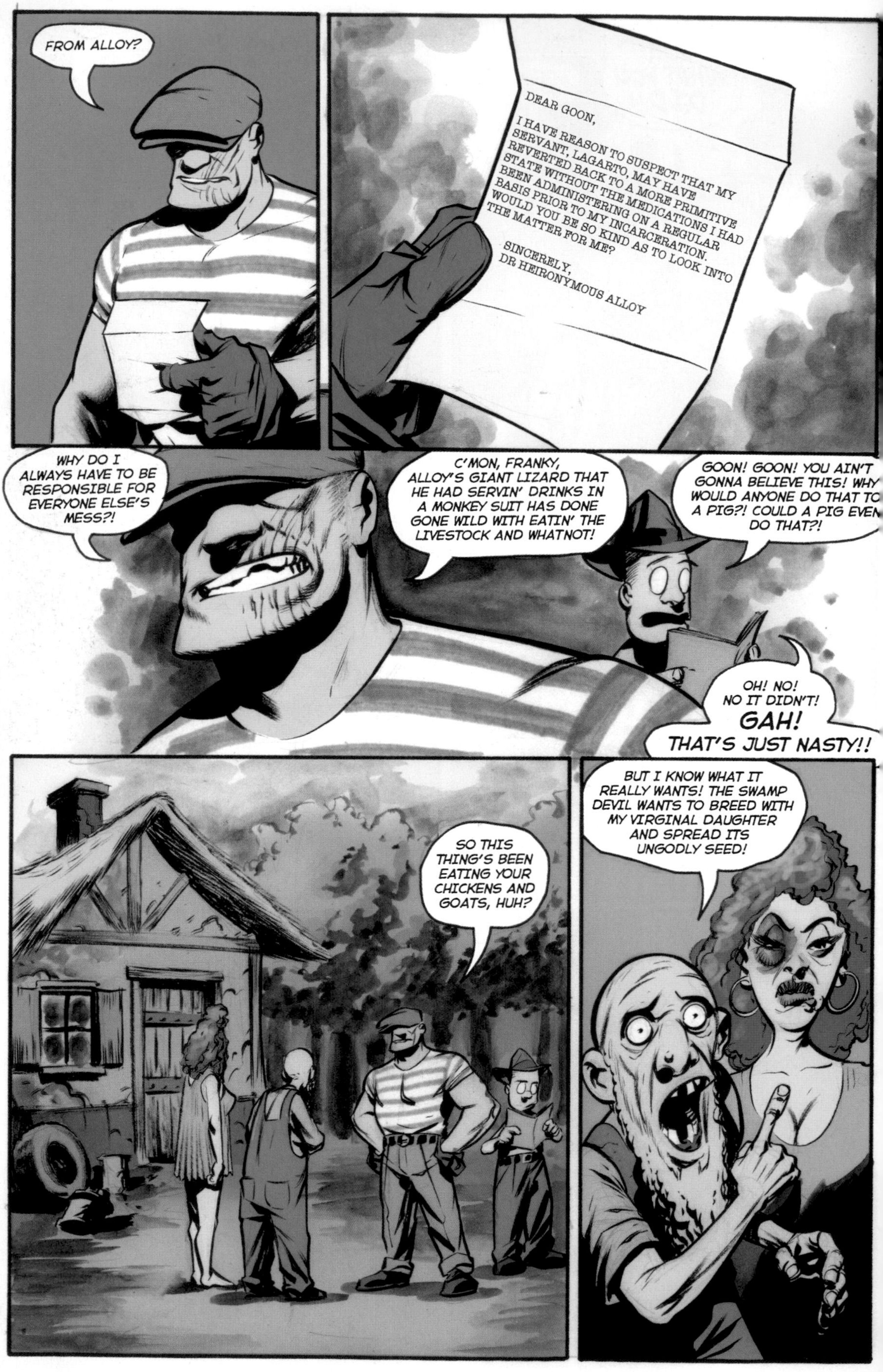
FROM ALLOY?
DEAR GOON,
I HAVE REASON TO SUSPECT THAT MY SERVANT, LAGARTO, MAY HAVE REVERTED BACK TO A MORE PRIMITIVE STATE WITHOUT THE MEDICATIONS I HAD BEEN ADMINISTERING ON A REGULAR BASIS PRIOR TO MY INCARCERATION. WOULD YOU BE SO KIND AS TO LOOK INTO THE MATTER FOR ME?
SINCERELY,
DR HEIRONYMOUS ALLOY
WHY DO I ALWAYS HAVE TO BE RESPONSIBLE FOR EVERYONE ELSE'S MESS?!
C'MON, FRANKY, ALLOY'S GIANT LIZARD THAT HE HAD SERVIN' DRINKS IN A MONKEY SUIT HAS DONE GONE WILD WITH EATIN' THE LIVESTOCK AND WHATNOT!
GOON! GOON! YOU AIN'T GONNA BELIEVE THIS! WHY WOULD ANYONE DO THAT TO A PIG?! COULD A PIG EVEN DO THAT?!
OH! NO! NO IT DIDN'T! GAH! THAT'S JUST NASTY!!
SO THIS THING'S BEEN EATING YOUR CHICKENS AND GOATS, HUH?
BUT I KNOW WHAT IT REALLY WANTS! THE SWAMP DEVIL WANTS TO BREED WITH MY VIRGINAL DAUGHTER AND SPREAD ITS UNGODLY SEED!

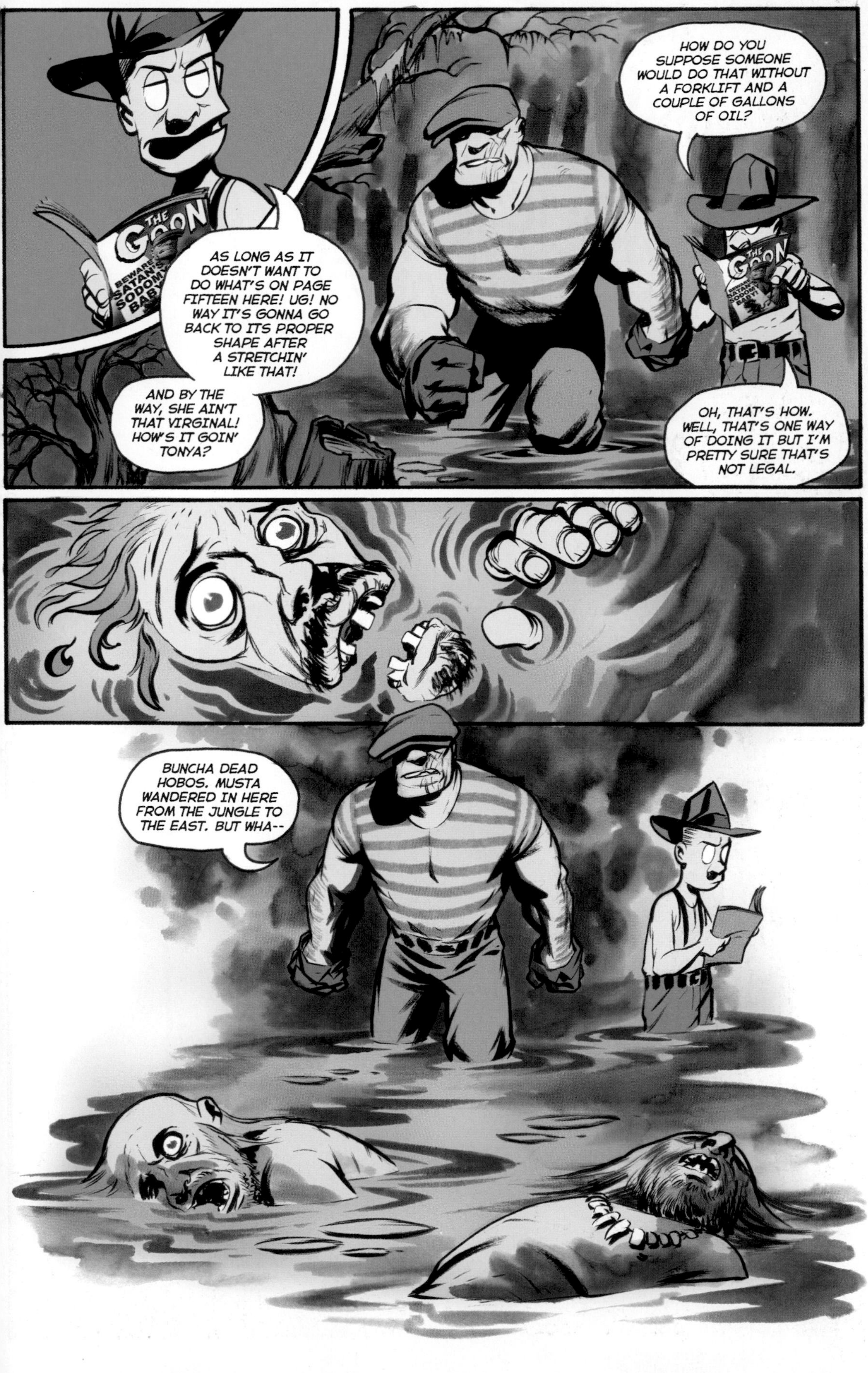
HOW DO YOU SUPPOSE SOMEONE WOULD DO THAT WITHOUT A FORKLIFT AND A COUPLE OF GALLONS OF OIL?
THE GOON
BEWARE SATAN'S SODOMY BABY!
AS LONG AS IT DOESN'T WANT TO DO WHAT'S ON PAGE FIFTEEN HERE! UG! NO WAY IT'S GONNA GO BACK TO ITS PROPER SHAPE AFTER A STRETCHIN' LIKE THAT!
AND BY THE WAY, SHE AIN'T THAT VIRGINAL! HOW'S IT GOIN' TONYA?
OH, THAT'S HOW. WELL, THAT'S ONE WAY OF DOING IT BUT I'M PRETTY SURE THAT'S NOT LEGAL.
BUNCHA DEAD HOBOS. MUSTA WANDERED IN HERE FROM THE JUNGLE TO THE EAST. BUT WHA--

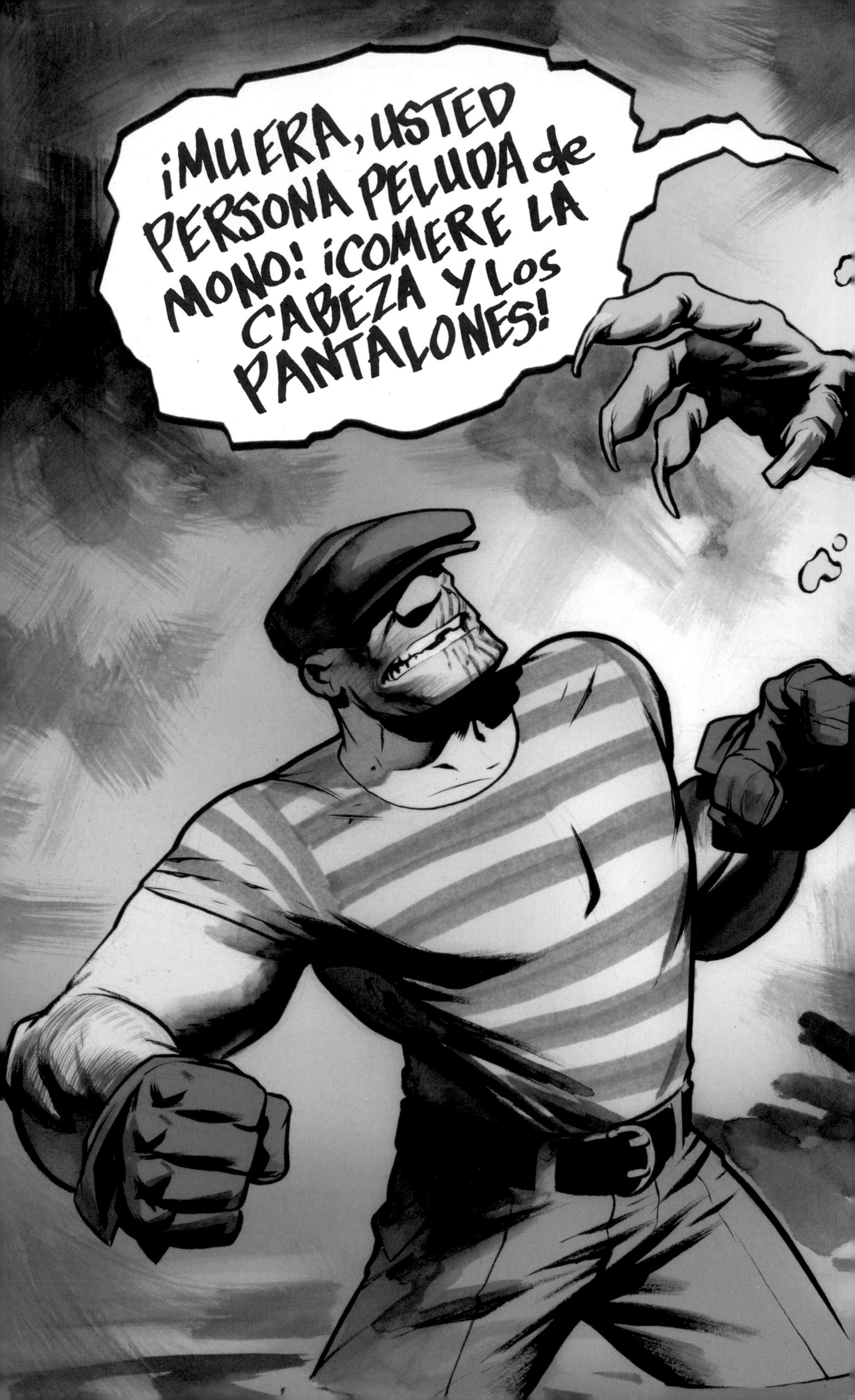
¡MUERA, USTED PERSONA PELUDA de MONO! ¡COMERE LA CABEZA Y LOS PANTALONES!

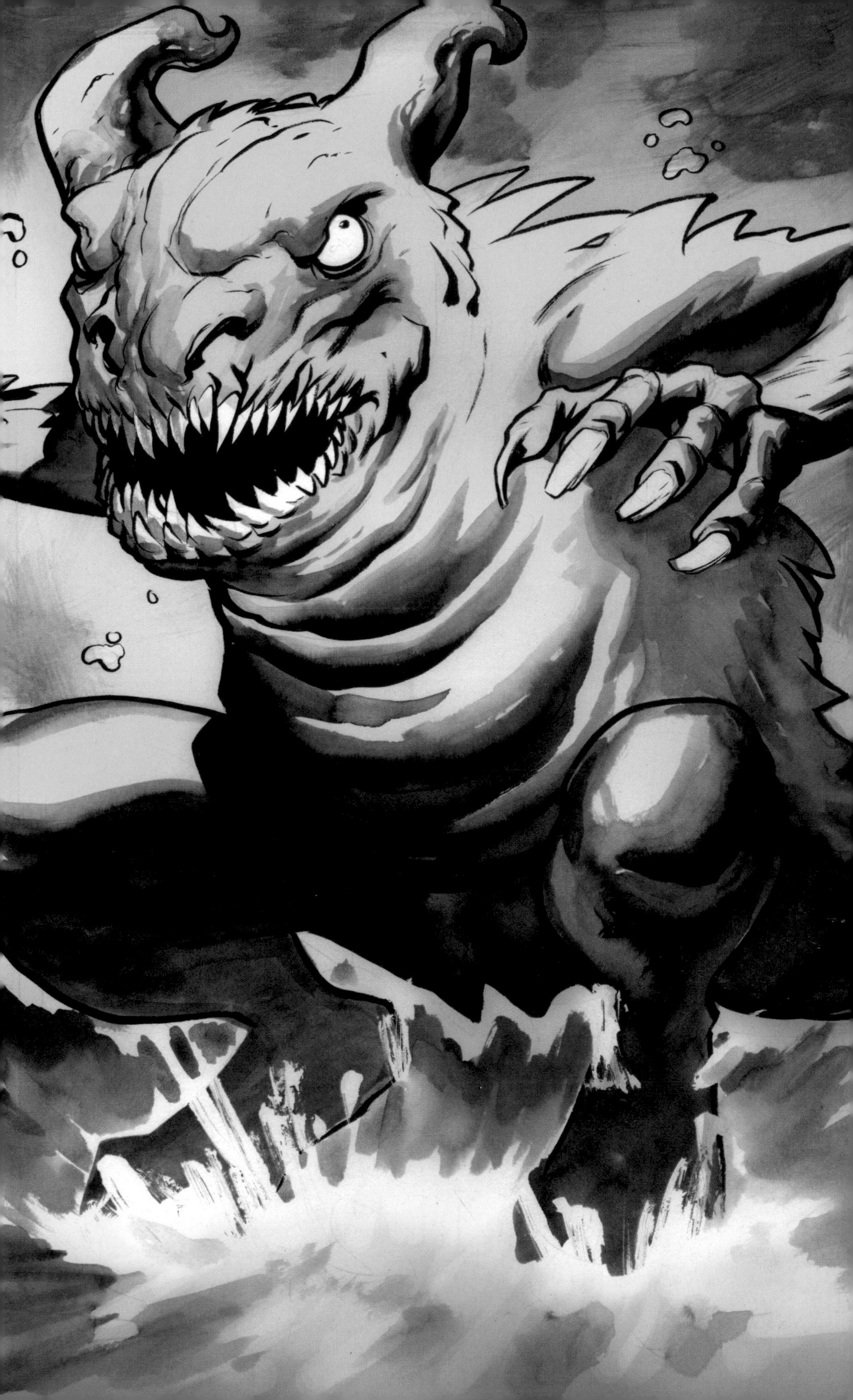

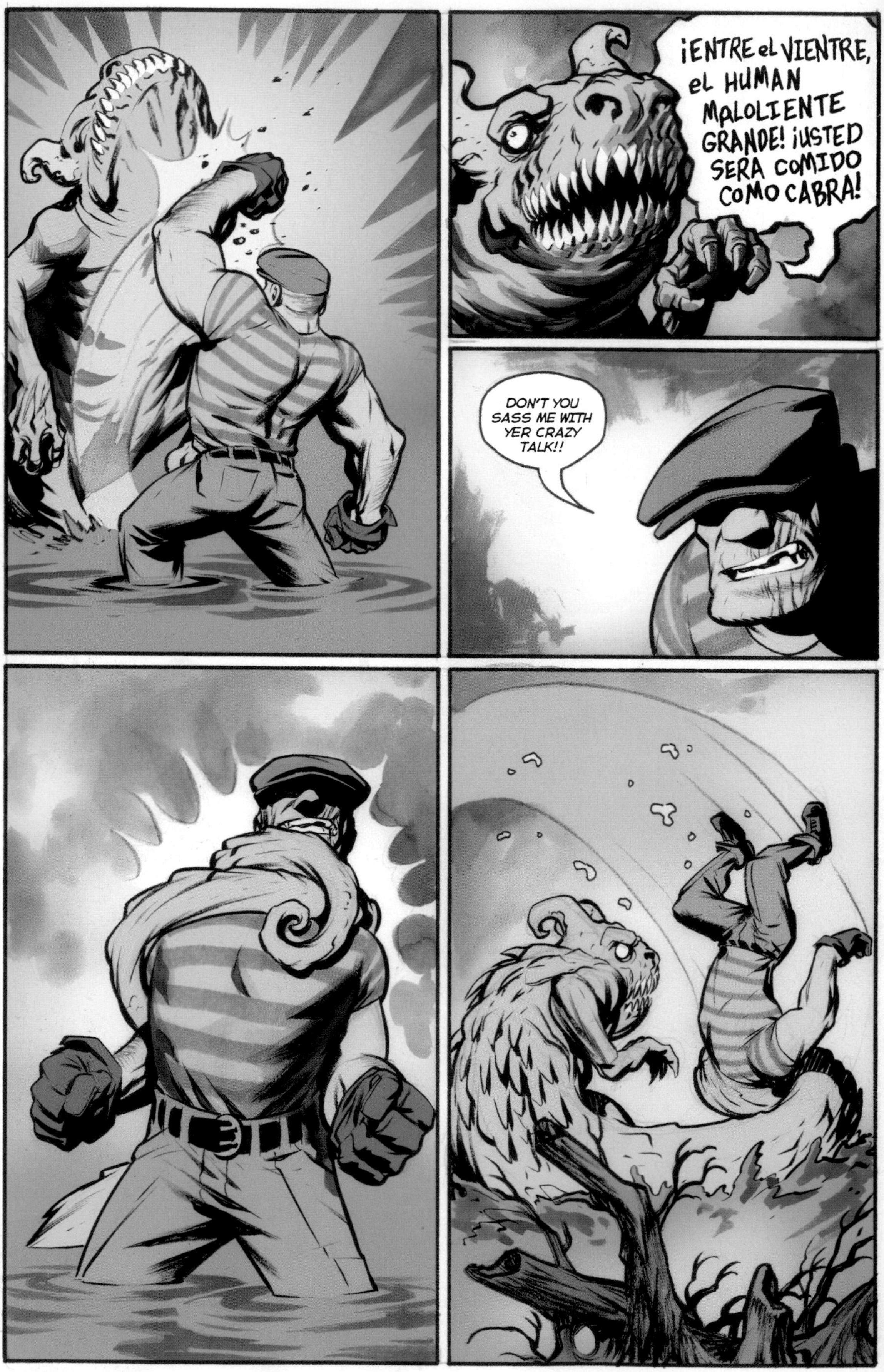
¡ENTRE el VIENTRE, el HUMAN MaLOLIENTE GRANDE! ¡USTED SERA COMIDO COMO CABRA!
DON'T YOU SASS ME WITH YER CRAZY TALK!!

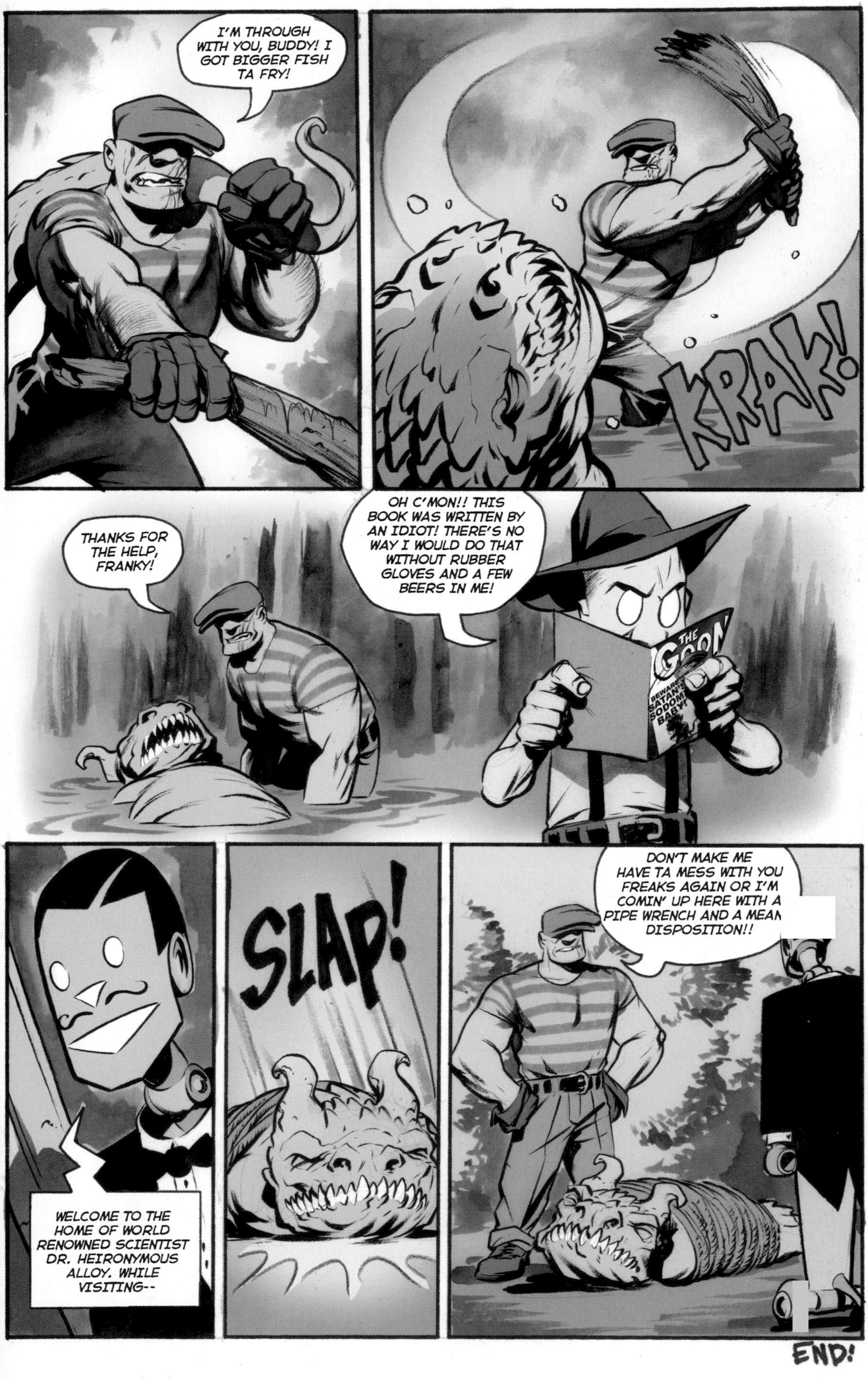
I'M THROUGH WITH YOU, BUDDY! I GOT BIGGER FISH TA FRY!
KRAK!
THANKS FOR THE HELP, FRANKY!
OH C'MON!! THIS BOOK WAS WRITTEN BY AN IDIOT! THERE'S NO WAY I WOULD DO THAT WITHOUT RUBBER GLOVES AND A FEW BEERS IN ME!
WELCOME TO THE HOME OF WORLD RENOWNED SCIENTIST DR. HEIRONYMOUS ALLOY. WHILE VISITING--
SLAP!
DON'T MAKE ME HAVE TA MESS WITH YOU FREAKS AGAIN OR I'M COMIN' UP HERE WITH A PIPE WRENCH AND A MEAN DISPOSITION!!
END!

THE GOON™

Short Stories

"Under the Sink"
story & colors by Eric Powell
art by Neil Vokes
letters by Nate Piekos

"Lagarto Diablo"
story & colors by Eric Powell
art by Kyle Hotz
letters by Nate Piekos

"Spike"
story by Tom Sniegoski
art by Michael Avon Oeming
colors by Eric Powell
letters by Nate Piekos

"It's All Fun and Games 'Til…"
story and art by Mike Hawthorne
colors by Eric Powell
letters by Jason Hvam

"Equine Twine"
by Tony Shasteen

Pinup
by Mike Allred

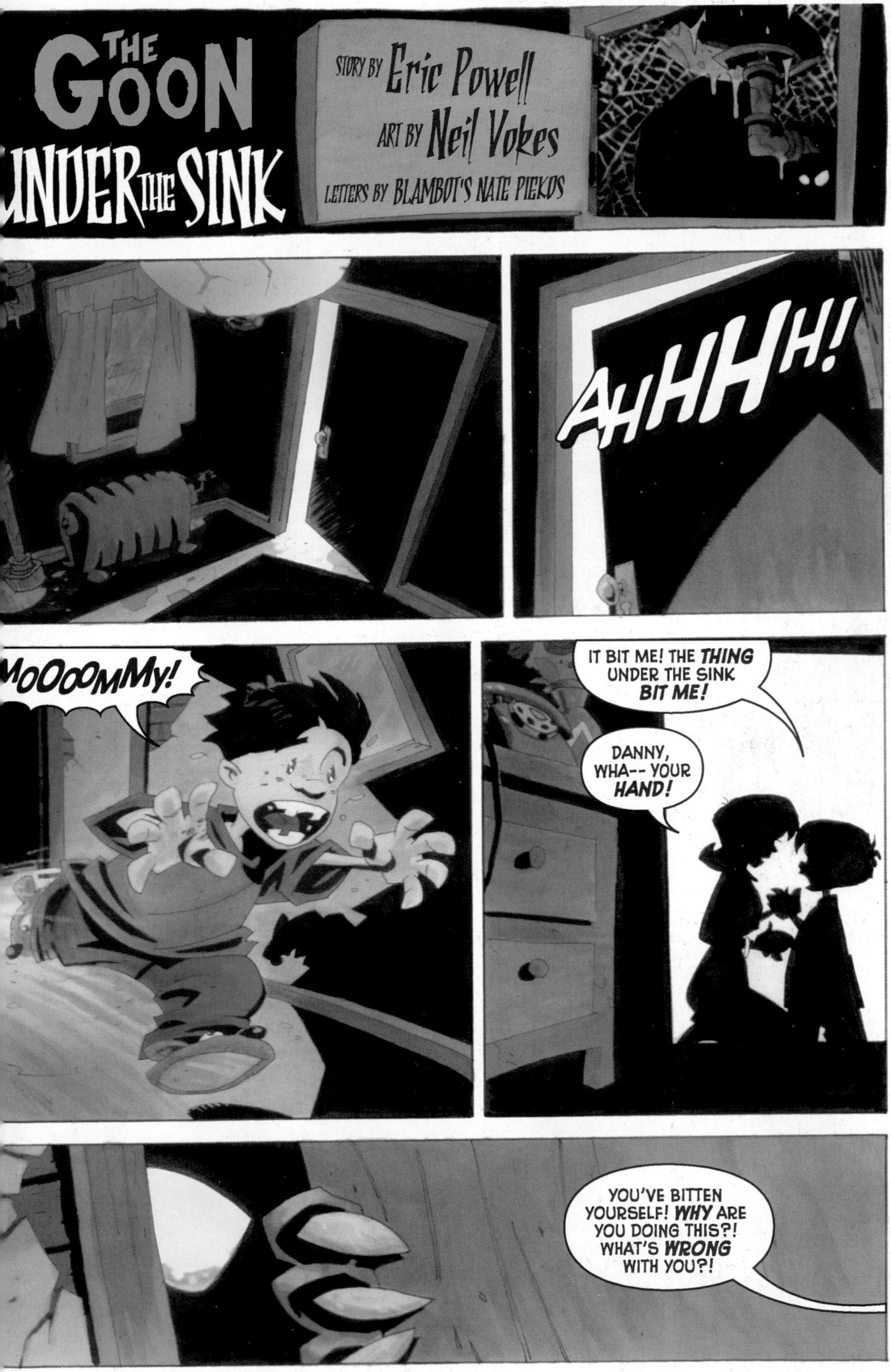
THE GOON
UNDER THE SINK
STORY BY Eric Powell
ART BY Neil Vokes
LETTERS BY BLAMBOT'S NATE PIEKOS
AHHHH!
MOOOOMMY!
IT BIT ME! THE THING UNDER THE SINK BIT ME!
DANNY, WHA-- YOUR HAND!
YOU'VE BITTEN YOURSELF! WHY ARE YOU DOING THIS?! WHAT'S WRONG WITH YOU?!

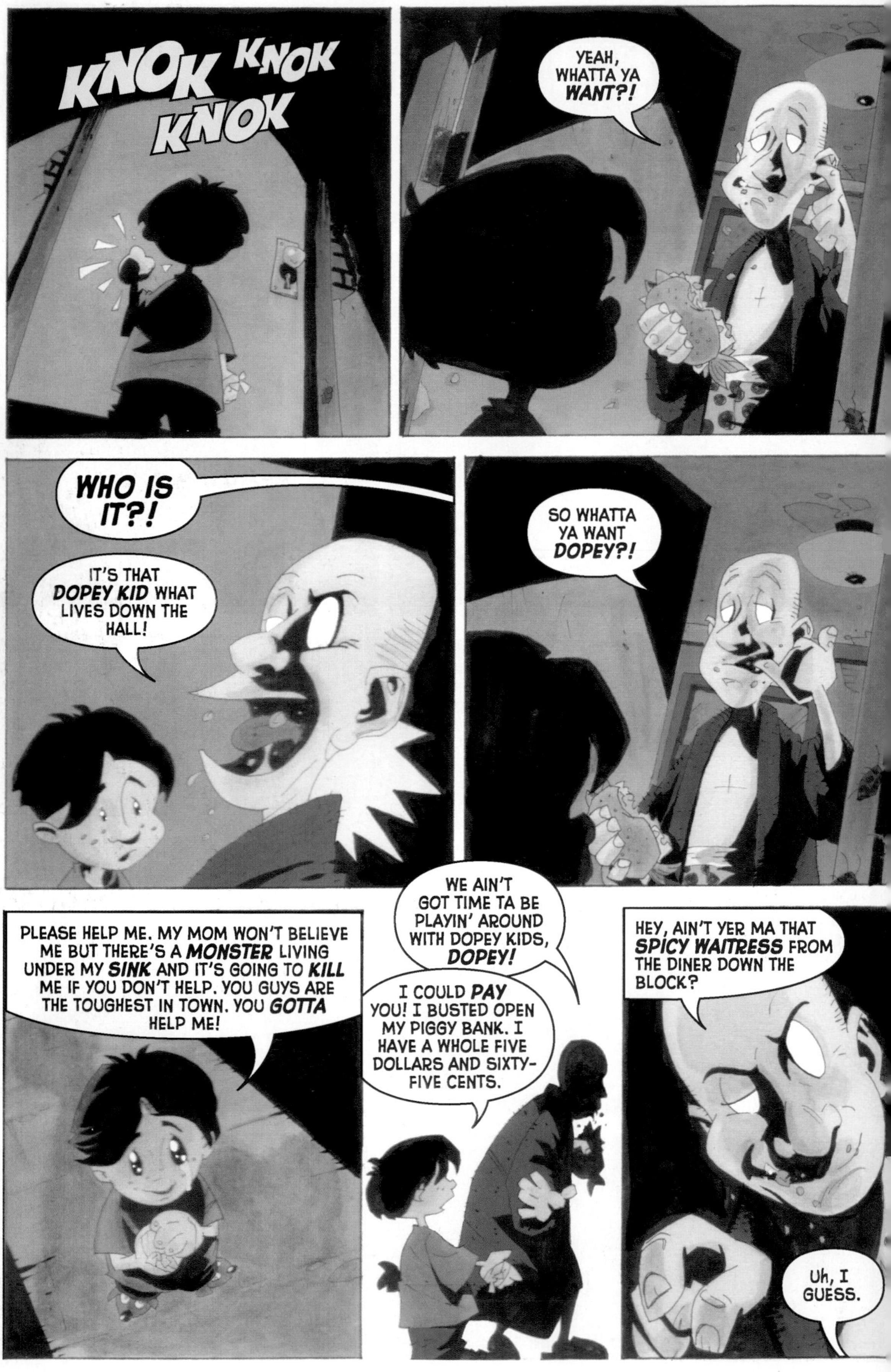
KNOK KNOK KNOK
YEAH, WHATTA YA WANT?!
WHO IS IT?!
IT'S THAT DOPEY KID WHAT LIVES DOWN THE HALL!
SO WHATTA YA WANT DOPEY?!
PLEASE HELP ME. MY MOM WON'T BELIEVE ME BUT THERE'S A MONSTER LIVING UNDER MY SINK AND IT'S GOING TO KILL ME IF YOU DON'T HELP. YOU GUYS ARE THE TOUGHEST IN TOWN. YOU GOTTA HELP ME!
WE AIN'T GOT TIME TA BE PLAYIN' AROUND WITH DOPEY KIDS, DOPEY!
I COULD PAY YOU! I BUSTED OPEN MY PIGGY BANK. I HAVE A WHOLE FIVE DOLLARS AND SIXTY-FIVE CENTS.
HEY, AIN'T YER MA THAT SPICY WAITRESS FROM THE DINER DOWN THE BLOCK?
Uh, I GUESS.

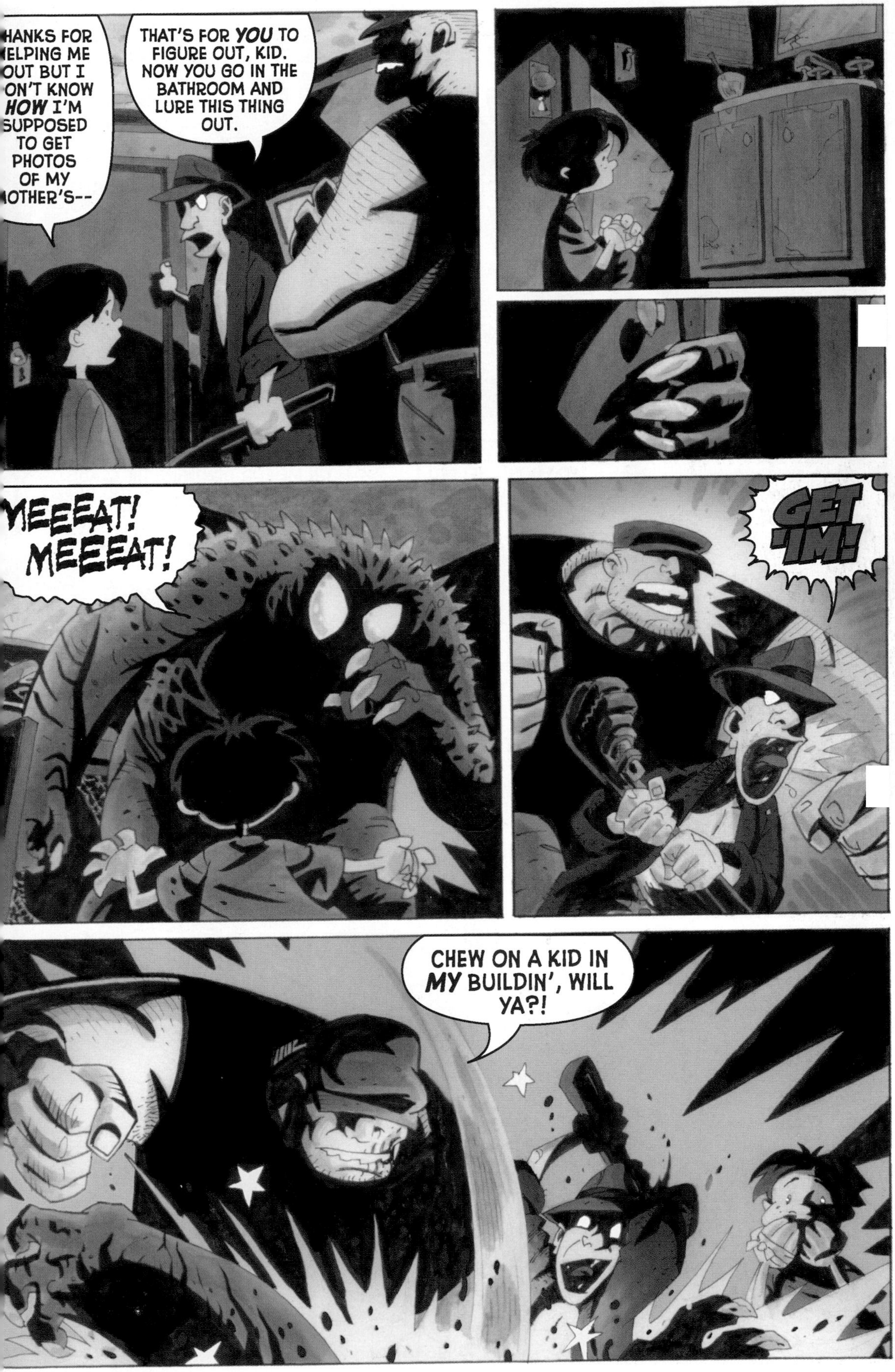
HANKS FOR ELPING ME OUT BUT I ON'T KNOW HOW I'M SUPPOSED TO GET PHOTOS OF MY OTHER'S--
THAT'S FOR YOU TO FIGURE OUT, KID. NOW YOU GO IN THE BATHROOM AND LURE THIS THING OUT.
MEEEAT! MEEEAT!
GET 'IM!
CHEW ON A KID IN MY BUILDIN', WILL YA?!

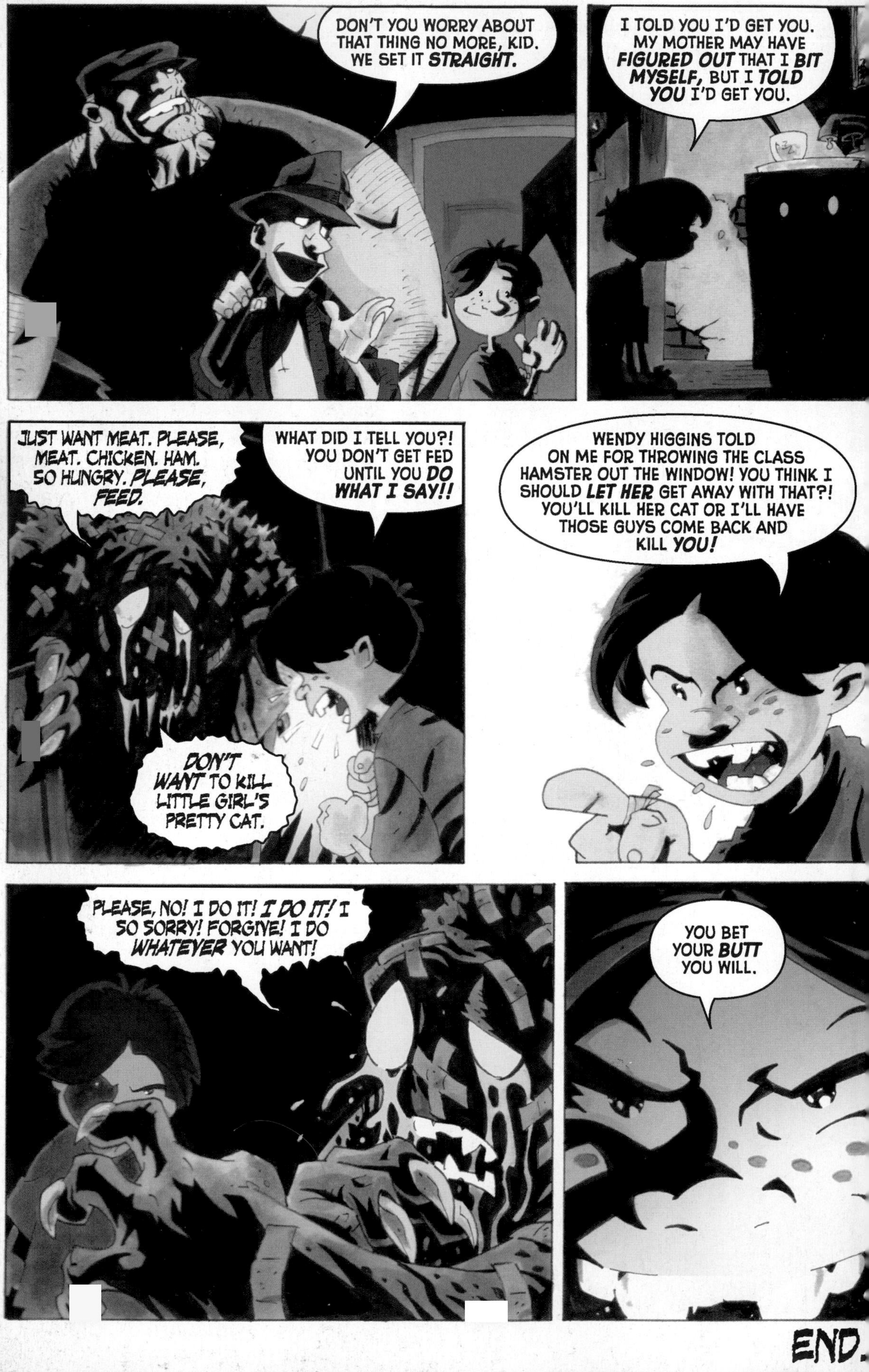
DON'T YOU WORRY ABOUT THAT THING NO MORE, KID. WE SET IT STRAIGHT.
I TOLD YOU I'D GET YOU. MY MOTHER MAY HAVE FIGURED OUT THAT I BIT MYSELF, BUT I TOLD YOU I'D GET YOU.
JUST WANT MEAT. PLEASE, MEAT. CHICKEN. HAM. SO HUNGRY. PLEASE, FEED.
WHAT DID I TELL YOU?! YOU DON'T GET FED UNTIL YOU DO WHAT I SAY!!
DON'T WANT TO KILL LITTLE GIRL'S PRETTY CAT.
WENDY HIGGINS TOLD ON ME FOR THROWING THE CLASS HAMSTER OUT THE WINDOW! YOU THINK I SHOULD LET HER GET AWAY WITH THAT?! YOU'LL KILL HER CAT OR I'LL HAVE THOSE GUYS COME BACK AND KILL YOU!
PLEASE, NO! I DO IT! I DO IT! I SO SORRY! FORGIVE! I DO WHATEVER YOU WANT!
YOU BET YOUR BUTT YOU WILL.
END.

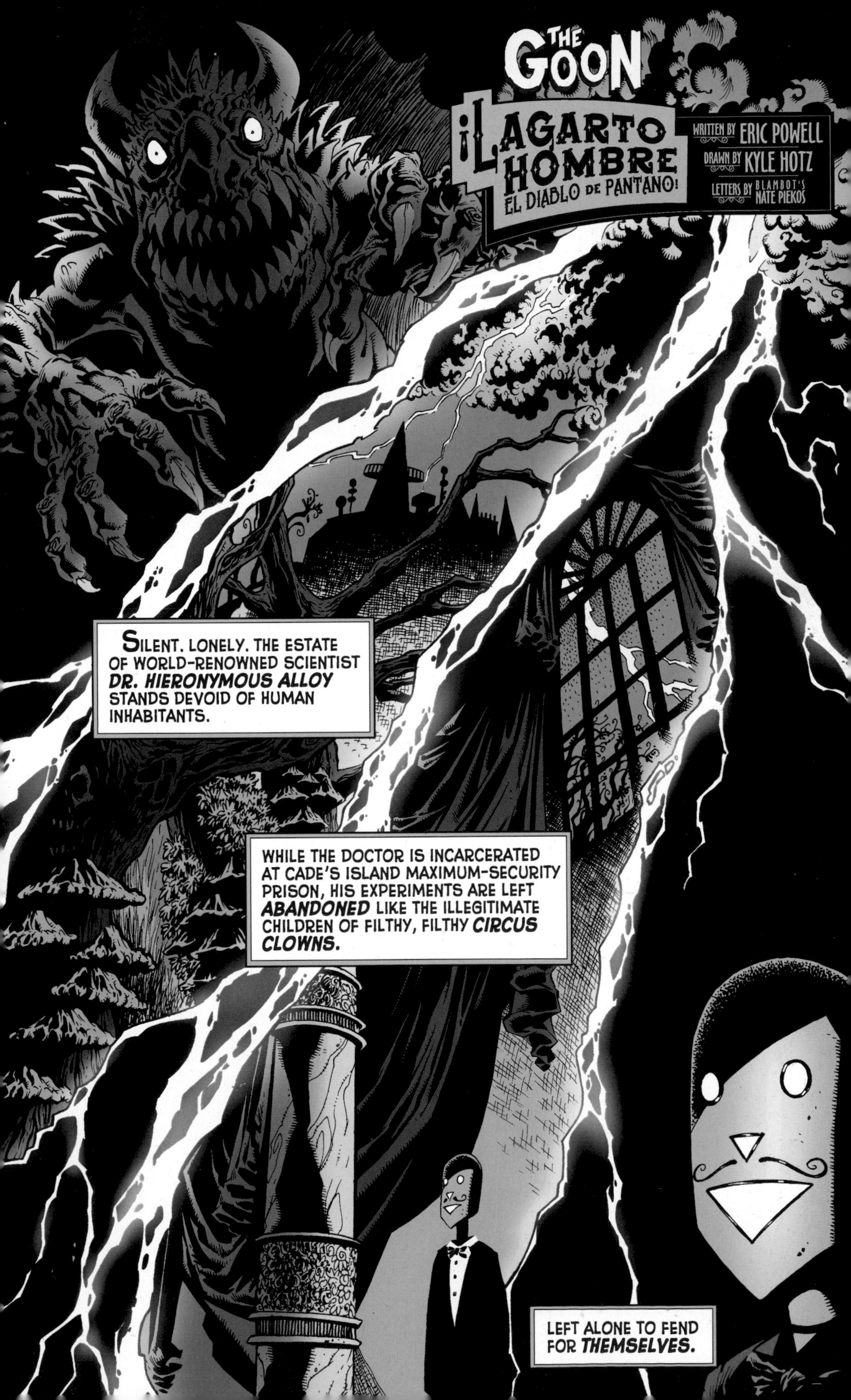
THE GOON
¡LAGARTO HOMBRE EL DIABLO DE PANTANO!
WRITTEN BY ERIC POWELL
DRAWN BY KYLE HOTZ
LETTERS BY BLAMBOT'S NATE PIEKOS
SILENT. LONELY. THE ESTATE OF WORLD-RENOWNED SCIENTIST DR. HIERONYMOUS ALLOY STANDS DEVOID OF HUMAN INHABITANTS.
WHILE THE DOCTOR IS INCARCERATED AT CADE'S ISLAND MAXIMUM-SECURITY PRISON, HIS EXPERIMENTS ARE LEFT ABANDONED LIKE THE ILLEGITIMATE CHILDREN OF FILTHY, FILTHY CIRCUS CLOWNS.
LEFT ALONE TO FEND FOR THEMSELVES.

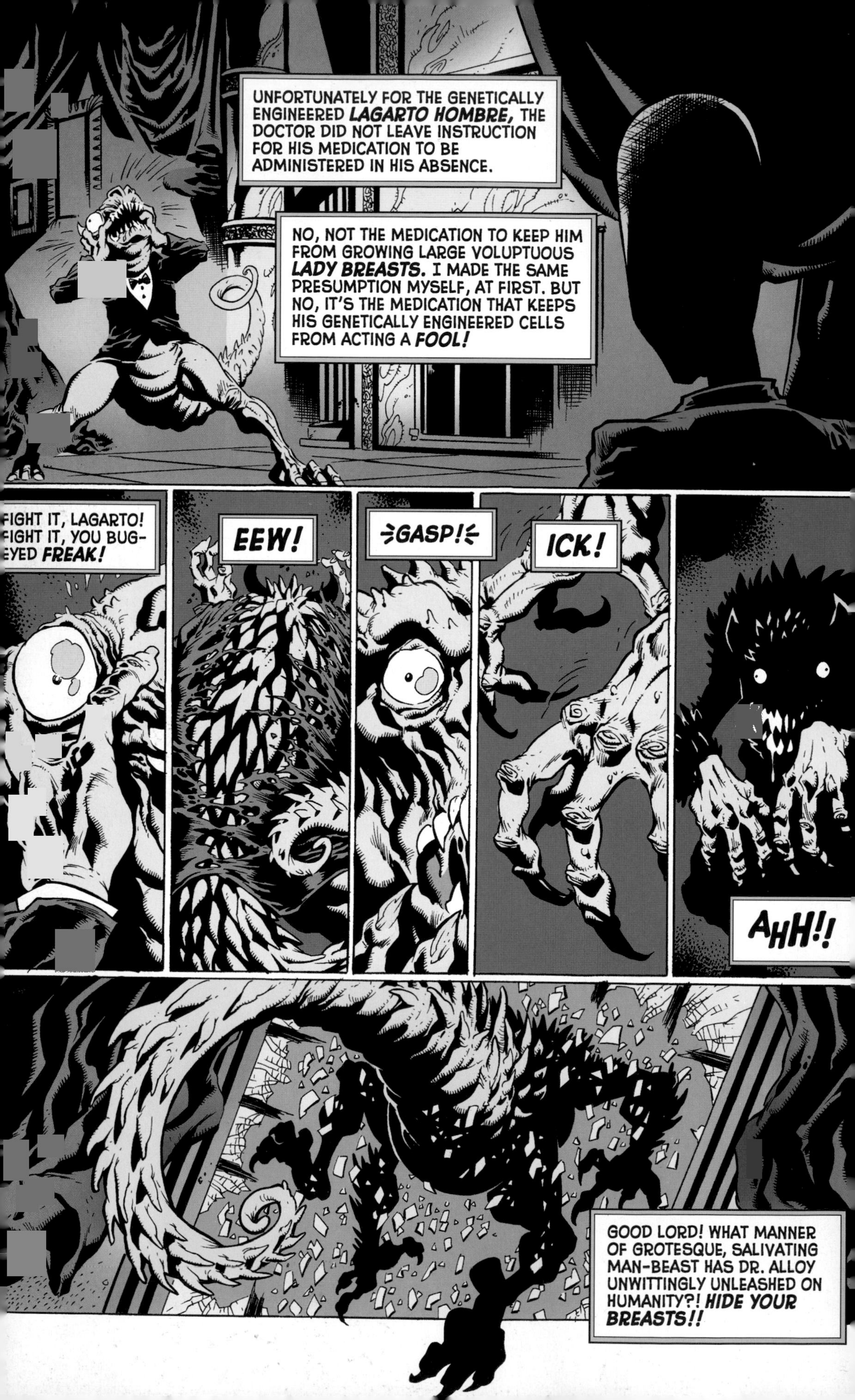
UNFORTUNATELY FOR THE GENETICALLY ENGINEERED LAGARTO HOMBRE, THE DOCTOR DID NOT LEAVE INSTRUCTION FOR HIS MEDICATION TO BE ADMINISTERED IN HIS ABSENCE.
NO, NOT THE MEDICATION TO KEEP HIM FROM GROWING LARGE VOLUPTUOUS LADY BREASTS. I MADE THE SAME PRESUMPTION MYSELF, AT FIRST. BUT NO, IT'S THE MEDICATION THAT KEEPS HIS GENETICALLY ENGINEERED CELLS FROM ACTING A FOOL!
FIGHT IT, LAGARTO! FIGHT IT, YOU BUG-EYED FREAK!
EEW!
GASP!
ICK!
AHH!!
GOOD LORD! WHAT MANNER OF GROTESQUE, SALIVATING MAN-BEAST HAS DR. ALLOY UNWITTINGLY UNLEASHED ON HUMANITY?! HIDE YOUR BREASTS!!

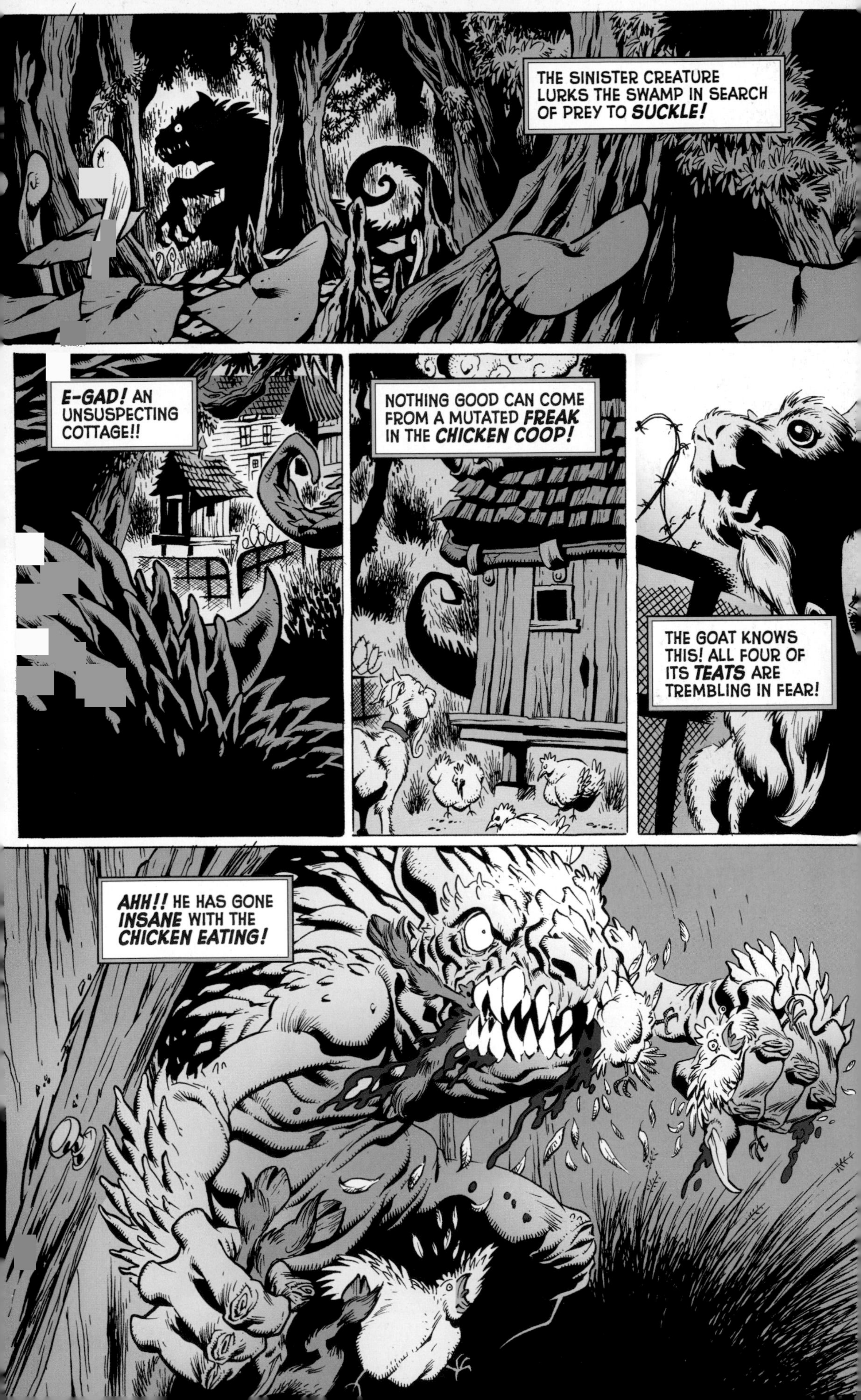
THE SINISTER CREATURE LURKS THE SWAMP IN SEARCH OF PREY TO SUCKLE!
E-GAD! AN UNSUSPECTING COTTAGE!!
NOTHING GOOD CAN COME FROM A MUTATED FREAK IN THE CHICKEN COOP!
THE GOAT KNOWS THIS! ALL FOUR OF ITS TEATS ARE TREMBLING IN FEAR!
AHH!! HE HAS GONE INSANE WITH THE CHICKEN EATING!

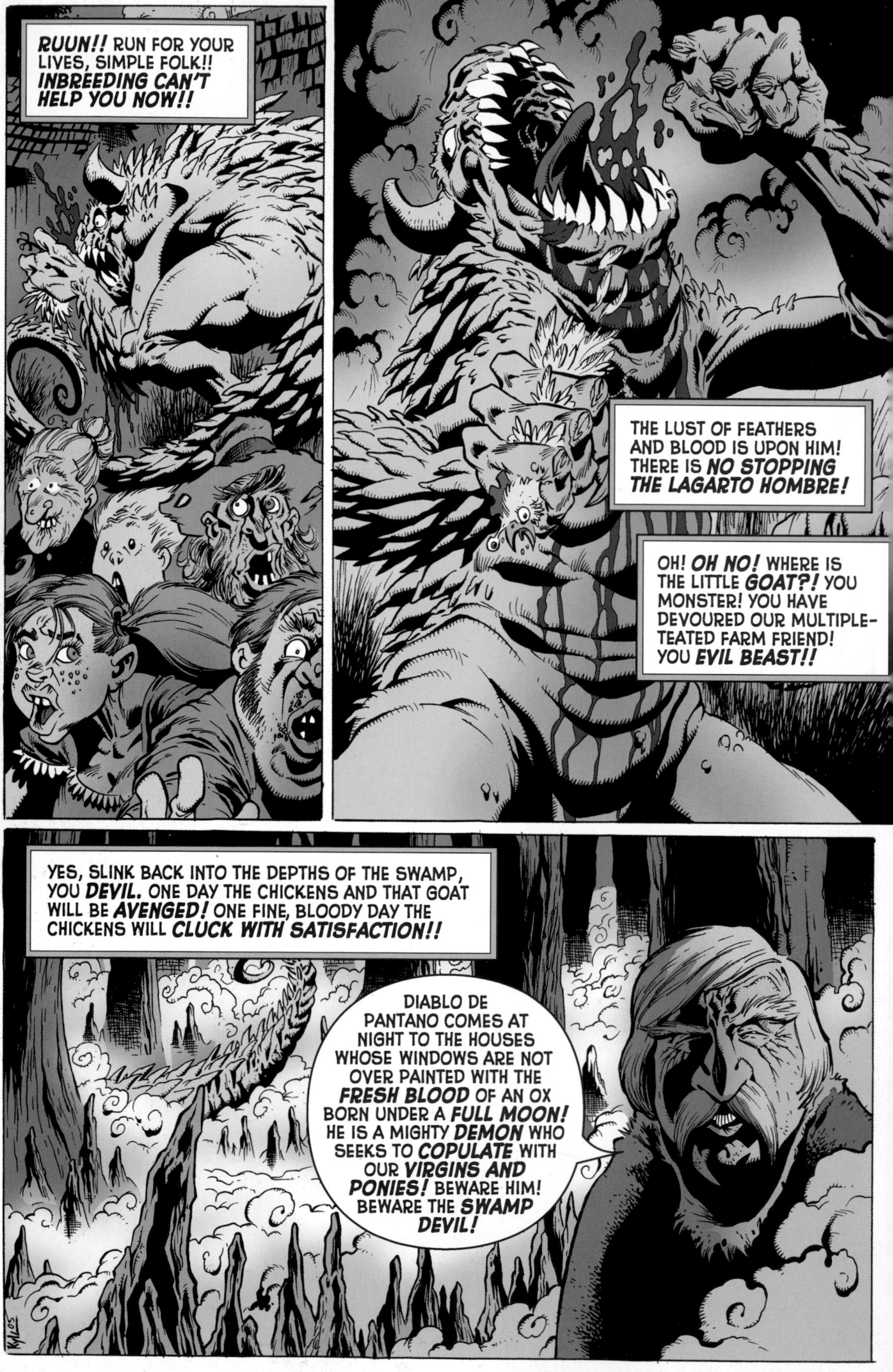
RUUN!! RUN FOR YOUR LIVES, SIMPLE FOLK!! INBREEDING CAN'T HELP YOU NOW!!
THE LUST OF FEATHERS AND BLOOD IS UPON HIM! THERE IS NO STOPPING THE LAGARTO HOMBRE!
OH! OH NO! WHERE IS THE LITTLE GOAT?! YOU MONSTER! YOU HAVE DEVOURED OUR MULTIPLE-TEATED FARM FRIEND! YOU EVIL BEAST!!
YES, SLINK BACK INTO THE DEPTHS OF THE SWAMP, YOU DEVIL. ONE DAY THE CHICKENS AND THAT GOAT WILL BE AVENGED! ONE FINE, BLOODY DAY THE CHICKENS WILL CLUCK WITH SATISFACTION!!
DIABLO DE PANTANO COMES AT NIGHT TO THE HOUSES WHOSE WINDOWS ARE NOT OVER PAINTED WITH THE FRESH BLOOD OF AN OX BORN UNDER A FULL MOON! HE IS A MIGHTY DEMON WHO SEEKS TO COPULATE WITH OUR VIRGINS AND PONIES! BEWARE HIM! BEWARE THE SWAMP DEVIL!

NEXT ISSUE: ***FART JOKES!***

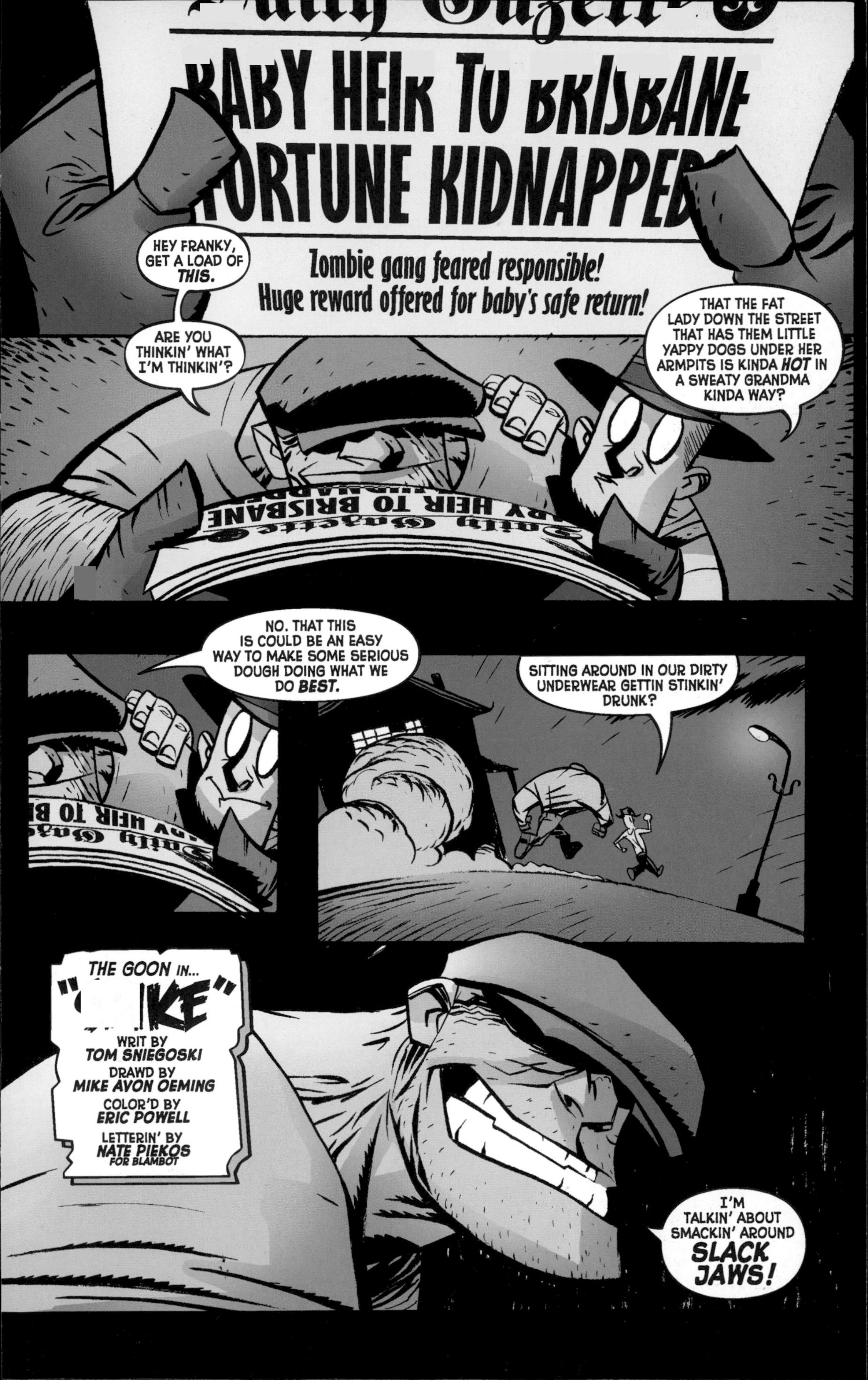
BABY HEIR TO BRISBANE
FORTUNE KIDNAPPED
Zombie gang feared responsible!
Huge reward offered for baby's safe return!
HEY FRANKY, GET A LOAD OF THIS.
ARE YOU THINKIN' WHAT I'M THINKIN'?
THAT THE FAT LADY DOWN THE STREET THAT HAS THEM LITTLE YAPPY DOGS UNDER HER ARMPITS IS KINDA HOT IN A SWEATY GRANDMA KINDA WAY?
NO. THAT THIS IS COULD BE AN EASY WAY TO MAKE SOME SERIOUS DOUGH DOING WHAT WE DO BEST.
SITTING AROUND IN OUR DIRTY UNDERWEAR GETTIN STINKIN' DRUNK?
THE GOON IN...
WRIT BY TOM SNIEGOSKI
DRAWD BY MIKE AVON OEMING
COLOR'D BY ERIC POWELL
LETTERIN' BY NATE PIEKOS FOR BLAMBOT
I'M TALKIN' ABOUT SMACKIN' AROUND SLACK JAWS!

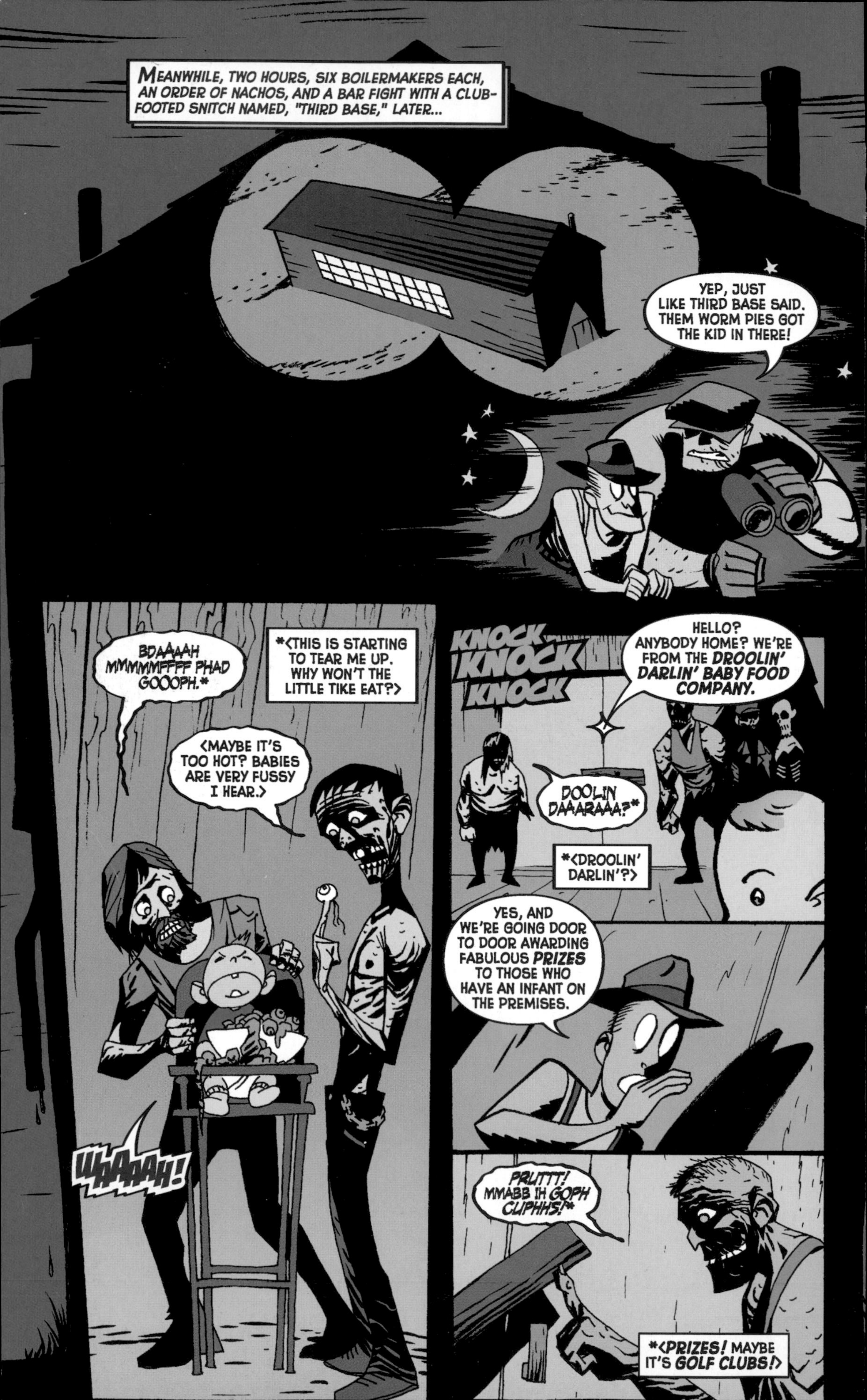
MEANWHILE, TWO HOURS, SIX BOILERMAKERS EACH, AN ORDER OF NACHOS, AND A BAR FIGHT WITH A CLUB-FOOTED SNITCH NAMED, "THIRD BASE," LATER...
YEP, JUST LIKE THIRD BASE SAID. THEM WORM PIES GOT THE KID IN THERE!
BDAAAAH MMMMMFFFF PHAD GOOOPH.*
*<THIS IS STARTING TO TEAR ME UP. WHY WON'T THE LITTLE TIKE EAT?>
<MAYBE IT'S TOO HOT? BABIES ARE VERY FUSSY I HEAR.>
WHAAAAH!
KNOCK KNOCK KNOCK
HELLO? ANYBODY HOME? WE'RE FROM THE DROOLIN' DARLIN' BABY FOOD COMPANY.
DOOLIN DAAARAAA?*
*<DROOLIN' DARLIN'?>
YES, AND WE'RE GOING DOOR TO DOOR AWARDING FABULOUS PRIZES TO THOSE WHO HAVE AN INFANT ON THE PREMISES.
PRUTTT! MMABB IH GOPH CLIPHHS!*
*<PRIZES! MAYBE IT'S GOLF CLUBS!>

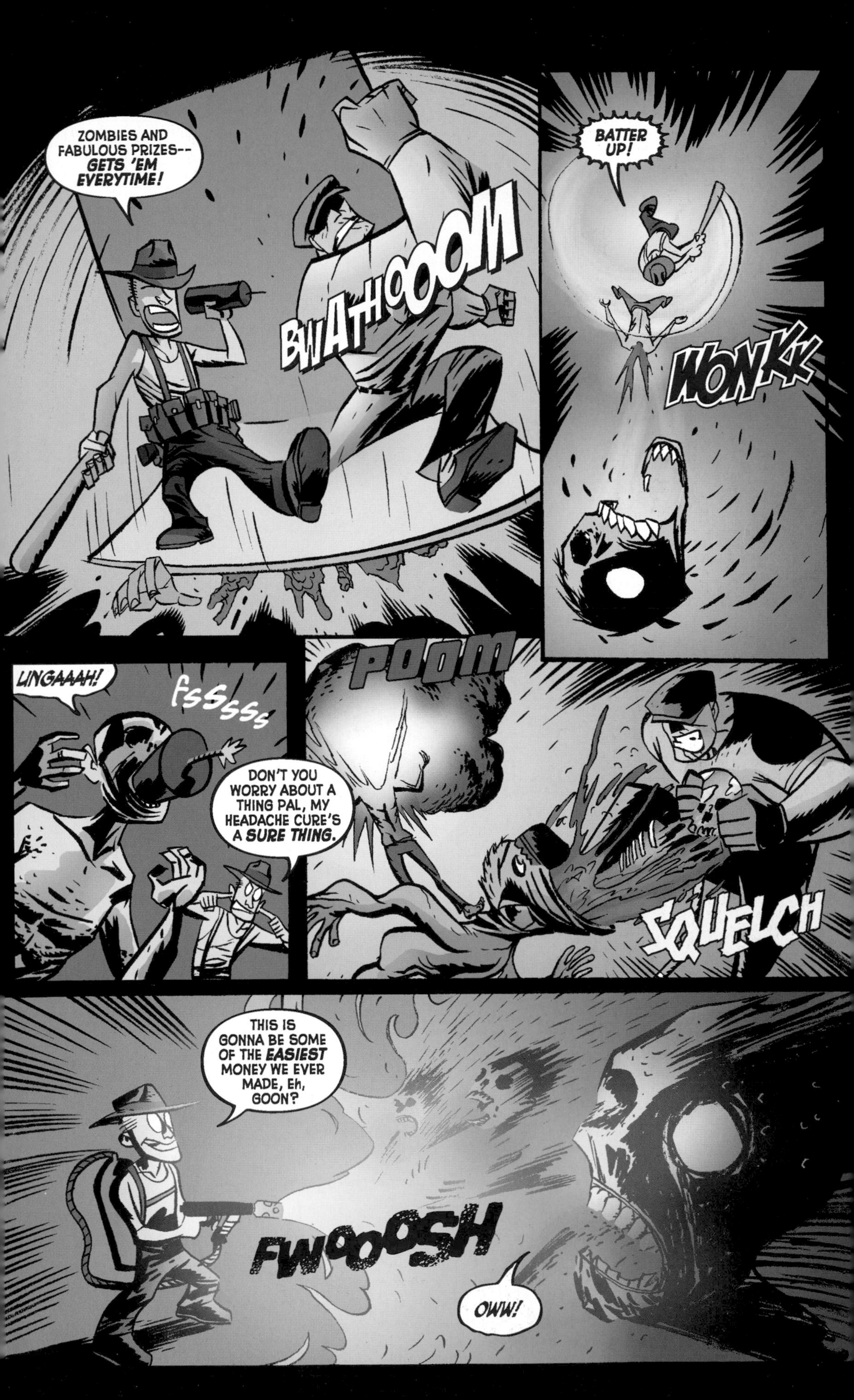
ZOMBIES AND FABULOUS PRIZES-- GETS 'EM EVERYTIME!
BWATHOOOM
BATTER UP!
WONKK
LINGAAAH!
FSSSSS
DON'T YOU WORRY ABOUT A THING PAL, MY HEADACHE CURE'S A SURE THING.
POOM
SQUELCH
THIS IS GONNA BE SOME OF THE EASIEST MONEY WE EVER MADE, Eh, GOON?
FWOOOSH
OWW!

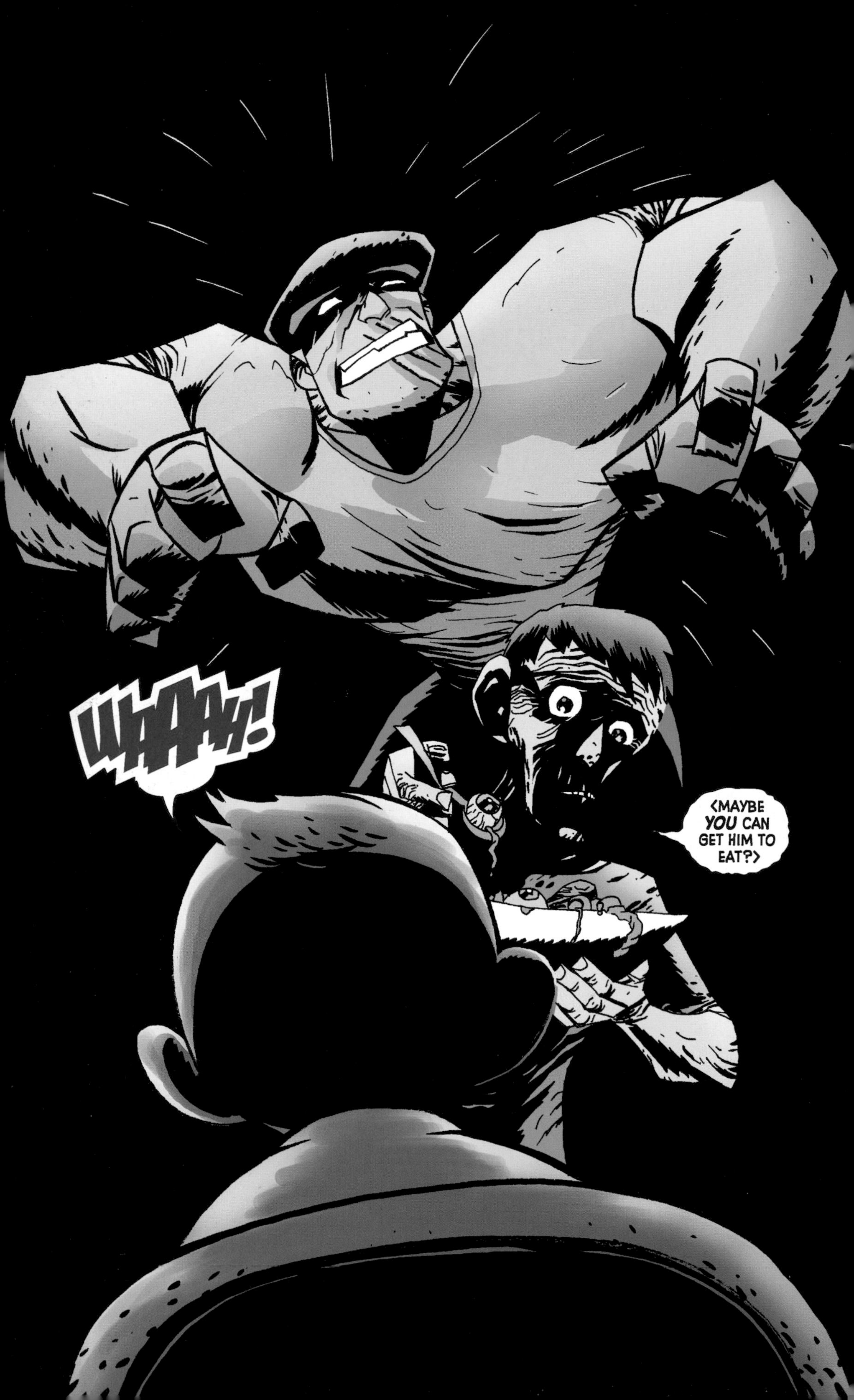
WAAAH!
<MAYBE YOU CAN GET HIM TO EAT?>

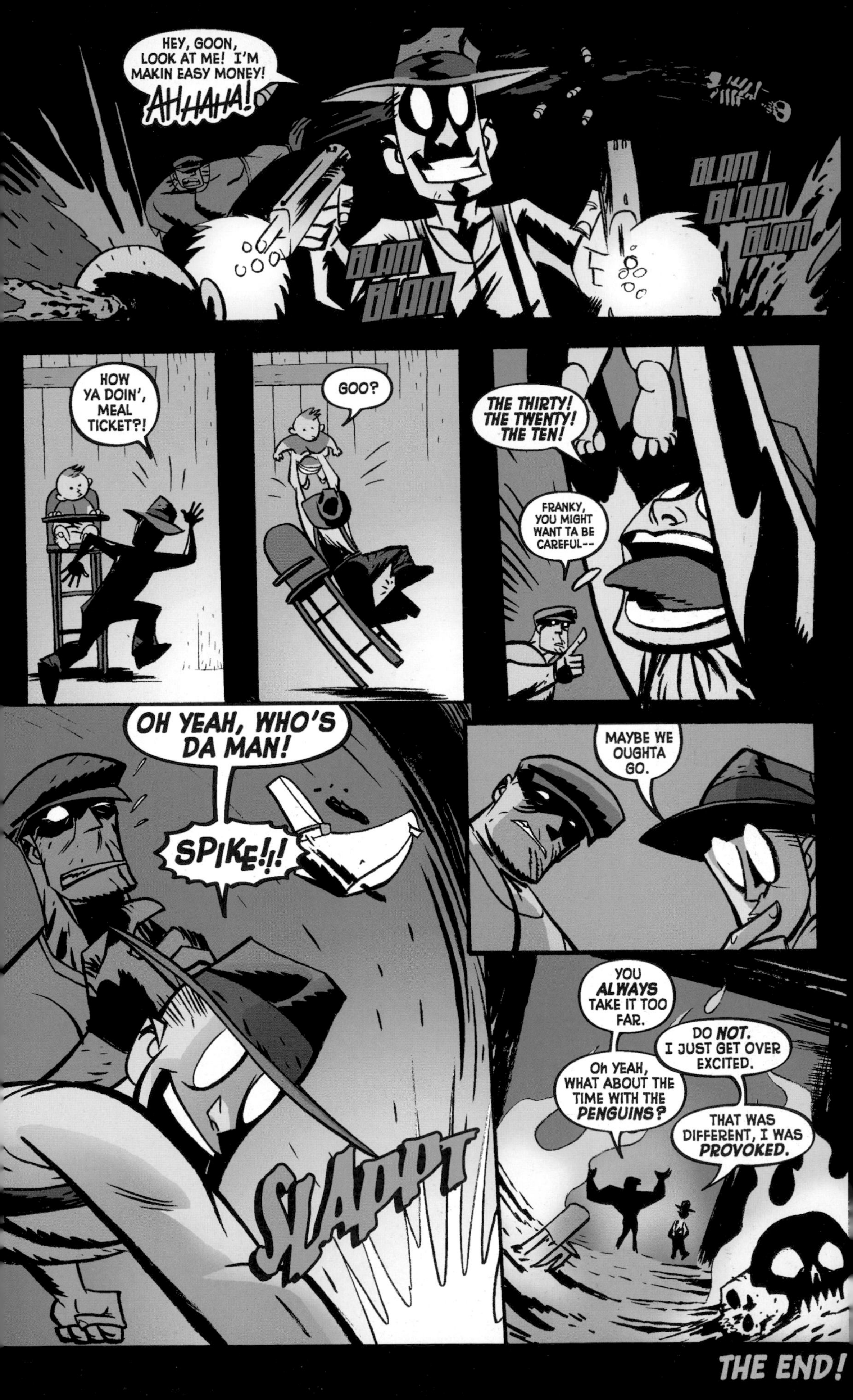
HEY, GOON, LOOK AT ME! I'M MAKIN EASY MONEY!
AH HAHA!
BLAM BLAM
BLAM BLAM BLAM
HOW YA DOIN', MEAL TICKET?!
GOO?
THE THIRTY! THE TWENTY! THE TEN!
FRANKY, YOU MIGHT WANT TA BE CAREFUL--
OH YEAH, WHO'S DA MAN!
SPIKE!!!
SLAPPT
MAYBE WE OUGHTA GO.
YOU ALWAYS TAKE IT TOO FAR.
DO NOT. I JUST GET OVER EXCITED.
Oh YEAH, WHAT ABOUT THE TIME WITH THE PENGUINS?
THAT WAS DIFFERENT, I WAS PROVOKED.
THE END!

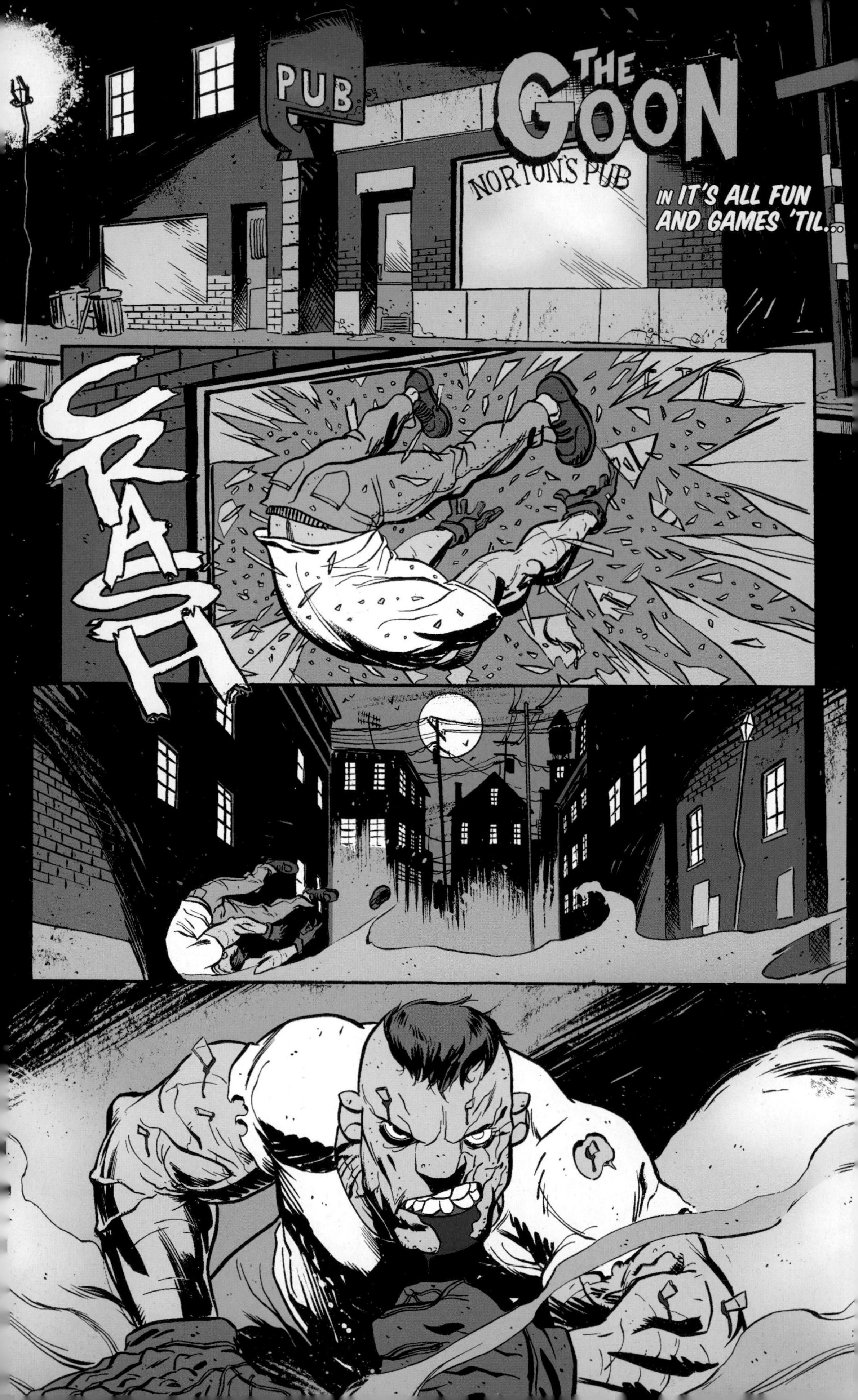
PUB
THE GOON
NORTON'S PUB
IN IT'S ALL FUN AND GAMES 'TIL...
CRASH

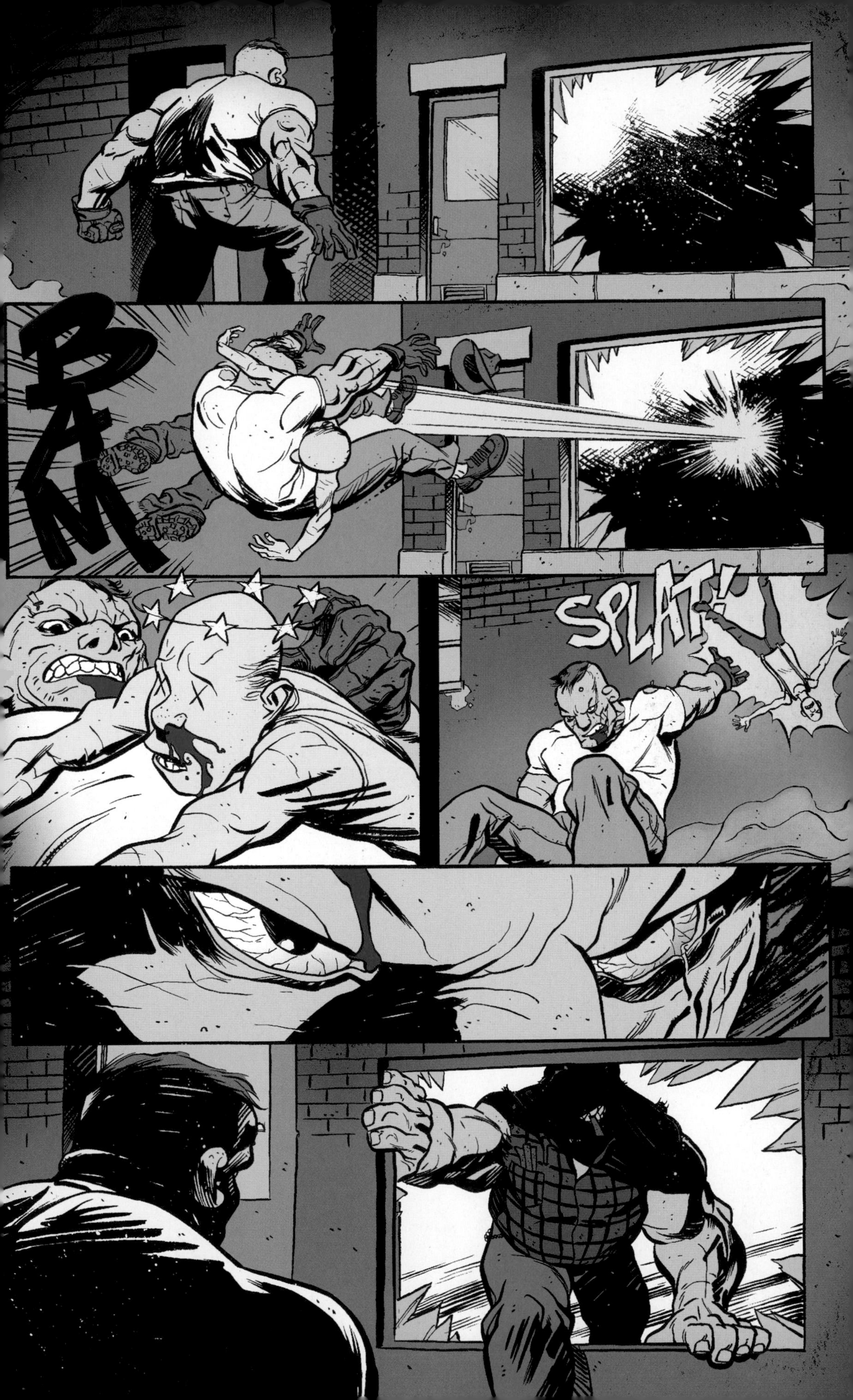
BAM
SPLAT!

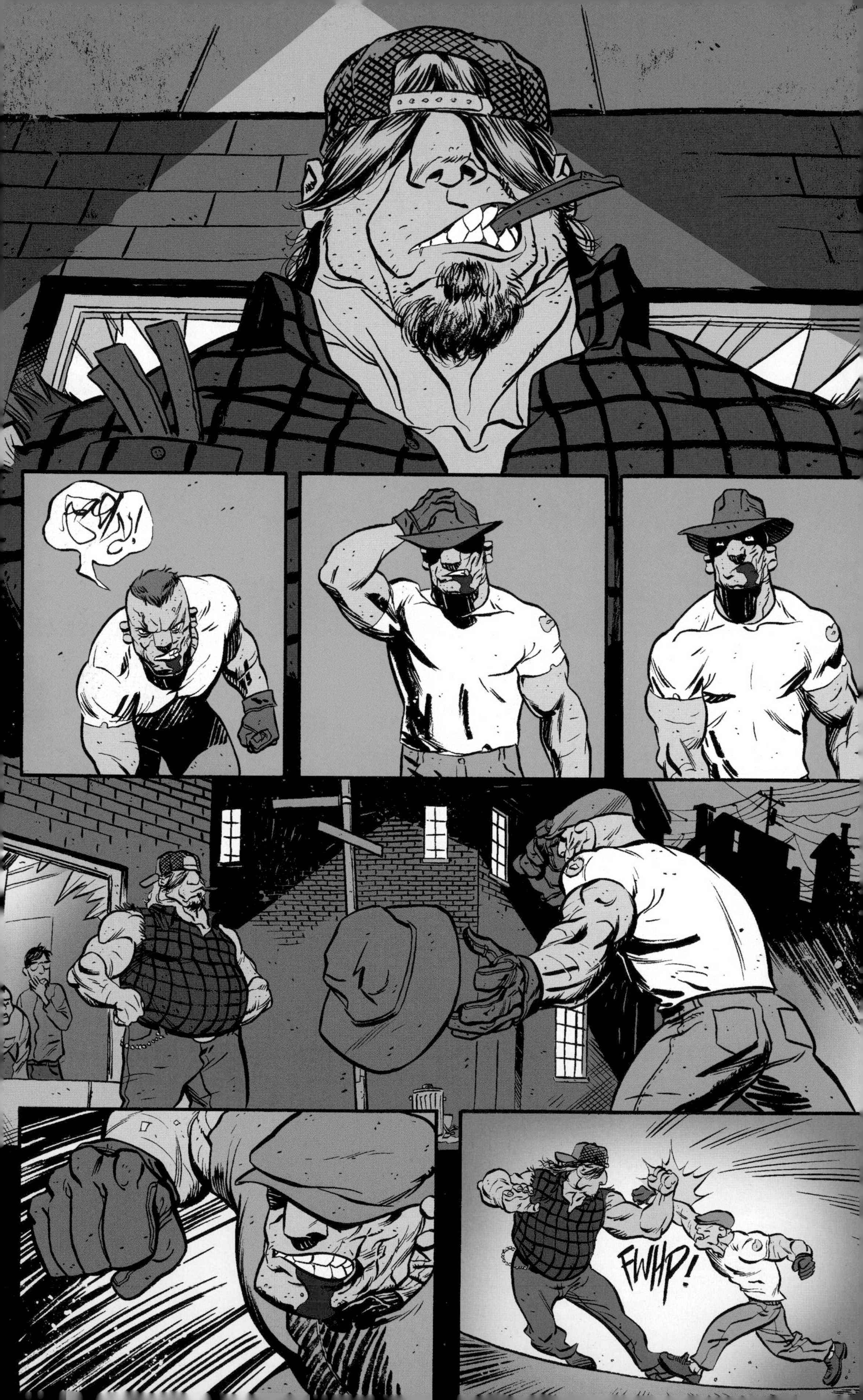
FWHP!

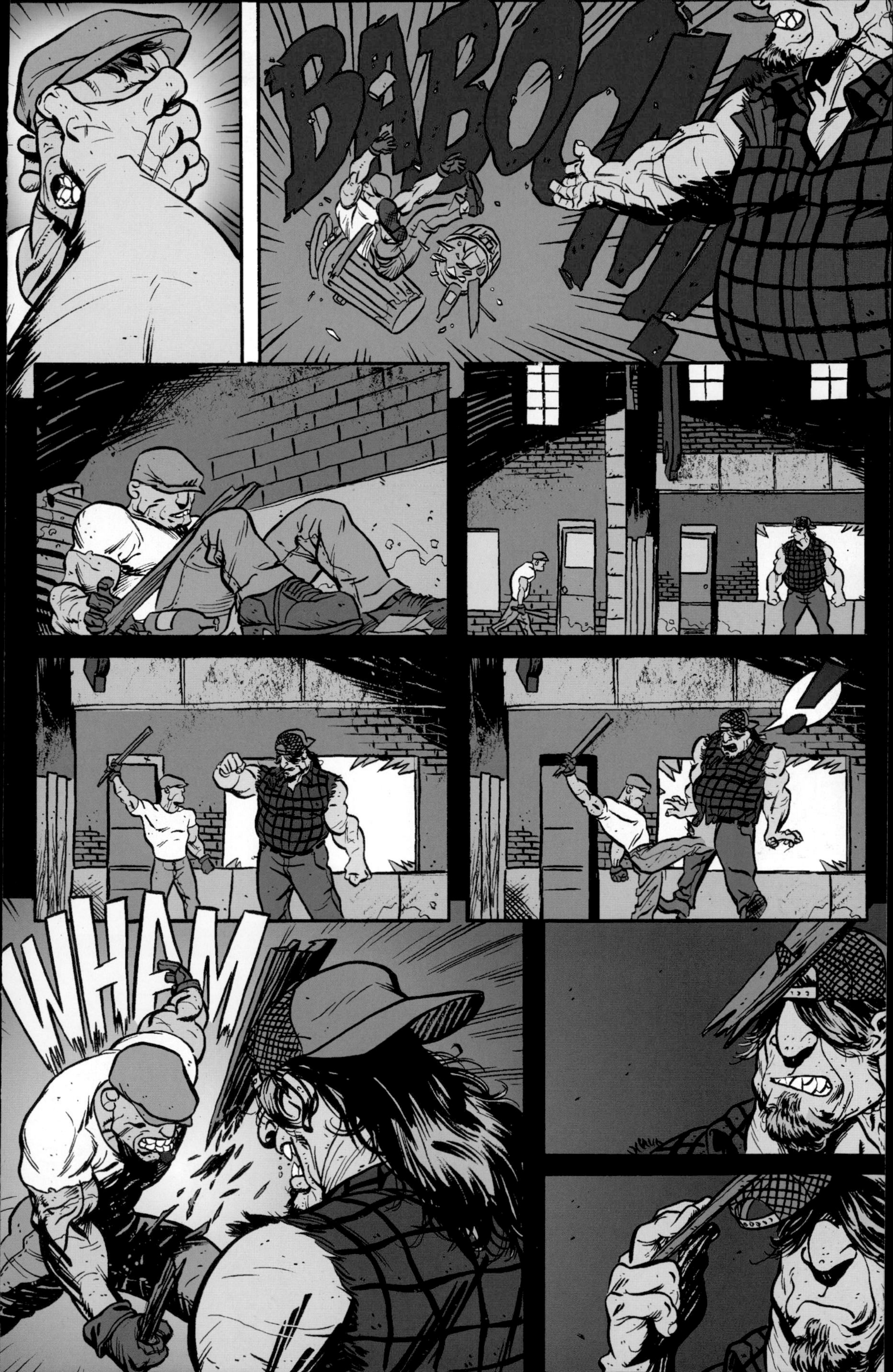
BABOOM
WHAM

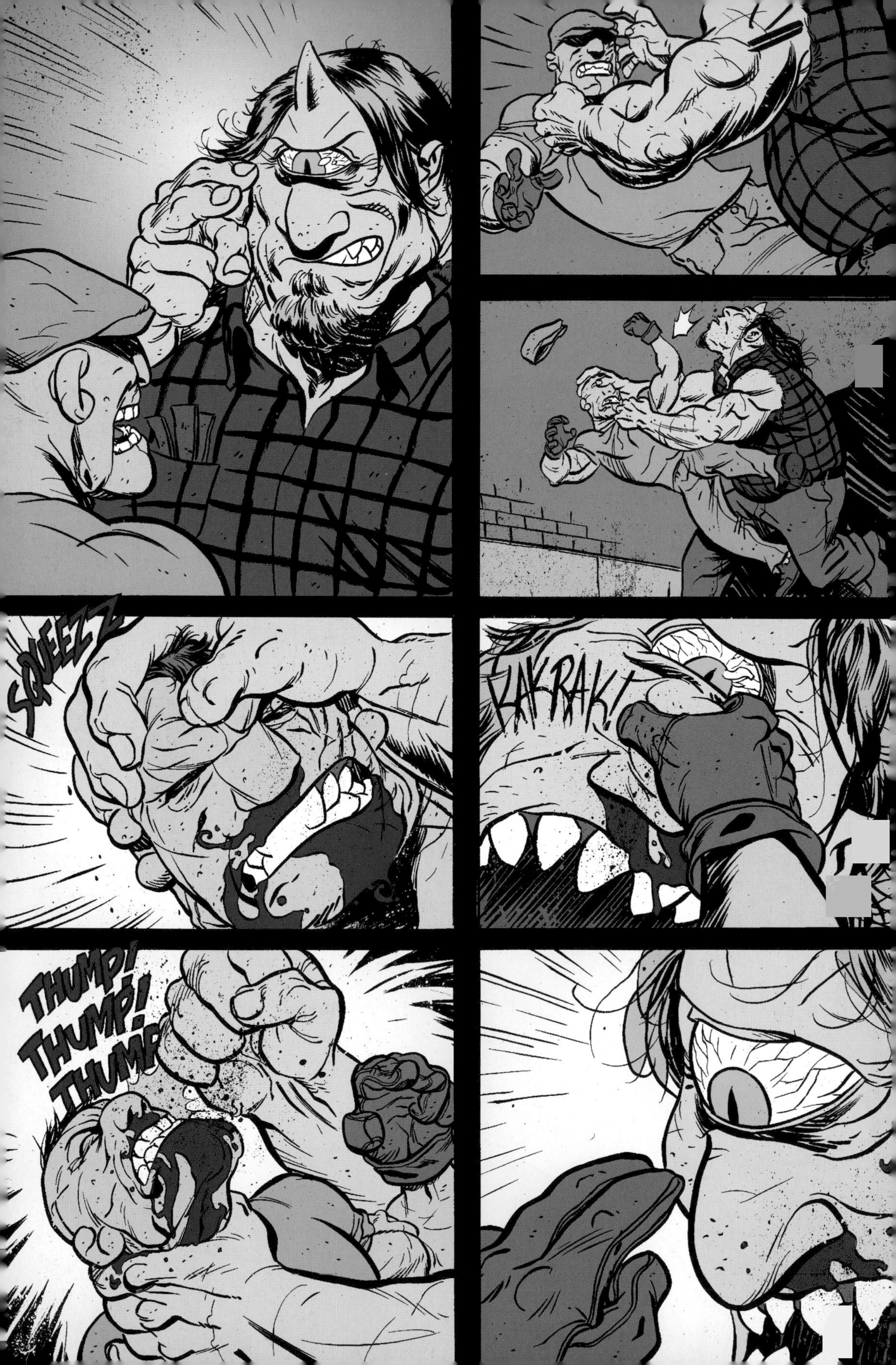
SQUEEZZ
KAKRAK!
THUMP! THUMP! THUMP

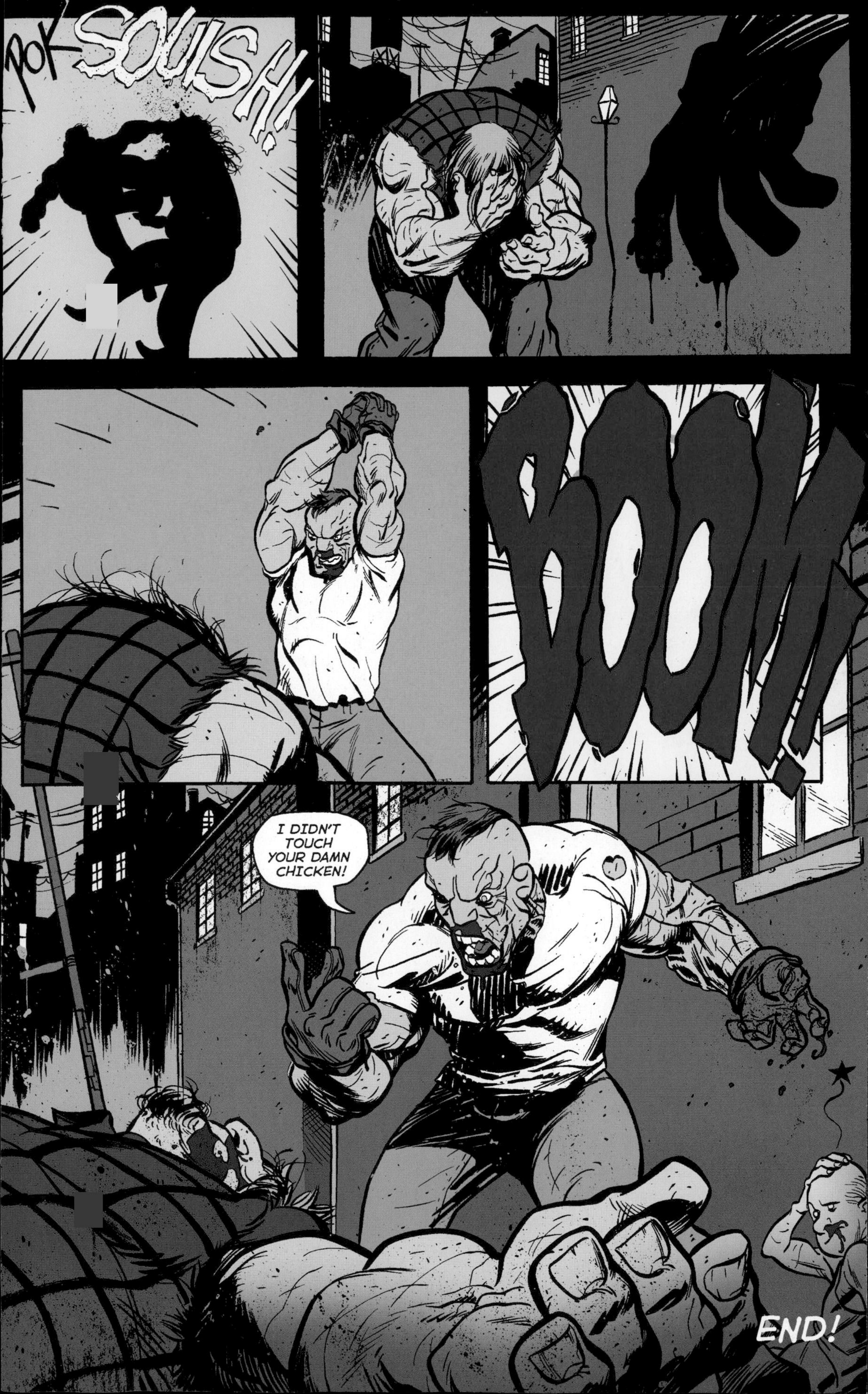
POK
SQUISH!
BOOM!
I DIDN'T TOUCH YOUR DAMN CHICKEN!
END!

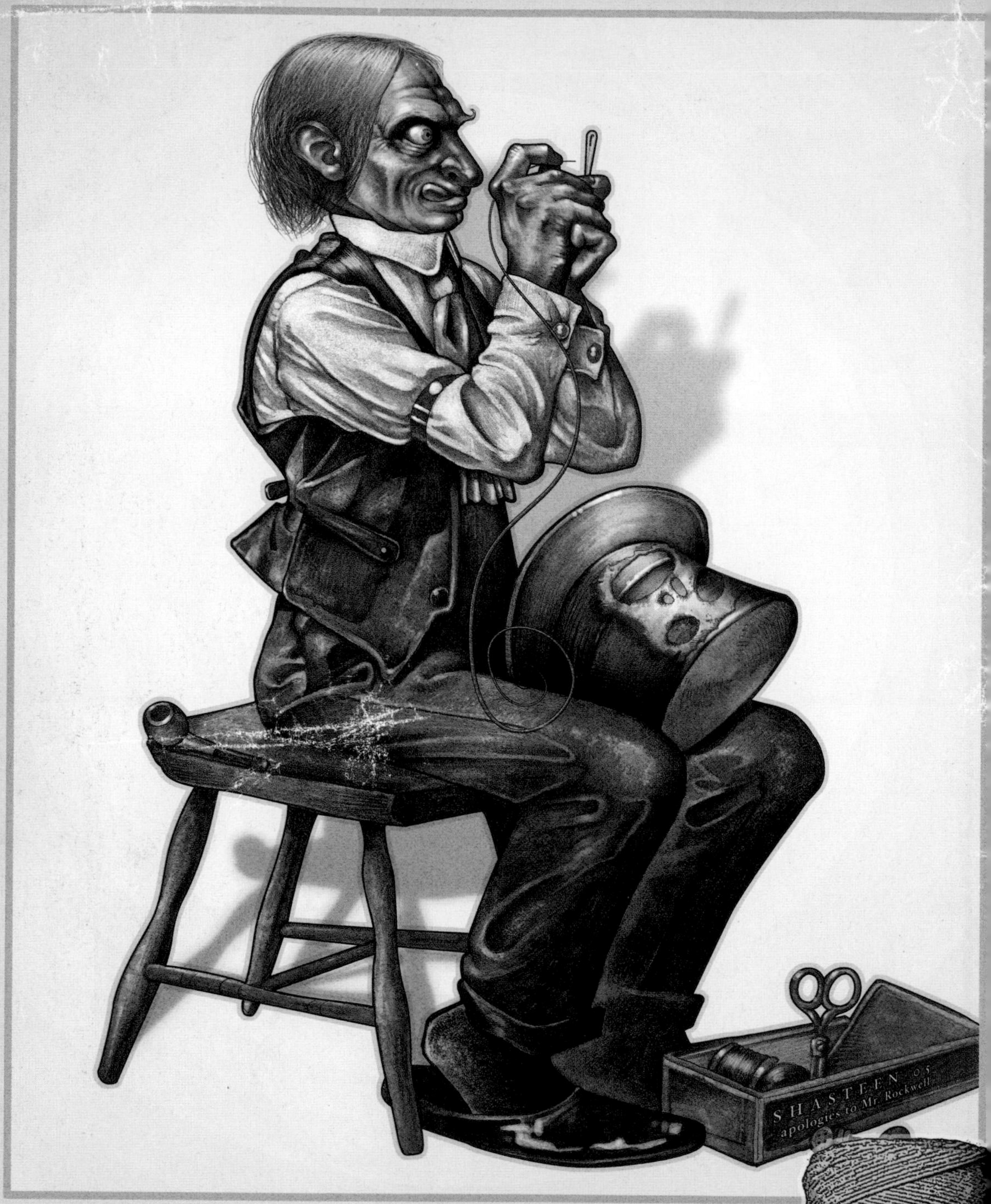
SHASTEEN 05
apologies to Mr. Rockwell

EQUINE TWINE®

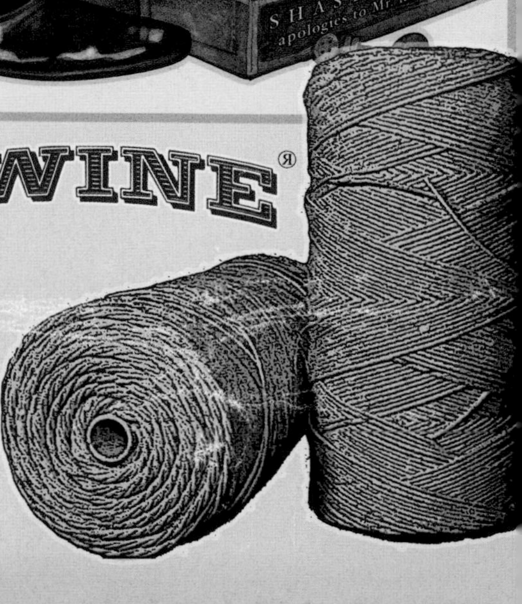

The all purpose twine spun from the finest stretched burro rectums and various post-processed innards! Strength tested & quality assured. Holds knots well, low stretch & does not melt on contact with hot wires. Absorbs a variety of liquids.

"I'd rather have a knife to the spine than use an inferior twine. Make mine Equine®!"

- the Zombie Priest

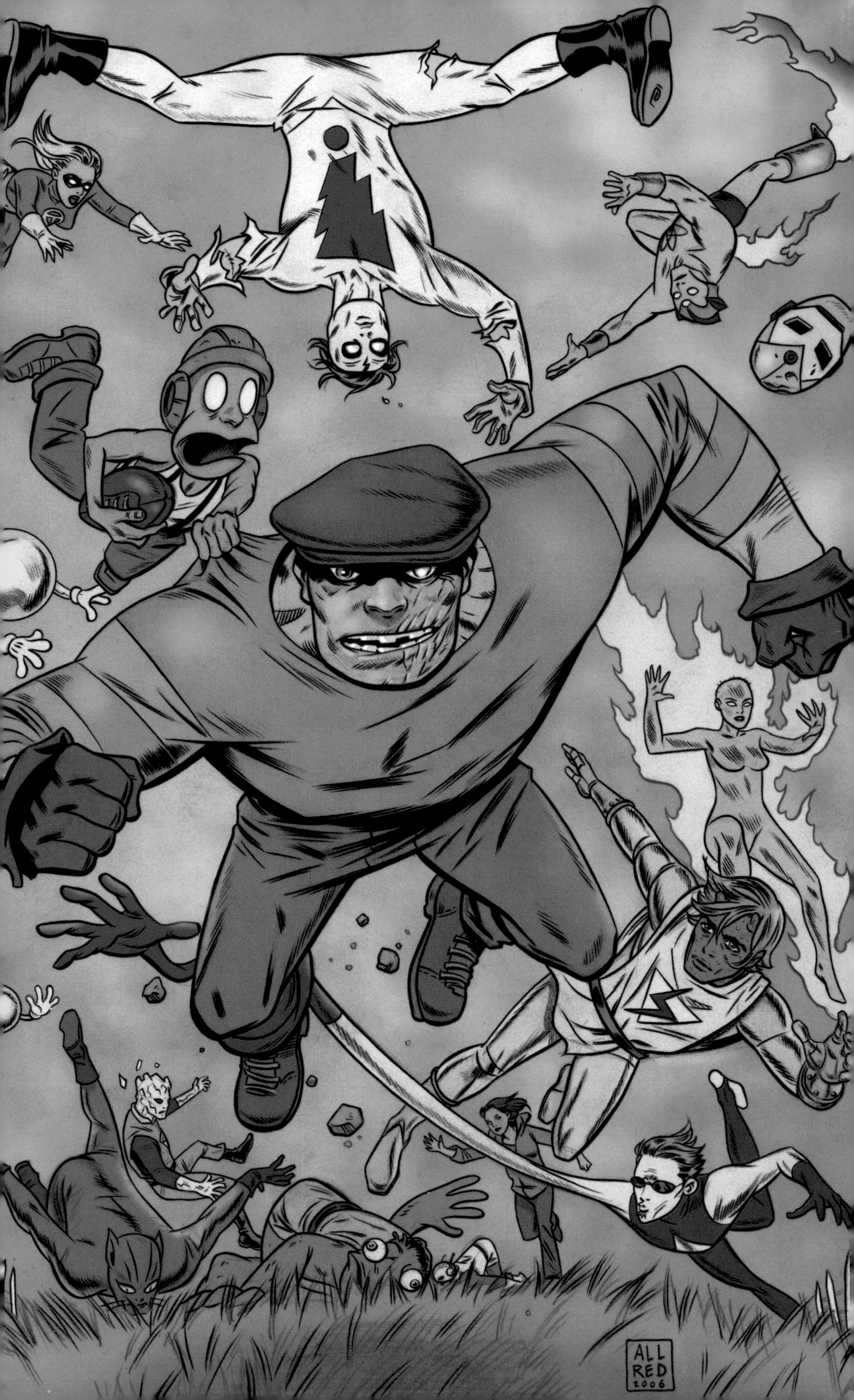
ALL
RED
2006

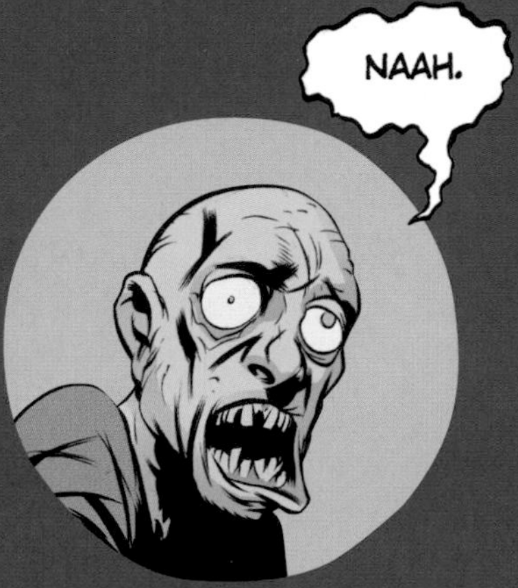
NAAH.

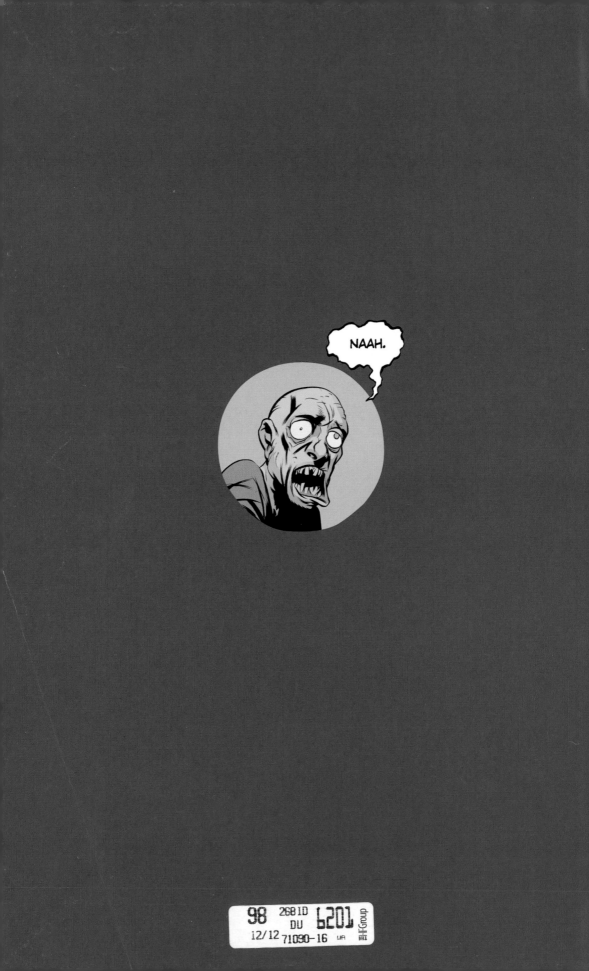